W9-BZG-844

Modern philosophy

An introduction

A. R. Lacey

Routledge & Kegan Paul
Boston, London and Henley

First published in 1982
by Routledge & Kegan Paul Ltd
9 Park Street, Boston, Mass. 02108, USA,
39 Store Street, London WC1E 7DD and
Broadway House, Newtown Road,
Henley-on-Thames, Oxon RG9 1EN
Set in Times, 10 on 11 pt by
Computacomp (UK) Ltd, Fort William, Scotland
and printed in the United States of America

Library of Congress Cataloging in Publication Data

Lacey, A. R. (Alan Robert)

Modern philosophy, an introduction.

Bibliography: p.
Includes index.
1. Philosophy.   2. Philosophy, Modern – 20th century.
I. Title.
B53.L29   190   81-8710
ISBN 0-7100-0935-6   AACR2

ISBN 0-7100-0974-7 (pbk.)

Contents

Preface

I have tried in this book to provide the general reader with two things: some insight into how a modern English-speaking philosopher sets about answering the questions he asks himself, and some appreciation of what sort of a subject philosophy is and where it has been going, at least in the English-speaking world, for the last forty years or so. These two aims occupy Parts One and Two respectively.

The bibliography is mainly confined to works quoted or referred to in the text, though I have added a few items of interest from time to time. It might give the impression that much of modern philosophy is done in the pages of *Mind* and the *Proceedings of the Aristotelian Society*. Excellent though these two journals are, however, the general reader should perhaps be warned that their predominance here may have something to do with the fact that they happen to be the only relevant journals that sit on shelves in my own office.

I am particularly indebted to Dr J. L. Watling for reading and discussing in detail with me the whole manuscript except for Chapters 9 and 10, to Mr D. A. Lloyd Thomas and Miss R. L. Meager for similar help with those two chapters respectively, and to Prof. D. R. P. Wiggins for reading two drafts of Chapter 6, Section II, and suggesting some considerable improvements, and saving me from a number of errors, both there and at the end of Chapter 2. Naturally I am alone responsible for the use I have made of their help. I am also grateful to Dr Ted Honderich for suggesting the project in the first place, and for various kinds of assistance in the early stages, to my colleagues in the Philosophy Department at Bedford College for allowing me a lightened teaching load during two terms, to the staff of Lambeth Palace Library and to Dr Edward Carpenter, Dean of Westminster, for tracing the reference to Archbishop Fisher's speech quoted in Chapter 9; and to Miss Felicity Doyle for her speedy and timely typing of a rather cramped and illegible manuscript.

March 1981. A. R. Lacey.

Introduction

Philosophy is a strange subject, and can even be a slightly embarrassing one for its practitioners upon occasion. Admitting that one is a professional philosopher can be something of a conversation-stopper. People perhaps think that one will constantly have one's mind on 'higher things', or that one's reactions to the vicissitudes of life will show a superhuman degree of 'philosophic' calm. They perhaps have dim memories of the (apocryphal) story of the Stoic slave-philosopher Epictetus (first–second century AD), who, on being rather brutally punished for some reason by his master, remarked, in a purely informative tone of voice, 'If you continue to twist my leg like that you will break it.' Stoicism, however, is not in fashion as a philosophy at the moment; and though the philosopher, during his working day, will probably have his mind on abstract things, whether they are any 'higher' than those, say, a mathematician will have his mind on is a moot point.

Rather more seriously embarrassing is the difficulty of answering the simple-sounding question 'What is philosophy?' If someone asks a historian 'What is history?' he might perhaps, after only a few minutes' thought, come up with something like this: 'The study of the past, so far as it involves or is affected by human actions, individual or collective.' This definition is at best rough and ready. If the Russians divert the river Ob with the intention and effect of flooding part of Siberia and altering the climate there, and if several centuries later a consequent change in the climate of New Zealand causes the extinction of a small and economically useless species of reptile, this event, even if its cause is known, will be felt to be a matter for zoology rather than history. On the other hand, purely passive human experiences, like the Black Death or the destruction of Pompeii, will rightly find a place in the history books. Still historians, I imagine, would generally agree with the definition as expressing at least the central thrust of their study. One would not expect it to divide historians into fundamentally different camps, which centred on their accepting or rejecting it.

It is much harder to provide even a rough and ready definition of

1

philosophy that would gain general agreement. This is at least partly because philosophers simply do not agree among themselves on what they are doing. They disagree not only about how to tackle their problems, but also about what problems to tackle. A phrase which neatly encapsulates the main effort of one school or period may be anathema to another. Some philosophers, for instance, have thought that philosophy is a purely theoretical and general study which is quite independent of, and so can ignore, any results of observation and experiment that the sciences may throw up; while others would say that to turn one's back on such results can only lead to unrealistic nonsense. What on earth then, the reader may ask, is this book supposed to be an introduction to? The short answer is: to philosophy as it is conceived by the mainstream of professional academic philosophers working currently or recently in English-speaking universities. However, the situation is not quite as desperate as the last few sentences may suggest. One reason for this is that philosophy as above defined is at present in a reasonably expansive and tolerant mood – much more so than a generation or so ago, as we shall see later. There are certain broad channels along which the mainstream is moving, but there are also many side-channels and lagoons whose explorers get a reasonably sympathetic hearing.

The popular image of the philosopher that I referred to above goes hand in hand with a distinction between knowledge and wisdom. It is a commonplace that a man can have much knowledge and no wisdom. It is not so obvious that he can have much wisdom and no knowledge, though the picture of the philosopher as unworldly, impractical and absent-minded suggests something of this sort. Knowledge does not bring wisdom, it is often said; but neither does wisdom bring knowledge. However, it may be that what wisdom does do is presuppose a certain amount of knowledge. Aristotle once remarked that a philosopher studies everything in general and nothing in particular (*Metaphysics*, 982a 8). But he was referring to the philosopher inside his study. He did not mean, and certainly did not suggest by his own life-style, that the philosopher, as a man, never had studied anything in particular. In fact he insists elsewhere (*Nicomachean Ethics*, 1095a 2) that political philosophy, anyway, is not for the very young, since they lack experience.

This issue is important, especially when we ask how philosophy is related to the sciences, and to the knowledge we acquire in ordinary life. Has philosophy a subject-matter, and if so, what is it? It is often said, as we have seen, that its subject-matter is abstract and general. In fact some people would perhaps define philosophy in just this way: it is the study of the most general and abstract questions that there are, while questions of detail and particularity are left to the sciences. But if we take this too seriously it will be hard to see how philosophy ever gets going as an academic study, a study, that is, that has a discipline of its own and proceeds by rational steps. Perhaps in fact it is too great an emphasis on pure generality that leads to the frothy waffle that too often disguises itself as philosophy in the murkier regions of the subject. To say the least the philosopher, if he is going to argue at all, must come to particular conclusions as a result of particular steps in his argument; he can hardly come to all his conclusions at once. This, however, is not the main point at the moment, which rather concerns his subject-matter. Many of the questions the philosopher asks are as general as can be. For instance the question 'What is there?' has been discussed in one form or another throughout the history of philosophy. It might be described as the central question of ontology (literally, study of being, or of what is). But not all the questions commonly regarded as philosophical are quite as general as this. Most people would probably say that the question 'Does God exist?' is a proper one for a philosopher, and it certainly concerns a particular subject-matter. Similarly, a philosopher might ask how a person differs from an animal, or how the meaning of a proper name differs from that of a common name like 'dog'. J. L. Austin (1911–60), one of the leading Oxford philosophers after the Second World War, spent a substantial amount of his time asking such questions as how doing something inadvertently is related to doing it involuntarily, accidentally or by mistake. Admittedly many philosophers now consider the zeal with which he pursued such questions rather excessive; but though philosophy has changed its mood in some respects here, no one would deny Austin the title of 'philosopher', and indeed that of being one of the most significant philosophers of his day. Of course, one could always say that Austin was concerned with meaning, and that meaning is a general topic. But one could as well say the biologist's subject-matter was general because he was concerned with life, or the chemist's because he was concerned with matter. Generality by itself then will not give us a key to the philosopher's subject-matter.

Rather similar remarks apply, though perhaps to a lesser degree, in the case of abstractness. Certainly the philosopher does not investigate the detailed structure of concrete material objects. He abstracts from things in space and time. But questions such as whether God exists, or whether we have freewill, are not obviously about abstractions, and in any case abstraction will not distinguish philosophy from mathematics.

It looks pretty clear then that philosophical questions cannot be defined as those which are general or those which are abstract; and we might add for completeness that the same sort of reasons seem to show that they cannot be defined as those which are both general and abstract, nor as those which have at least one of these properties without perhaps having the other. None of this stops us from saying that philosophical questions have a strong tendency to be both general and abstract. But we are looking for a definition of the subject-matter of philosophy, and this is what we have not yet found.

Some years ago, about the time that Austin was writing in fact, it was widely held that the proper business of philosophy was something called conceptual analysis, i.e. the analysis of concepts. What this means is roughly that the philosopher is concerned with the meanings of words; but this is not very accurate as it stands, for synonymous words in the same or different languages are words for the same concept; indeed this is what makes them synonyms. If, say, 'sagesse' is the French for 'wisdom', then one can give the meaning of one of them by saying the other. But to analyse the concept of sagesse, which, given the sameness of meaning, is also the concept of wisdom, involves more than this. It involves saying what it is to be wise, or when it is correct to apply the terms 'sagesse' or 'wisdom' to something. We shall see more about this later, but a few preliminary things must be said to show why this will not provide a simple answer to our question. In the first place, not any old concept was supposed to be relevant. The philosopher was not expected to say what it was that distinguished being a lion from being a tiger, or how the meaning of the word 'lion' and its synonyms differed from that of 'tiger' and its synonyms. And so in any case we could not say simply that the philosopher's subject-matter is concepts. We still have the problem of deciding which concepts. But there is a further objection, because unless we artificially restrict philosophy by fiat there are other questions which it seems to cover. I have already mentioned the question whether God exists. This no doubt involves asking what we mean by 'God' anyway; but that by itself is hardly all that we are asking. Again, suppose we ask whether every event has a cause. Naturally we shall want to know what is meant by 'cause', what it is to be a cause; but we shall then want to go on and ask whether every event does have a cause.

What all this suggests is that philosophy is not limited either to explaining the meanings of words or to discovering essences, in the sense of answering questions of the form 'What is it to be such-and-such?' One of the most eminent of all philosophers, Immanuel Kant (1724–1804), once remarked that morality only made sense if we assumed the existence of God, freedom and immortality. The questions whether these do exist are typical of questions that through the ages have been thought to belong to the philosopher's province, and they clearly go beyond the analysing of concepts.

Another suggestion about the proper subject-matter of philosophy is akin to some of the main ideas of existentialism, an outlook recently and currently popular on the Continent, though the suggestion also has roots in the philosophy of Kant. This view, to put it very briefly and crudely, separates consciousness from the world, and gives to philosophy as its subject-matter the gap between the two, the world itself being the subject-matter of science. Consciousness is of the world but not in it. It is related to the world, and indeed apart from this relatedness it is nothing at all, so that it does not itself form a third subject-matter to be studied. To be conscious is to be conscious of something. The proper topics of philosophy therefore are things like knowledge, language, action, and in general those spheres wherein consciousness and the world are brought together, as it were – though we must not be misled into thinking of consciousness as existing separately and independently of the world, as this way of putting it might suggest.

As a description of some of the topics of philosophy, and as representing a way of looking at those topics, this view may have some validity. But as a definition of philosophy's subject-matter it seems to be too narrow. It seems anyway that only by stretching it rather could one include questions about God; or about categories, in the sense of ultimate divisions of things that exist; or about the relations between matter and space and time.

The failure of these attempts to define the subject-matter of philosophy does not mean that no attempt could succeed. We can certainly say some things about its subject-matter, if only negative ones. Plainly there are vast numbers of questions which are not philosophical, but belong to the sciences, the arts and crafts, the purely subjective sphere of individual preference, and so on. More positively, we can list some of the questions that do belong to philosophy. Apart from those already mentioned we have such questions as whether everything that is real consists of matter, as materialists of one kind assert; or what conditions must be satisfied if a person's claim to have knowledge of something, and not mere opinion about it, is to be allowed; or whether all the things that we call good or beautiful or true have something in common in virtue of which we call them so. The list could be extended indefinitely, and the longer it becomes the harder it gets to find some common subject-matter for all the items on it.

But perhaps it is time to try another tack. Perhaps philosophical questions are to be distinguished not by their subject-matter at all but by the type of question they are, and by the methods appropriate for answering them. One thing which suggests this is the history of the subject. The word 'philosophy' has not always covered what it now covers, as we can see if we look at the more or less obsolete term 'natural philosophy', which is now limited to physics, though originally it applied to the natural sciences in general. It contrasts with 'moral philosophy', which covered not only ethics but also the study of behaviour, and so the study of the mind in general, and included what we now call psychology ('mores' is the Latin for customs or ways of life). Throughout its history, in fact, philosophy has shed subjects one after another, like offspring that leave the nest when they become fully fledged and can fly by themselves. Becoming fully fledged has usually with these subjects meant becoming able to reach definite answers to their respective questions by definite methods, and in particular by methods involving systematic use of observation and experiment. In other words, the subjects in question have become sciences. Philosophy itself meanwhile remains in the nest, forever unable to fly.

It may seem an unhappy irony for the philosopher that as soon as he becomes able to answer his questions with assurance and rigour they promptly slip away from under him and cease to be philosophical questions at all. But we do seem to have hit on a real feature of philosophy, one that can be amply illustrated from its history. It is virtually within living memory in fact that the last of the sciences so far to go, psychology, flew from the nest. (In my own College the Departments split asunder in 1944, and the journal *Mind*, founded in 1876 as 'a quarterly journal for psychology and philosophy', dropped the word 'psychology' from its title only in 1974, though psychology had disappeared from its contents long before.) Philosophy does not use the methods of observation and experiment, and here it differs clearly from the sciences. The method of philosophy is reflection. It is an *a priori* method and not an empirical one, which means that philosophy, like mathematics, does not derive its conclusions from experience of the world, but gets them prior to experience and independently of it. It might be worth noting before going on that 'a priori' as a philosophical term means prior to experience in general, i.e. to any and all experience, not just prior to a particular investigation on hand, as when a detective investigating a murder says, 'I don't know yet if the beneficiary under the will was in the house that night, but I know *a priori* that money is a motive for murder.'

So far, so good. But to say that philosophy is an *a priori* subject is not to say that it is the only such subject, and so can be defined in that way. What about mathematics, which we compared it with above? Mathematics is certainly abstract and general enough for anybody's liking. In fact the most obvious way in which it seems to differ from philosophy is in its rigour. Its conclusions are *par excellence* subject to proof, and it is well supplied with what are called algorithms, i.e. definite procedures which can be guaranteed to produce, or check, relevant results after a finite number of steps; the procedures for long division, or extracting a square root, are algorithms. It does in fact seem to be this definiteness or rigour that separates mathematics from philosophy. Mathematics seeks conclusions that can be rigorously proved. It builds on these conclusions by generalising them and linking them together in various ways, and assesses the significance of its conclusions largely by whether they are amenable to this sort of development. But always the emphasis is on rigorous proof.

It is interesting at this point to compare the position of logic, which has always stood somewhere between mathematics and philosophy. Philosophy is an argumentative subject, and pays much attention to kinds of argument and to their bases. Since logic mainly studies the nature and basis of valid argument, the two subjects have always been closely connected. Philosophy relies heavily on logic, and one part of logic forms an undoubted, and indeed centrally important, part of philosophy itself. This part is in fact called philosophical logic, and it is the more speculative part in the sense that it does not contain algorithms. The other part of logic, which it contrasts with, is called formal logic, or, especially in its more advanced stages, symbolic logic; this name refers simply to the fact that, like mathematics, it uses special symbols rather than ordinary language, which would be impossibly cumbrous here. Formal logic sets out to organise the rules of valid inference systematically. It is used by, and indeed is indispensable to, both philosophical logic and philosophy in general. But it has always been felt to stand at the edge of philosophy itself, and again this seems to be because of its use of algorithms and rigorous proofs. Indeed the gap between it and philosophy is widening rather than closing, and its study now occurs as much in departments of mathematics as in those of philosophy. This is simply because it is becoming increasingly dependent on technical knowledge. In the old days, up till roughly the end of the last century or a bit earlier, formal logic consisted mainly of a fairly circumscribed body of doctrine, which had remained largely unchanged for centuries and could be absorbed by the philosopher as a preliminary before he turned to his real muttons in philosophical logic and the rest of philosophy. The change is perhaps best dated to George Boole (1815–64), the inventor of Boolean algebra, though it took some time to have the effects I have mentioned, and many other writers contributed to the process.

After saying all this, some caveats are necessary. For one thing we must not exaggerate the role of algorithms in mathematics and other subjects. It is easy to train people, and even computers, to use algorithms; in fact computers normally use nothing else. But computers do not become mathematicians or scientists any more than they become philosophers. We must distinguish between heuristics and checking. Heuristics is the art of discovery, and in particular the art of discovering that which needs insight to discover. It transcends the merely mechanical. This is true of philosophy, mathematics and science alike. Indeed if it were not it would be much easier than it is to produce first-rate scientists and mathematicians. But there is no guaranteed way of getting bright ideas, whether we are looking for a philosophical theory, a scientific hypothesis or a mathematical proof. Where the difference comes is in checking. Once a mathematical proof has been proposed there is normally a definite procedure for checking whether it is a valid one, though sometimes admittedly a controversial axiom is involved, and standards of rigour have developed over time. Something similar applies with scientific hypotheses, though the matter is less simple there. But with philosophical theories the situation is much more fluid. Sometimes a theory can be shown to be simply inconsistent, either in itself or with positions no sane man would want to give up. But usually matters are less clear cut, and all sorts of different arguments have to be used, with nothing approaching a standardised procedure, and no cut-off point after which a theory is damned beyond recall.

A second caveat concerns the independence of philosophy from the sciences. The method of philosophy is *a priori* and that of the sciences is empirical, in that they appeal in the last resort to experiment and observation. Philosophical problems cannot be solved by these empirical methods, but this does not mean that philosophy can entirely ignore the results of these sciences. A typical philosophical problem, one belonging to the branch called epistemology or theory of knowledge, would be what it is to see something, and what sort of things we do see. Do we see material objects, or only parts of their surfaces, or only images of them on our retinas, or even only our own brain cells? (Bertrand Russell held at one time a view rather like this last.) No experiment in a laboratory will give us the answer; but without experience of seeing (or at least of other people's seeing, if we happen to be blind) we shall not have the faintest idea what it is we are trying to analyse. Empirical considerations also come in because we constantly rely on what ordinary people in fact say about seeing, on when they allow that someone sees something and when they refuse to allow this. For instance, would people accept my claim to have seen the Queen if I have only seen her on television? Such questions involve facts about the use of language, in this case about how the word 'see' is used, and we can hardly discover such facts without observing the world around us, from which we ourselves learned our language, though we may also have to reflect on what such observation tells us.

There are many other ways in which philosophy relies on observation. We could not get far in discussing the nature of space and time if we ignored completely the mathematicians' discovery of non-Euclidean geometries or Einstein's theories of relativity. In ethics we could not say much of value about the nature of justice if we ignored popular intuitions about it. In philosophy of science our accounts of the role of induction in proper scientific method would be impoverished if we ignored what scientists actually do in their laboratories, and the circumstances in which hypotheses are in fact accepted and rejected. But though in all this the philosopher uses data that have been acquired by his own or others' observation, he does not rely on observation when he constructs his philosophical theories on the basis of this data, nor when he judges theories offered to him. The point is admittedly a subtle one, and the reader will, I hope be better able to appreciate it after reading Part One, where we shall do some actual philosophising. Perhaps for the moment we can best put the point by saying that in philosophy the role of observation is only indirect or suggestive. It may suggest conclusions to the philosopher, but he can never discover his conclusions through it, nor verify them by it. I must add that not all philosophers would fully accept this, I think. Furthermore, it does not follow that it is always possible to draw a sharp line between philosophical questions and scientific ones. Sometimes, for example, with certain questions about space and time, it may be impossible to decide whether the role of observation is direct enough to put the question into physics rather than philosophy. In fact, it is because of this that philosophy has been able to shed sciences in the way I have described. To continue with our picture, though of course it is only a picture and not an argument, there need be no definite moment when a bird is first flying from the nest rather than cavorting around on its edge.

In modern universities philosophy usually counts as an arts subject and mathematics as a science one. Such classifications have a mainly practical function. Mathematics is vital for most of the sciences, and usually of little use to historians or classicists. Philosophy, like mathematics, is clearly distinguished from the sciences by not using laboratories; but, unlike mathematics, it is not an essential preliminary in a scientific training. The more reflective among scientists will no doubt be interested in at least the branch called philosophy of science, but the main debt is the other way round. The philosopher, if he is wise, observes the scientist and describes and draws out the basis of what the scientist does; he does not tell him what he ought to be doing. Of course he can criticise the doings of an individual way-out scientist, but only on the basis of what the scientific community as a whole is doing.

But how far is philosophy really an arts subject? This raises a profound issue which it would be premature to do more than touch on. The issue is simply this: does philosophy seek truth? This may seem an odd question for a philosopher to ask, until one reflects on how hard truth is to come by in this area. Is not philosophy notorious for going round in circles and never getting anywhere? And don't philosophers in effect admit this in the great attention they insist on paying to their own history? Ptolemy, Copernicus, Harvey, Dalton are names the scientist bows respectfully to as he enters his laboratory before getting down to his day's business. But Aristotle, Descartes, Hume, Kant form a substantial part of an undergraduate course in philosophy, and are constantly referred to in the most up-to-date writings. Remembering the remark of the philosopher A. N. Whitehead (1861–1947) that the history of philosophy is nothing but a series of footnotes to the philosophy of Plato, one might well wonder whether philosophy has really made any progress since Socrates drank his hemlock in 399 BC. Some philosophers react to all this by saying that each age has to seek its own philosophy, or perhaps that each age has to express the eternal truths of philosophy in its own terms. Here we do indeed have a reference to truths, but the emphasis is on re-expressing old ones rather than on discovering new ones. It is hard to see anything that could be called long-term progress on such a view. The philosopher would study his predecessors to extract from them the truths which he would seek to re-express in idioms suited to his own age, and philosophy would hardly be a cumulative subject in the sense that the sciences seem to be.

There is another feature of philosophy which suggests the same conclusion. The student of philosophy is not expected to learn a mass of facts, apart from some historical ones. He is rather being trained in a way of thinking. He is being taught to adopt a certain approach to the relevant questions, these being, of course, the ones to which the approach is thought suitable. This has much in common with what happens in a pure arts subject like classics. The student of Latin learns facts, such as that 'ut' takes the subjunctive in final and not in consecutive clauses. But what he is really aiming at is facility in the art of translation out of or into Latin, and lists of words and rules are things he will, to speak roughly, meet only in the early stages. The interesting part comes when he is acquiring something called 'Latinity', the art of

10

expressing oneself in Latin, and appreciating the expression of the Romans themselves, at a level of idiomaticness and not mere gross adequacy.

If philosophy is like this it is indeed a pure arts subject. But philosophy involves argument, and argument implies the possibility of classifying moves or inferences as right or wrong. Which branch of philosophy one takes up, what questions one starts by asking, will largely depend on taste, no doubt helped by fashion and other considerations. But once one has chosen one's field the steps one takes through it are certainly not matters of taste but are subject to the same discipline as all intellectual reasoning. This vital point, which is largely what distinguishes philosophy from pseudo-philosophy, is perhaps all we need at this stage.

Again, however, one or two qualifications are needed to what I have been saying. I have talked of 'pure' arts subjects, but I don't wish to imply that all arts subjects are of this kind. History, for instance, may well be classified as fundamentally truth-seeking, and so are at least parts of subjects like classics or English. For one thing they involve the analysis of concepts, such as romanticism, and here they approach what we saw was one part, though only one part, of philosophy. In fact the second qualification is that again the borderline between philosophy and other subjects is a fuzzy one. Romanticism as a historical phenomenon belongs to the student of literature. But romanticism as a general idea could well be studied, along with such ideas as tragedy, or art in general, by the branch of philosophy known as aesthetics.

Let us mention one final feature of philosophy before we go on to do some. Philosophy is a very self-conscious subject. It is not just that the philosopher is always worried about where he is going, but that he considers it part of his business to examine his own tools and what he is doing with them. To introduce a bit of jargon, philosophy is its own meta-subject. 'Meta' here means 'after'. 'Metaphysics' is a familiar term, and refers to the study of the concepts that appear in physics (i.e. natural science in general, which 'physics' originally meant). For instance, the scientist asks what causes what; the metaphysician asks what it is to cause something. Similarly, whether Brutus killed Caesar belongs to history, but whether history is a science belongs to metahistory. Questions about philosophy, such as those we have been asking, belong to metaphilosophy. But whereas metaphysics is not a part of physics (or science), nor metahistory a part of history, metaphilosophy is a part of philosophy, and so indeed are the other 'meta'-subjects. Metaphysics is more familiar than the others, and occupies a higher status, simply because of its general and all-embracing nature.

Those who know philosophy only from the outside are constantly asking what philosophy is, and where it is going, and very often they are critical of where they think it is going, and they think it ought to be going somewhere else instead. The mathematician or physicist, or even the student of Icelandic sagas, is pursuing a technical subject and can be left to his own devices; but the philosopher is dealing with problems that are felt to be common property, problems about the existence of God, the meaning of life, the foundations of value, or what have you. If he goes too far away from these problems he is likely to be accused of failing to fulfil his proper role as a philosopher, or even of betraying a trust which has been laid upon him.

In the rest of this book I want to try to cater for this concern by combining the two aspects of the subject, namely, doing philosophy and reflecting on it.

We have already found some difficulty in reflecting on philosophy before doing some, and several questions have had to be put aside until later. Admittedly we have already done some philosophy in discussing what philosophy is, since metaphilosophy is part of philosophy; but this has not been the kind of philosophising usually thought of as the most central and obvious kind, and anyway was very limited in scope.

So now it is time we turned to some run-of-the-mill problems. In Part One we shall take a circular tour of these problems, though perhaps 'circular' is a bit of a euphemism: the tour will in fact be rather twisting and figure-of-eightish. This is deliberate, because I want to cover a fairly wide range of problems, and also to give some idea of how the different parts of philosophy are linked together, even when they might seem to be very distant from each other. Normally each problem will arise fairly naturally out of its predecessor, and this in itself, I hope, will show something of these links.

At the end of all this the reader may feel a little dizzy, and wonder where it has all been leading. In Part Two we shall pause for rest and refreshment, and take stock of what has been happening. We shall survey by helicopter the course we have hacked with the machete, and map out the landscape into its main regions. Then we shall return to the nature of philosophy, and take up some of the questions we have had to put aside about what sort of a subject it is, where it has recently been and where it is now going, and also about some of its pervading features, the '-isms' that are so widespread and recurrent, and can be so perplexing in the way they suddenly appear in unexpected guises in regions remote from what might be thought their homeland; I mean terms like idealism, pragmatism, Platonism, nominalism.

We could start almost anywhere. But it seems best to start with some problem the reader has probably already been puzzled about in his reflective moments, and so, rather at random, I will begin the discussion with whether the will is free.

Part One

1 Freewill

Most people have probably felt at some time in their lives that whatever happened to them was going to happen to them anyway, irrespective of anything they did about it. If the bullet has your name on it, then that's it, chum, and nothing you do will deflect it. This outlook is known as fatalism, and elevated to a philosophical theory it says that the course of events in the world unfolds according to a pre-ordained pattern, and that human desires and actions have no effect on this course of events. The pre-ordaining may be done by God, Fate, or just 'the nature of things'.

In this form, however, the theory has almost certainly never been seriously held. In fact it is not even easy to state it with any plausibility. For one thing, it is hardly possible to say that actions have no effect. If I chop your head off, you die, and Fate would be hard put to it to save you. One might try limiting the doctrine to desires, taking these to cover wishes, intentions, and in general all those things that seem to go on inside oneself without having any direct effect on the outside world until they are manifested in action. Perhaps these are idle and destined to be frustrated. But how many of them? Not all of them, unless either no actions ever occur, which is plainly false, or else all actions are independent of desires, etc. and would occur anyway. Now the relations between actions on the one hand and desires, wishes, intentions, etc. on the other form a substantial branch of philosophy in themselves, sometimes called the philosophy of action. But it would be clearly absurd to say that actions and desires, etc. are totally independent of each other. In fact one might rather say that anything not connected in any way with a desire or intention, etc. would not be an action at all, except in that weaker sense in which we talk of 'reflex actions' like the knee-jerk, or the 'action' of rain on the rocks.

A more viable line for the fatalist would be to say not that desires as such are irrelevant but that only those desires will come to fruition whose objects are in accordance with what Fate has ordained. This is certainly nearer to the form fatalism usually takes in fact, especially if it is allowed that Fate may leave large areas of the world free from any ordinances at all. Oedipus was fated to kill his father, but Fate need not have been concerned with whether he used a knife or a riding-whip, and still less with what he had for breakfast that morning.

As a philosophical doctrine this has certain disadvantages, quite apart from whether it is true, and perhaps this is why it is found more often in literature than in philosophy. For one thing, it does not say anything interesting about desires or actions as such. It throws no light on what sort of thing a desire or action is. This is not fatal to it, since we saw earlier that philosophy is not limited to the analysis of concepts. But it does narrow the doctrine's appeal. Second, it is hard to see how we could say whether something was fated or not, without simply waiting to see whether it happened; and even then it might not have been fated, if Fate only ordains in some regions. The standard way of finding out has been by consulting oracles. But oracles are few and far between in real life, and seldom as explicit as the one predicting the action of Oedipus; normally they clothe their predictions with a prudent ambiguity, which makes a scientific study of them rather difficult. Third, the philosopher is more interested in what the world must be like or can be like than in what it happens to be like. If oracles were commoner than they are, and made substantive predictions which turned out correct more often than chance would allow, this would be interesting to scientist and philosopher alike. To the philosopher its interest would lie in its suggesting that really, and despite appearances, the future must already exist in a disguised form, somehow wrapped up in the present or past; or else it might lie in the discovery that it was possible for a non-material force or spirit to influence material events, although it had no material body or limbs at its disposal. But such oracles are rare.

Fatalism as so far described is of minor interest to the philosopher. But there is one form of it of rather greater interest, usually called logical determinism. The argument goes like this: Sometimes people drown. Suppose Smith is unfortunate enough to do so, one Monday at noon. Then anyone who said at noon on Monday 'Smith is drowning' would speak truly, and so would anyone who said afterwards 'Smith drowned at noon on Monday'. But suppose Jones on Sunday had said 'Smith will drown at noon on Monday': surely he too would have spoken truly. He might not have been able to support what he said by any reasons, and in that case he could hardly complain if nobody believed him. But still, if Smith does drown on Monday, surely Jones can then claim to have spoken truly. 'Never mind how I knew,' he might say, 'or even if I knew. Maybe I spoke quite at random, or was looking for some proposition to place a small bet on. The point is that what I said was true. I said Smith would drown, and he did.' Jones would certainly win his bet. But if Jones spoke truly when he said on Sunday that Smith would drown, then it was true on Sunday that Smith would drown. Nor would it do Smith any good to take a crash course in swimming on Sunday evening. For how could anything Smith did after Jones spoke truly have the effect that Jones did not speak truly after all? We are concerned here only with whether Jones spoke truly, not with whether Jones, Smith, or anyone else could be in a position to know that he did. Either I shall drown one day or I shall not. Since I don't know which, it might seem rational for me to learn to swim, just in case. But on the present argument this cannot be so; for if it is true that I shall drown, learning to swim will not help me, while if it is true that I shall not drown, learning to swim will be superfluous.

The argument looks like a trick. But if it is one, it is tricky enough to have engaged the serious attention of a philosopher as great as Aristotle, to whom we owe the first recorded discussion of it. Since I have the advantage over Aristotle of having dipped into two thousand years of philosophy written since his time, I feel fairly convinced that the argument is indeed fallacious, but it is not easy to say just where the fallacy lies, and whatever answer we give may have important repercussions on our other philosophical views. But before we discuss any answers let us note that the problem the argument raises is a quite general one, concerning all statements about the future. The future will be what it will be, and it can't at the same time not be what it will be. *What* it will be we perhaps don't know, but that makes no difference; we can always find out by waiting to see. The future therefore is fixed, and that not by 'Fate' or a lot of odd gods and godlets, but simply as a matter of logic; hence the name 'logical determinism'.

The most obvious answer to try would perhaps be this: 'It is true, I hope, that I shall not drown; but this is only because it is also true that I shall learn to swim.' Suppose I am right about both these statements; what follows? Ought I to contact the nearest swimming teacher straight away? But why should I bother? After all, I am going to learn to swim anyway. No doubt this is only because I am going to contact the swimming teacher, but the same argument applies: if I am going to contact him anyway, why should I bother to take any steps to do so? Pursuing the argument further we shall come to some step which it is true that I am going to take now, such as reaching for the telephone. Since it is true, we suppose, that I shall do this, then I do indeed do it, and we might be inclined to assume I do it in the normal way, i.e. after deciding to do it. But now we reach a puzzle. Either it is true that I shall decide to reach for the telephone or it is true that I shan't, and I know this. Therefore surely I must regard the outcome as already certain, so

19

how can I go through any process of deciding? How can one possibly take a decision about something unless one regards it as open to decision? I cannot 'decide' to grow older, or to hit the ground after falling from a cliff – unless I can somehow con myself into thinking that the result is not inevitable.

Still, perhaps the trouble is that I have been corrupted by philosophy. No normal person thinks of the outcome of his impending decision whether to reach for a telephone as already fixed. Let us then take two steps to amend our example. Let us transfer it from the first person to the third person and from the future to the past. The trouble with the first person case, where I am both participant and commentator, is that I know of the case for logical determinism, which hinders me as participant, and do not know the outcome of the still future situation, about my drowning, which hinders me as commentator. Let us return to Smith, who is blissfully free from any tincture of philosophy, and who will, since we have so constructed the example, in fact drown; the reader can perhaps substitute someone who really did drown through not being able to swim. Smith, we suppose, did decide not to learn to swim, perhaps through laziness. Since Smith is ignorant both of philosophy and of his impending doom there is nothing to stop him going through the process of deciding in the ordinary way. But what, we as commentators may ask, did it matter whether he did so or not? After all, it was already true that he would drown, so how could anything he did after it was true make any difference? Was not his deciding a mere illusion, a going through the motions like a puppet? Of course it may well have been true that if he were to learn to swim he would escape drowning. But since it was true that he would drown it must also have been true that he would not learn to swim. He might have said to himself, and said truly, 'If I learned to swim I should escape drowning,' but for us these words must represent a mere idling, not an open option for him.

Obviously something is wrong. What we want to say, we feel, is that it may on Sunday have been true that he would drown on Monday, but it was not fixed or determined. Sunday did not stretch out tentacles to hold Monday in its clutches. Similarly, there will be a day on which I shall die. Suppose this sad event occurs on 1 January 2000, which we will call Z-day, for short. It will on Z-day be true that Z-day is the day of my death, and so it is presumably true now. But if it *is* true now, how can it possibly not be fixed or determined? What is added to saying that something is true when we say that it is fixed?

In many cases the move from 'true' to 'fixed' does not worry us very much. It is true that Napoleon died on St Helena, and fixed as well, in that it is not an open question, but he definitely did. Admittedly historians might come to doubt this one day, but the point is that they would only doubt that it is fixed or unavoidable that he died there by doubting that it is true that he did. Similarly it is true, and also fixed and unavoidable, that today, as I write these words, is Wednesday. But the trouble comes with statements about the future. How can we allow them to be true without making them, or what they describe, unavoidable?

Perhaps the answer is a simple, if at first surprising, one: they are not true. They will be true when the time comes round, but they are not true yet. Nor are they false. They simply cannot be called either true or false. There could, on this view, be some statements about the future that are true or false now: namely, those that are so as a matter of logic. It is true that either I shall drown tomorrow or I shall not. This is unimpeachable, and would be generally accepted by philosophers. But does it follow that either it is true that I shall drown tomorrow or it is true that I shall not? It might look at first sight as though it obviously must follow. But we must be careful. There are other cases of a superficially similar form where the inference equally obviously does not hold. For instance, 'It is true that everyone is either male or female' clearly does not imply 'Either it is true that everyone is male or it is true that everyone is female'. Here the distinction arises because of the way the word 'everyone' works. 'Everyone' is not a name, like 'Smith'. What the first sentence says is not something about a person or collection of people called 'everyone', but simply that in the case of each person the question what sex that person is can be given one of two answers, though different answers may apply in the case of different people. (Cf. p. 38 below.)

But if this holds for words like 'everyone', perhaps something like it also holds for words expressing tenses, so that the inference we are discussing may not hold in the case of sentences in the future tense.

There are at least two objections to this line of escape. First of all, we often want to say non-logical things about the future, and it is hard to see how we can do this without at the same time saying, or at least being committed to not denying, that what we say is true, and that its opposite is false. If I say 'There will be an eclipse of the moon tomorrow', or 'Smith will come to the party tomorrow', I am surely committed to holding that it is true that there will be an eclipse, or true that Smith will come. Could one reply that I am only committed to holding that these things will be true, not that they are true now? But this will simply lead to the question whether the statement that they will be true is itself true now; and if it itself merely will be true, then the same question recurs about that statement, namely the statement that it itself merely will be true; and so on. Furthermore, a sentence in the future tense could at no time be true, for when the event it describes does come about it will no longer be correct to use the future tense in describing it.

One could try to avoid some of this by saying that only some statements about the future cannot be true or false now. Indeed we have already seen that logical statements, like 'I shall either drown or not drown', might be allowed to be true now, though it might be argued that these are hardly 'about' the future, or anything else, in any meaty sense. The obvious place to draw the line would be between statements about events involving human freewill and statements about the natural world. We could then at least make predictions about eclipses. But could we? Who knows what secret machinations are going on at Cape Kennedy? And anyway, either there are some statements of the relevant kind, i.e. statements about the future which are nevertheless true or false now, or there are not. If there are, then the same objections will apply to them as applied originally: there will be some parts of the future, even if now only some parts, which as a matter of logic, and not of deficient technology, we shall be unable to interfere with. Even if we can, then, divide statements about the future up in this way, this solution does not seem very satisfactory. It does not go deep enough.

This in fact is the second objection. The proposal to debar a whole class of statements from being true or false, when they are statements we commonly make, and when there would be no point in our making them unless we thought they could be true or false, gives too much away to the logical determinist. It in effect accepts the contention that if we say that a statement about the future is true now, this involves saying that the future is indeed already fixed and determined in the sense in which we normally think it is not. As we have seen, the temptation to say this leads to obvious paradox only in the case of statements about the future, because we don't mind the past and present being fixed, at least in the sense of being now unavoidable. When an event is fixed or determined this is normally because it is caused by something which happened previously, and to say that it is not fixed is to say that there is still time to prevent it. Only in the case of statements about the future do we have an apparent clash between two things we want to say, that if the event does occur the statement saying that it will is true now, and that there is still time to prevent it occurring. But how real is this clash? What exactly is the relation between saying the statement is true now and saying it will be true then? Are we really saying different things? 'It is true (now) that Smith will drown tomorrow' contains both a present and a future tense. I put the 'now' in brackets because it may or may not be included in the sentence; it could be dropped. Let us compare another sentence with both these tenses in it: 'The world is (now) such that Smith will drown tomorrow.' Does this mean that something about the world today is forcing (causing) Smith to drown tomorrow? Or does it mean simply that the history of the world, taken as a whole, contains Smith's drowning tomorrow? The second interpretation, which is surely different from the first, is the one we would probably intend if we uttered the sentence without the 'now'. This 'now' certainly suggests the first interpretation, but it does not actually compel it.

Let us compare a different example. 'England is (here) such that Cornwall is west of Devon.' What is the effect of the 'here', which I would not normally put in? I am writing this in Bromsgrove, a good hundred miles from Cornwall or Devon. With 'here' the sentence suggests that in Bromsgrove, though possibly not in neighbouring Redditch, some mysterious process is going on which forces Cornwall to be west of Devon. Normally, and without 'here', the sentence would mean simply that it is a fact about England that Cornwall is west of Devon. But England is what it is in all parts of itself, including Bromsgrove. So surely I *can* say, even though it would be rather misleading, that England is *here* such that Cornwall is west of Devon. If it is such, it is so everywhere else as well, of course, including for that matter in places outside England. The inclusion of 'here' suggests that this is not so, and that is why it is misleading, as well as superfluous. One more example: Is twice two four this week? Well yes, presumably. But adding 'this week' misleadingly suggests that it might not be so last week or next week. What we really want to say is that twice two simply *is* four, timelessly.

In the case of Cornwall a geological cataclysm might at some time shift it to the east of Devon. But take the statement 'Cornwall is west of Devon in 1977'. This is true, and never was nor will be false. In this respect it resembles 'Twice two is four'. If it is true at all it is true once and for all. Its truth cannot vary with time. What does vary is the way in which it is proper to express this statement. In 1978 the proper way would be 'Cornwall was west of Devon in 1977'. What might be described neutrally as Cornwall's being west of Devon in 1977 is a feature of the universe as a whole. The 'is' in the previous sentence is plainly the sort of timeless 'is' that appears in 'Twice two is four'. This suggests the same treatment for 'is' in the phrase 'it is true that ...', for Smith's drowning on Monday, or my drowning tomorrow, if I do, are equally features of the universe as a whole. On this view then the 'now' in 'It is true now that I shall drown tomorrow' is as superfluous and misleading as the 'here' in 'It is true here that Cornwall is west of Devon'.

Here then is our second line of escape. Logical determinism, in this version anyway, says that any event which occurs is fixed beforehand by something which exists beforehand: namely, the truth of the statement describing it. But I have argued that this truth does not in any substantive way exist beforehand. So even if it is true (now, because always) that I shall drown tomorrow, it by no means follows that it is now fixed or determined that I shall. Of course, anyone who now says something true will now be speaking truly; but this is because speaking, whether truly or otherwise, does take place in time. Another version of logical determinism might say that anything that happens is necessary when it happens. But here I think a confusion may be in the offing. 'Necessarily if something happens it happens' is a logical truism. But 'If something happens it necessarily happens' is quite different, and cannot be defended by merely being confused with the truism.

So far this seems a reasonable solution to our problem, though I will mention an objection in a minute. But a few points need to be cleared up before we go any further. In the last paragraph I talked of something being 'true now, because always'. Really I was trying to say something negative: it is not true now in any other sense except that in which it is true always; i.e., it is not true now as opposed to at some other time. But it seems better to say, when talking more strictly, that it is true neither now nor always, but timelessly, just as twice two is four timelessly, and orange is between red and yellow timelessly. The 'is' in these examples is often called the 'timeless present tense'. This use of the present tense, which is as free from any reference to today's date as it is from any reference to Bromsgrove, is important in logic and philosophy generally.

A second point springs from an objection the reader has probably made to himself: surely we do, and very frequently, talk of things being true at one time and not at another, or even at one place and not at another. We say things like 'It is true now, though it wasn't a century ago, that New York is bigger than London', or 'It is true in England, but not in France, that cricket is a national sport'. This, however, may be because what is said to be true at one time or place but not at another is not strictly the same thing. The 'is' in 'New York is bigger than London' is a tensed 'is', and therefore anyone uttering the sentence now would be saying something different from anyone uttering the same sentence a century ago. The original sentence could be rephrased like this: 'It is (timelessly) true that New York is (timelessly) bigger-than-London-in-1977, but it is (timelessly) not true that New York is (timelessly) bigger-than-London-in-1877'. The cricket example is rather similar in nature, though perhaps here it is 'national' rather than 'is' that carries the covert ambiguity: national to which nation? The sentence could be translated into 'It is (placelessly) true that cricket is a national sport in

England, but not true that it is so in France'. A full translation would have to refer to the relevant time as well; cricket might go out of fashion in England and come into fashion in France in the next century. However, the reader must be given a warning here. Sentences which are free from tenses and similar tacit references to the time or place or circumstances of utterance (like personal pronouns) are called eternal sentences, a name given them by the American logician W. V. O. Quine. An eternal sentence is such that if one person uttering it on one occasion speaks truly then anyone else uttering it on any other occasion must also be speaking truly. I have been taking certain sentences with tenses, etc. in them and translating them into eternal sentences. The warning is that it is controversial whether such translation is always possible. If it is not, our solution to the problem of logical determinism may need to be revised, but how radically I must leave open.

The point of our solution lies in the nature of truth. We want to apply truth to the future because we want to talk about the future, predict it and make claims about it. Yet it seemed that to say now that a statement about the future is true is the same as saying that the statement is true now, and that this in turn is the same as saying that something exists at present in the world which fixes and determines the future in the way that only a cause could do, if anything could. To avoid this we have suggested that the second of these three things we might say (that the statement is true now) is acceptable only if it is taken as simply another way of saying the first, and as not equivalent to saying the third. This has involved us in saying something about truth, and as truth is a major topic of philosophical investigation it seems natural to go on now to say some more about it.

But before doing so we must tidy up one or two loose ends about freewill. We have discussed two views: fatalism, where the future will ride rough-shod over human wishes and intentions; and logical determinism, where the future will be what it will be, and we can do nothing to alter it, because in a way it already is there, lurking in the shadows like an actor waiting offstage to deliver his pre-set lines. But determinism takes other forms too, and in fact the doctrine normally known by that name says outright, and not by tacit implication or confusion, that the future is fixed and unalterable because its causes already exist. Human wishes, etc. are not now irrelevant; they play their part in the causal chain, but they are themselves caused. Determinism takes various forms. For instance, the causes in question may or may not be limited to physical causes, as against psychological causes such as Freud thought in terms of. Also determinists differ among themselves about whether their doctrine excludes or is compatible with freewill.

'Hard' determinists say freewill is an illusion, while 'soft' determinists (also called compatibilists) say freewill is compatible with, and perhaps even presupposes, the view that human actions and decisions are as much the effects of causes as are any other events. But these are issues we must leave aside.

2 Truth

What sorts of thing can be true or false? Jack may be a true friend, even though he has false teeth. But this is pretty clearly not the main sense of 'true', though it is probably connected with it. A true friend is a real friend, someone who is really and not just apparently a friend. False teeth are not really 'teeth' at all, or anyway not natural ones, though they look rather like natural teeth and serve the same function. But a false sentence is every bit as much a sentence as a true sentence, for where 'false' is applied to sentences a thing has to be really a sentence in order to be a candidate for being true or false at all. In this sense of 'true', which is the main sense philosophers are interested in, 'true' does not mean 'real' or 'genuine'. What it does mean is highly controversial; but before saying something about that let us look a little further at what sorts of thing can be true or false in this sense.

I have just taken the example of sentences, and they seem a fairly obvious candidate. For truth and falsity seem to belong to things we say, so that if there were no language there would be nothing to be true or false. But there are some difficulties. When do we have one sentence and when another? To take an example made famous in another connection by the philosopher of language Noam Chomsky, 'Flying planes can be dangerous' can mean two quite different things, according as 'flying' is taken as an adjective agreeing with 'planes' or as a verb governing it. Have we one sentence or two here? Most people would probably say two, and perhaps such examples are manageably few, and can be catered for. But what about the sentence 'The cat is black'? Here there is first the problem whether we have one or more sentences according as 'the cat' refers to the species (as in 'The cat is a mammal') or to some particular cat; and here there is no grammatical ambiguity to help us to decide we have two sentences. But more important, if we take 'the cat' to refer to some particular cat, then which cat? We can hardly say we have

27

a different sentence for each cat that might be referred to, including fictional cats. Which cat, for instance, was referred to in my own use of the sentence when I first introduced it above? But which cat, if any, is referred to will clearly make a difference to whether the sentence is true; again, was it true when I first introduced it above?

The truth of a sentence will clearly depend on which cat, if any, the speaker is referring to, to say nothing of the time at which he is speaking: a black cat might fade in its old age. So perhaps it isn't really sentences at all that are true or false, but the thoughts we use them to express.

Perhaps then it is thoughts, judgments, beliefs or opinions that are true or false. One advantage of this is that it shows why it sounds absurd to ask whether 'The cat is black' is true when it is used simply as a philosophical example, as I have been using it.

Still, the suggestion won't do quite as it stands. First, something doesn't have to be actually believed by somebody in order to be true. Probably at one time everyone on earth believed that 'The earth is round' was false, and they might easily have gone on doing so; but 'The earth is round' would have been none the less true if they had. Perhaps we should replace beliefs by possible beliefs, and limit the list in the last paragraph to thoughts. Whether a thought is actually believed or not seems irrelevant to whether it is true. The point is that it could be believed. But must what is true be an actual thought? That is, must someone actually entertain it or think it? Some philosophers hold that they must, because the question of something's truth never arises until it has been put forward as someone's opinion or at least as possibly someone's opinion. But it is surely possible to talk of truths that have not yet been discovered, or even contemplated, and perhaps never will be. Truth seems to belong to the object of an act of judging or a state of believing rather than to the act or state themselves, and the same applies in the case of entertaining: it is the object entertained rather than the entertaining itself that can be true or false, and if that is so, why should it matter whether it ever actually is entertained? Of course we cannot *call* something true without entertaining it, or somehow referring to it, if only as what Smith said yesterday. But we can, as I suggested above, talk in general terms of truths (and falsehoods) as yet unadumbrated. An alternative would be to say these merely possible beliefs are also merely possible truths. Should we adopt this? I suggest not, though the reader may well disagree.

It might seem that what are primarily true or false are acts of judging or asserting, or states of believing, because we talk of true or false judgments, assertions and beliefs, and of judging, etc. truly or falsely. But words like 'belief' are ambiguous, and can refer to either the state someone is in when he believes something or to the thing believed. To believe truly is surely to believe something which is true. We can hold a true belief, but the holding itself is not called true, though it might be called correct or justified. Language works in a slightly complex way here. Why do we talk of believing truly, but not of contemplating truly, nor of disbelieving truly? (We talk of truly contemplating, or truly disbelieving, but that is different; 'truly' means 'really' there.) We talk of believing, contemplating, or disbelieving correctly. But only in the case of believing is the correctness of our attitude always ensured by the truth of its object. It seems to be for this reason that in the case of believing, but not in the other two cases, 'true' and 'truly' denote the correctness of the attitude as well as the truth of its object.

All this suggests that the things that are primarily true or false are neither sentences nor human attitudes, but the objects of the relevant attitudes and what the sentences can be used to state. We can call these statements, where this means things stated, not acts of stating, though this usage is perhaps commoner in philosophy than in ordinary English. They are sometimes called propositions. Both 'statement' and 'proposition' are used in many ways, and there are many problems associated with each of them, such as that of individuating them, i.e., deciding when we have one statement and when we have another. Also it is not clear, as I said above, whether a statement, in this sense, can always be formulated in a neutral way; that is, whether a formulation can be found that could be used by anyone, regardless of who he was or when or where he was speaking. A formulation like 'Tomorrow is Thursday' clearly won't satisfy this condition, since it will represent a different statement on every day it is uttered. This is the problem of 'eternal' sentences in the sense I mentioned earlier, i.e., sentences which say the same thing each time they are used. These problems we shall have to pass over, and simply assume that the notion of a statement as I have described it is a viable one. We do, after all, say things like, 'Jack and Jill said the same thing', however hard it may be to decide just when it is true that they did. But if statements are what are *primarily* true or false, we can still call other things true or false sometimes as a matter of convenience. In particular we can call sentences true or false, if we assume that any ambiguities are laid aside and a definite interpretation chosen, and if the sentence is an eternal sentence. A sentence like 'I am hot' or 'Today is Tuesday', which is not an eternal sentence, can be called true if what we mean is that what it is being used to say on the occasion in question is true. This is important, since the only way we can get at a statement in speech or writing is to use some sentence to represent it. I shall in fact often use 'sentence' or 'statement' rather indifferently in what folows.

So much then for the question what sorts of thing can be true or false. Our answer is, what is said, thought, believed, disbelieved, etc., to which we have given the name 'statements'; though our answer is by no means free from difficulties.

II

Now let us turn to what has historically been the main problem concerning truth: namely, what it is, or what the word 'true' means. When we say that something is true, what are we saying about it?

Almost certainly the most famous theory of truth has been the correspondence theory. Strictly this term covers a number of different theories, which cannot easily be reduced to a single one, but it is convenient as well as traditional to use the singular when we are talking about them in general, or about what they have in common. To say that something is true if it corresponds to the facts seems a natural piece of common sense. The correspondence theory can be regarded as an attempt to take seriously this way of talking.

We can start then by saying that correspondence is a relation relating statements, or some of them, and facts. But what is a fact? And what is it for a statement to correspond to a fact? A fact should presumably be something with a structure similar to that of the statement that is going to correspond to it, so that each bit or feature of the statement somehow goes together with a bit or feature of the fact. The situation would be like what happens when we draw a picture or a map of a landscape. The bit of paint on the left represents the house on the left, or the black blob at the top represents the town in the north.

Here we have already a distinction between different ways of representing something. The bits of a picture represent the bits of the landscape largely by resembling them, though the resemblance must have its limits; if it hadn't, we would have a duplicate landscape, not a picture. Such representation is called iconic. Maps are more abstract. A milestone may be represented by the symbol 'MS', which doesn't look much like a milestone. However, the difference is one of degree. Pictures are often less iconic that they seem (compare different versions of a colour photograph: which is the 'correct' representation?). And maps have certain iconic features. For instance, in an ordinary map nearness between places on the ground is in general represented by nearness between the symbols representing them on the page. In fact it is hard to avoid the iconic altogether. A symbol need not at all resemble what it symbolises, but when symbols are combined according to a rule to symbolise something complex, the resulting complex symbol will presumably resemble − have something in common with − the structure of the thing symbolised. Even in a case like the French sentence 'Je ne fume pas' and its English translation 'I do not smoke', where the translation is not word for word, the two sentences have something in common: they both consist of three elements, subject, verb and negation.

If a statement corresponds to a fact, then, we would expect to find some structural resemblance between them, so that parts of the statement go together with parts of the fact. But what sort of parts can a fact have?

Take the stock example of a statement, 'The cat is on the mat', and assume that for some given cat, mat and time it is true. The statement seems to contain three main elements, 'the cat', 'is on', and 'the mat'. So presumably the world should contain three things to correspond to them: a cat, the relation of on-ness, and a mat. The world does of course contain such things in profusion; there are plenty of cats and mats and there is a relation of on-ness. But this is not enough. On-ness must relate the cat and the mat. The statement contains two noun-phrases and a relation-phrase, where this latter is not just mentioned but is put to work in linking the noun-phrases. So the fact should presumably contain two objects, a cat and a mat, and the relation of on-ness linking them.

So far this seems reasonable. After all, the world does, we suppose, contain the cat on the mat. But now take the phrase 'The cat being on the mat', as it might occur in a sentence like 'Imagine the cat being on the mat'. Does not this phrase equally well correspond to the fact in the way we have sketched? Yet it does not say that the cat *is* on the mat, for it does not say, or assert, anything at all.

We might tackle this by dividing our original statement into two parts, the bit that does the asserting and the bit that says what is asserted, so that we get something like this: 'The cat being on the mat: yes'. Following the Oxford philosopher R. M. Hare we can call the first bit, which gives the content asserted, the phrastic, and the second bit (the 'yes') the neustic. 'Phrastic' and 'neustic' come from Greek words meaning roughly 'propound' and 'assent', and there are many other neustics besides 'yes'. Then we might say that a statement is true if there is a fact to which its phrastic corresponds. It will be false if there is no such fact.

The statement we have considered so far was an affirmative one, 'The cat is on the mat'. What happens with a negative one, like 'The cat is not

31

on the mat'? Does the world contain a negative fact, the cat not being on the mat? Such a fact seems stranger than the affirmative one when we try to give its structure. Not-on-ness seems an odd relation.

Before going any further, let us look at two ways out. Perhaps 'The cat is not on the mat' is made true by the existence of some fact incompatible with its being on the mat, such as its being in the larder drinking cream. But there are two objections to this. It is not at all clear how correspondence will come in now; what will correspond to what? And shall we not have to add a clause saying that being in the larder *is* incompatible with being on the mat? For this is not obvious. Some aberrant housemaid with a grudge against the family might have put the mat into the larder to facilitate the cat's activity. The second way out is to say that the negation belongs not in the phrastic but in the neustic, so that the statement is analysed not as 'The cat not being on the mat: yes', but as 'The cat being on the mat: no'. The statement will now be false if there is a fact corresponding to the phrastic, and true if there is none. But there is an objection to extending the notion of a neustic in this particular way, deriving from the German logician G. Frege (1848–1925). What our way in effect does is to treat asserting and denying as two activities on the same level, which we engage in according as what we way is affirmative or negative. But Frege pointed out that we often say something negative in a way which does not involve doing any denying. For instance, the negative might come in the antecedent of a conditional statement: 'If the cat is not on the mat, the cream is in danger.' Here we have neither asserted nor denied that the cat is in fact on the mat. Frege concluded that negation belongs to the content of what we say, and not to something we do, like denying, when we say it. To deny is for him simply to assert something negative. This argument may or may not be conclusive. To investigate it would take us too far afield. But it is forceful enough to be discouraging.

In the simple example we are considering ('The cat is not on the mat') the correspondence theorist's best bet is probably to take the bull by the horns and say that not-on-ness, or off-ness, is in fact a relation. We must not be misled by supposed features of picturing, he could say. We might think it hard to draw a picture of the cat not being on the mat, because the mat would not appear in the picture. But it would, only at a distance from the cat. Of course the picture must show the mat at *some* distance from the cat, and cannot *just* show the cat as not being on the mat. But so of course a picture cannot just show the cat as being on the mat; the cat must be either standing or crouching or sitting or ...

But what about more complex examples, where the mat does not appear? 'The cat is not on any mat' is as good a statement as 'The cat is not on the mat'. General statements like this do seem to raise a difficulty, and they do so too when affirmative. What is the structure of the fact that the cat is on some mat? 'Some mat' does not name an object in the world in the way that 'the mat' may. And anyway the cat is not on two mats, so if it is the same mat that makes 'The cat is on some mat' true as makes 'The cat is on the mat' true, then what is the difference between these statements? Yet they surely state different truths, even when they are both true. It looks as if cases like this will have to be accounted for by adding to the requirement of correspondence. 'The cat is on some mat' will have to be true, not if it itself corresponds to a fact, but if some statement does so of the form 'The cat is on ... mat', where the dots are filled by a description of some definite mat, such as my aunt Tabitha's. Any one of indefinitely many statements about particular mats would do; there is no definite one of them that must be true for 'The cat is on some mat' to be true, but one of them must. If 'The cat is on some mat' is true because 'The cat is on aunt Tabitha's mat' is true, we shall have to distinguish these sentences by saying that the former, but not the latter, would have been true had the cat been on some other mat.

Still this, it may be said, merely complicates the theory and does not destroy it. But there is a more serious objection. I have already referred briefly to the difficulty of saying what a statement or proposition is, once one disengages it from the sentence used to express it. The sentence has a grammatical structure, and in a simple case like 'The cat is black' it is tempting to transfer this to the statement and think we have got the structure of the statement, and so must look for a fact with a corresponding structure. But what happens if instead we say, cumbrously but not impossibly, 'The cat has blackness', or 'Blackness belongs to the cat'? We need not in fact confine ourselves to current English. We have so far referred to the cat by means of a noun, but we could easily use an adjective or verb instead, and say, 'Blackness is feline here', or 'Blackness cattifies here'. Similiarly as alternatives to 'The cat is on the mat' we might have 'The mat is under the cat', 'The mat is adjacent to the cat and between it and the strongest centre of gravity in the region', 'On-ness relates the cat to the mat', or 'On-ness catmatifies'. Some modern poet perpetrated the following lines:

> Onness catmatifies peaceful fierinear.
> Snoozing-purring cattifies. Cream-fullness is here.

Such a language does not seem unintelligible, though admittedly there could be difficulties, which we must pass by, over whether it could be anyone's *first* language. Languages of this type are called 'feature-placing'.

How many statements have we got in all this? If, for 'The cat is on the mat' and its alternatives, we have just one, what is its structure? If we have more than one, how are they related together? And on the other side of the correspondence relation how many facts have we got?

The difficulty about statements goes beyond the theory of truth, and we must leave it, with one final remark: perhaps we should think of statements in terms of the uses, roles or functions of sentences, rather than as independently existing things. 'Statement' is a noun, but so are 'sake' and 'mistake'. But we are not tempted to think of sakes and mistakes as part of the furniture of the universe.

But to return to facts, what does the world really contain in this area? It seems to contain situations or states of affairs, and these sometimes consist in cats sitting on mats. But whenever we want to talk about situations we naturally have to use words to do so. We can pick out a situation only by uttering a set of words and perhaps also pointing, etc. Situations seem related to facts rather as phrastics are related to statements. The cat's being on the mat is a situation. That the cat is on the mat is, or may be, a fact. But in either case we can *say* what a statement or phrastic corresponds to only by clothing the fact or situation in words. This perhaps suggests that facts and situations, considered as parts of the world in the way that cats are, are less useful to us than they looked. Furthermore situations may be actual or possible, and only actual ones could be part of the world.

Is it not possible that the world does not contain facts and situations in quite the same way that it contains cats, mats, and cats sitting on mats? Perhaps facts and situations are things that we construct when we look at the world and talk about it. We have a choice about how we divide the world up, which features we pay attention to and which we ignore, and there is no way in which we have to divide it up – though of course there are many ways in which we cannot divide it up, because it does not allow of them; these ways involve statements that are false or otherwise inadequate. We talk of 'discovering' facts, which suggests they were already there to be discovered. But they need not have been there in the sense that America was. We might try comparing the way that facts are in the world with the way that slices of bread are in an uncut loaf. The slice as such only results from our cutting, but the bread which now forms the slice was already in the loaf. We can slice the loaf in many ways and there is no one 'correct' way, but there are limits to our powers; we cannot produce a twenty-inch slice from a ten-inch loaf, nor a brown slice from a white loaf.

If this idea has any merit we cannot accept the correspondence theory in the form we have so far considered it in. A statement will not be true by having a structure which mirrors the structure of an independently existing fact. A statement may 'state a fact', but this will be like our 'cutting a slice' from a loaf. Was the slice there already? Yes in one way, no in another.

I started by saying that the correspondence theory gained plausibility from the way we talk. We say something is true if it 'corresponds to the facts'. But this linguistic usage perhaps supports the theory less than it seems to at first. For what we usually say is something like this: 'Smith's statement corresponds to the facts' — not that it corresponds to *a* fact. This suggests that we are not thinking of some single entity which his single statement corresponds to, but that we are talking in a much looser way, where 'facts' need no more be existing objects than amends are when we 'make amends'. The linguistic usage might rest on something like this (though it is for the historian of language to say what it does rest on): 'His statement corresponds to the facts, i.e. to those statements anyone would make who spoke truly on the matter in question.'

But if our everyday use of 'correspondence' does not support a 'meaty' correspondence theory of the kind we have discussed, it may still suggest that in a looser sense what we say is true if it corresponds to the way things are. Many modern writers have developed theories of this looser kind, which is sometimes said to go back to Aristotle. One such theory is that of J. L. Austin, a leader of the post-war 'linguistic philosophy' school (who, incidentally, uses 'statement' for an act of stating rather than as I am using it). Austin distinguishes two kinds of convention. First there are descriptive conventions, which link words or sentences with the types of situation in which it is correct to use them. 'The cat on the mat' is, according to the conventions of English, suited for use when one wishes to indicate the situation of a given cat being on a given mat. Then there are demonstrative conventions, which link statements, rather than sentences, with actual (or as Austin says, historic) situations in the world. Austin gives the example of a traffic sign, where the descriptive conventions are embodied in the design on it, and the demonstrative conventions are embodied in its siting. A 'Give way' sign at an entrance to the Brighton Road tells you to give way on entering the Brighton Road. The red triangle or white lines tell you what to do, while the fact that they are where they are tells you to do it *now*, before entering the Brighton Road. Austin then continues (G. Pitcher (ed.), *Truth*, p. 22):

A statement is said to be true when the historic state of affairs to which it is correlated by the demonstrative conventions (the one to

which it 'refers') is of a type with which the sentence used in making
it is correlated by the descriptive conventions.

This is a weak correspondence theory because it leaves quite open
what form the correlating conventions take. There is no insistence on
parts of a statement corresponding to parts of some entity like a fact in
the world.

However, even this theory has been criticised, notably by P. F.
Strawson, who holds that what Austin has done is tell us not simply
what it is to call a statement true, but also what conditions must be
satisfied if we are to formulate the statement correctly. To call something
true, Strawson thinks, is not to say anything about conventions, in the
way the above quotation does, though no doubt certain conventions
must be satisfied if we are to be right (see especially §IV in Strawson's
second article in the Pitcher volume).

The criticism may seem rather subtle. It stems from a different theory
of truth, known as the redundancy theory or 'no-truth' theory, that to
call a statement something true is not to say anything *about* it, but is
simply to repeat it. Strawson added that to call a statement true is not to
state a fact about it but to do something to it, such as agreeing with it, or
confirming it, or conceding it; or else it is to make the statement itself,
but in a way which is only possible in certain contexts, such as where
someone else has already made it. Later, in the article last mentioned, he
agreed with Austin that to call something true does include saying
something about it, but he interpreted this widely, so that 'Smith's
statement that Brutus killed Caesar is true' means 'Brutus did, as Smith
states, kill Caesar', where the words 'as Smith states' count as saying
something about Smith's statement. But he still insisted that it does not
include saying anything, even in this wide sense, about the conventions.

Analyses of this kind, which analyse a word's meaning in terms of the
actions it is used to perform (confirming, conceding, etc.) are called
performative analyses. One can object to them in the way that Frege
objected, as we saw, to analysing negation in terms of the activity of
denying. Strawson's concession to Austin may partly enable him to
avoid this. For he can analyse 'If it is true that Brutus killed Caesar' as
something like this: 'If Brutus did, as has been (or: as might be)
suggested, kill Caesar.' But it is not clear that the performative element in
the analysis is still kept here.

Anyway the redundancy theory really seems too thin to do everything
we want. It is not clear what it would do with a remark like 'Always
search for the truth'. To analyse this as 'Always search for how things
are' is to move back to a weak correspondence theory, and Strawson's

concession, though he insists that it still keeps within the spirit of the old redundancy theory, in fact seems to move too towards a weak correspondence theory. And can the redundancy theory really do justice to the demand we naturally make that statements can be divided into two sets, the true and the false (perhaps more than two if we include the indeterminate, which we will come to later)? Perhaps the performative theory might divide them into those to be agreed to and those to be dissented from, though it might be doubted whether this is still a pure performative theory. To talk about statements that are *to be* agreed to is not to do any agreeing, and prompts the question why the statements are to be agreed to. Is it not in virtue of something, for example, that they say things as they are? But then we are again back with a weak correspondence theroy.

There is one particular form of weak correspondence theory which we must look at because it has played an important role in recent theories about meaning. This is the theory of A. Tarski, who calls it the 'semantic conception of truth', because semantics is the study of certain relations between linguistic expressions and the objects or situations they 'refer to'. The basic idea is simple and may even seem trivial, but the actual development of the theory becomes quite technical. The sentence 'Snow is white' is true if and only if snow is white; and so is the sentence 'La neige est blanche'. We can think of the theory as trying to generalise a single example like this so as to cover all cases of truth. But this is harder to do than it might look. We cannot just say that any sentence is true if and only if that sentence, because this does not make sense. One suggestion, though cumbrous if not grotesque, would be simply to list all indicative sentences and state for each of them the conditions under which it would be true. We should be giving an extensional definition, that is, one that exhibits the extent of what 'true' applies to. Extensional definitions are seldom illuminating because they don't tell us why the items have been grouped together. To define the UK extensionally as England, Wales, Scotland and Northern Ireland would be correct, but would tell us nothing of what those areas had in common. However, we cannot list the infinitely many indicative sentences anyway.

A way of dealing with this would be to give truth-conditions of a finite number of sentences, i.e., say under what conditions they would be true, and then give rules for generating the truth-conditions of other sentences from this basis. For instance, if p and q are sentences we know that the sentence 'p or q' will be true if and only if at least one of p and q is true. Given the truth-conditions of p and q separately we can work out those of 'p or q'. Again, the truth-conditions of not-p are obvious when we know those of p, so we could re-apply the same procedure to get the truth-conditions of 'not-(p or q)' and then those of 'not-p or not-(p or q)', and so on. A procedure like this, where we begin with a finite number of items to get yet further items, is called a recursive procedure. As an even simpler example, we could pick out someone's ancestors recursively by saying they include his parents and the parents of anyone already shown to be an ancestor of his.

This is indeed the way Tarski adopts; but immediately he meets a problem, which we can illustrate by comparing the sentences 'My pen is red or black' and 'Everything is red or black'. 'My pen is red or black' is short for 'My pen is red or my pen is black', and its truth-conditions can be constructed from those of 'My pen is red' and 'My pen is black' taken separately. But 'Everything is red or black' is not short for 'Everything is red or everything is black'. The sentence 'Everything is red or black' in fact cannot be analysed into component sentences, but needs a more complex analysis. Tarski extracts from it something called a sentential function and then analyses this into component sentential functions. He then introduces a notion called 'satisfaction', which stands to sentential functions rather as truth stands to sentences. Finally he defines truth in terms of satisfaction. He thinks in fact that sentences are a special case of sentential functions, and that truth is a special case of satisfaction. Let me now explain all this a bit further.

In mathematics 2x is called a function of x, and so is 3x + 7, or log x. The point is that the value of 2x is given automatically once we are given a value for x. Similarly in logic 'x is white' is called a function because, at least in principle, its truth-value (i.e., whether it is true or false) is given when we give a value for x, i.e., replace x by an object or stuff, like snow or my pen. (Strictly we replace the symbol 'x' by the name of the object, 'my pen'. Quote-marks round a symbol or phrase or sentence here signify that we are mentioning or talking about it rather than using it or asserting it.) '2x' is called a numerical function because when we replace 'x' by the name of a number we get the name of another number. Similarly 'x is white' is called a sentential or propositional function because when we replace 'x' by the name of an object we get a sentence or proposition. (We need not distinguish these here, since in formal logic we normally ensure that a sentence is associated with only one proposition.) The function 'x is white' can also be called an open sentence, which becomes closed when we replace 'x' by a name of something; ordinary sentences are closed.

A notion important to modern logic is that of quantification. It was first properly formalised by Frege, who used it to solve long-standing problems about sentences containing different kinds of generality (cf. the sailor example below). Roughly, quantification tells us how big a proportion of the things we are talking about have a certain property, much as qualification tells us which sort among the things we are talking about has a certain property. A symbol specifying a quantity in this sense is called a quantifier. Quantifiers can be multiplied indefinitely, but in practice only two are normally used, and even they can be reduced to one, by defining one in terms of the other. These two are the universal quantifier, meaning 'all' and symbolised as '( )' or '($\forall$)', and the existential (or particular) quantifier, meaning 'some' or 'at least one' and symbolised as '($\exists$)'. ('Some' is assumed for convenience to include the case of exactly one.) An expression like '(x)(x is white)' is read as 'For all x, x is white', or 'Whatever x may be, x is white'; i.e., it says that everything is white. '($\exists$ x)(x is white)' is read as 'For some (or at least one) x, x is white', or 'There exists an x such that x is white'; i.e., it says that something is white. 'x', as we have been using it, is called a variable. When it occurs in a bracket after a quantifier also containing 'x' it is said to be 'bound' by that quantifier. In all other cases it is called free, including cases where it occurs in a bracket after a quantifier containing another variable, e.g. 'y', but not in a bracket after one containing 'x'. For example: '($\exists$ x)(y)(x is bigger than y and hotter than z)' is read as 'There is an x such that, for all y, x is bigger than y and hotter than z'; i.e., 'There is something which is bigger than everything (including itself) and hotter than z'. Here 'x' and 'y' are both bound but 'z' is free. Note incidentally that it makes a difference which order the two quantifiers at the beginning come in; consider the two possible ways of taking 'Every nice girl loves a sailor': the same sailor? A sentence is open if it contains at least one free variable. Our sentence about being large and hot is therefore an open sentence, or a sentential function, even though two of its three variables are bound.

We can now explain how 'Everything is red or black' differs from 'My pen is red or black'. The proper analysis of 'Everything is red or black' is '(x)(x is red or x is black)' and not '(x)(x is red) or (x)(x is black)'. It is the sentential function, 'x is red or x is black', that is composite, and not the sentence.

The next idea to introduce is that of satisfaction. A sentential function like 'x is white' is said to be satisfied by anything that *is* white, e.g., snow. Sentential functions with more than one variable are satisfied (if at all) by ordered pairs, triplets, quadruplets, etc., of things. 'x killed y' is satisfied by the ordered pair <Brutus, Caesar>, but not by the ordered pair <Caesar, Brutus> (since Caesar did not kill Brutus). When the order of items in a set is relevant, angle-brackets are used, as above. When it is irrelevant squiggly brackets are used. ' <Brutus, Caesar> ' means 'Brutus and Caesar, taken in that order'. '{Brutus, Caesar}' means

'Brutus and Caesar, taken in any order'. Some convention must be adopted to align the order of terms within the bracket with that of the free variables within the sentential function. The most obvious convention is to take the variables in the function in alphabetical order; the terms in the bracket are, of course, taken in the order in which they appear in it. A further convention will ensure we need not keep specifying the number of terms in the ordered set. Suppose the sentential function we are considering has n different free variables (any of them may of course occur more than once in the function; 'x loves x more than y' has two free variables, one of which occurs twice). We shall need an ordered set (also called a sequence) with at least n terms. But a sequence with more than n terms will do; we can simply agree to take the first n of them, and ignore the rest as irrelevant. In particular we can confine ourselves to infinite sequences, and then instead of talking of a sentential function as being satisfied by certain ordered pairs or certain ordered triplets, etc. we can simply talk of it as being satisfied by certain infinite sequences. A function satisfied by an infinite sequence beginning with, say, a certain ordered pair will clearly be satisfied by any other infinite sequence beginning with the same ordered pair. Similarly a function not satisfied by an infinite sequence starting in a certain way will not be satisfied by any other infinite sequence starting in the same way.

Now we come to what many may consider rather a technical dodge. All the terms in the infinite sequence beyond the relevant number of initial ones were irrelevant. But a (closed) sentence, as against a sentential function, has no free variables, and so the relevant number of initial terms in the sequence, i.e., the number of terms which make a difference to whether the sequence satisfies the sentence, is zero. All the terms in the sequence are merely idling, and the sentence is either satisfied by all infinite sequences or by none of them. This gives Tarski his definition of truth. A sentence is true if it is satisfied by all infinite sequences, and false if it is satisfied by none of them. Of course, this gives us no way of finding out whether it *is* true; for that we must look to the relevant subject-matter. It is simply a device yielding a definition which fits in with Tarski's general outlook on truth as I described it earlier. It is in fact a common complaint against the definition that it throws no light on the nature of truth. The validity of this complaint perhaps depends on how much we expect a definition to do for us.

Be that as it may, there are some further complications in Tarski's theory which we must look at before leaving it. We have so far talked about such things as snow being white. But if the theory is to apply generally it should apply for all predicates, including 'true' and 'false' as well as 'white'. Now consider this example ('iff' is the standard abbreviation for 'if and only if'):

'THE SENTENCE IN CAPITALS ON THIS PAGE IS FALSE' is true iff the sentence in capitals on this page is false.

There is only one sentence in capitals on this page, so to find out whether it is true we must follow the instructions given, which, however, tells us that it is true iff it is false. If it is true, it is false; and if it is false, it is true. This paradox is known as the Liar, because one of its many versions asks whether someone who says 'I am now lying' is lying (where to lie is just to say something false, whatever one believes or intends). The paradox goes back to ancient Greece, but apparently only in this century has it been taken seriously, along with a whole lot of other paradoxes, known collectively as the logical paradoxes; the Liar itself in fact is important particularly because it is relevant to Tarski. (For technical reasons the term 'logical paradox', used in a narrower sense, is sometimes limited to some only of these paradoxes, not including the Liar.)

Tarski's response to the Liar is momentous. He uses a device which derives from one invented by Bertrand Russell shortly before the First World War and called the theory of types. Its effect is to split the language we are using into a whole hierarchy of levels. First there is the level containing words like 'snow' and 'white' and in general the vocabulary we need for talking about the world around us, but not including any terms used for talking about language itself, such as 'true', 'false' or 'sentence'. This is called the object language. Words like 'true', etc. which are used to talk about it, form part of what is called the metalanguage; words used to talk about the metalanguage are sometimes said to belong to the metametalanguage. But often the term 'object language' is used relatively, for whatever language we are talking about, and 'metalanguage' for the language we use to talk about it. The main point is that the language we use to talk about a language contains terms that do not appear in the language talked about. The object language can form part of the metalanguage, and it is often convenient to let it do so, but it cannot form the whole of it. Names of words or sentences in the object language themselves belong only in the metalanguage. A convenient way of forming the name of an expression is to enclose it in quote-marks, as we have been doing. The word 'snow' belongs in the object language, but ' "snow" ' belongs only in the metalanguage. Note that the quote-marks in the first case and the outer ones in the second signify that I am talking about what they contain.

41

What I am talking about is the unadorned word in the first case and the word plus the inner quote-marks in the second.

A feature of this system is that words like 'true' are defined afresh for each level, and mean something different in the case of each level, though of course their meanings are systematically related. If we call the object language L_0 and its metalanguage L_1, then 'true-in-L_0' will belong in L_1, 'while true-in-L_1' will belong in L_2, and so on.

As a result of all this the Liar paradox cannot arise, because the term 'false' in our original capitalised sentence must be replaced by 'false-in-L_n' for some value of 'n', and then the capitalised sentence as a whole will belong in L_{n+1}, and so cannot be the sentence referred to by the words 'THE SENTENCE ...' within the capitalised sentence. In fact, in this case there will be no sentence for those words to refer to, for the only sentence given is in L_{n+1} and no sentence of L_n has been given. The capitalised sentence will therefore suffer whatever fate we assign to sentences which include referring phrases referring to nothing, like 'The present King of France is bald' (to take an example made famous by Russell).

Tarski constructed his theory to apply to formalised languages, where the relevant differences of level can be built in as required. Such languages are constructed for many purposes in logic, and for mathematics and some of the sciences. The essential thing about a formalised language is that it is completely specified. It has none of the vagueness and ambiguity of ordinary language. Also it cannot change or develop without becoming a different language. Tarski thought his theory could apply to natural languages only approximately, to the extent to which they could be crammed into the straight-jacket of a formal system constructed for the purpose. We have seen, for instance, the complexity that he introduces into what we normally think of as the single and unitary concept of truth, even though a unitary definition could be constructed in his terms. Attempts have been made to apply the theory to natural languages in all their vagueness and instability, and we shall have a brief look at some of the significance of this later. But for the moment it seems that Tarski has taken a remarkably large sledge-hammer to crack a remarkably hard nut, with unhappy results for the table on which it was lying.

There are other theories of truth, notably the coherence and pragmatic theories, which we have no space to discuss. But as well as theories about what truth is there are also further questions, which have come into some prominence recently, about what things are true. We have already discussed the question what kinds of thing are true, and I have suggested that statements are the primary bearers of truth and falsity.

But is everything of the right kind to be true or false in fact true or false? Could some statements be neither?

III

A little while back I mentioned Russell's sentence 'The present King of France is bald'. Russell thought this was false, because it entailed that there is a present King of France. Since there isn't, he would argue, everything which entails that there is must be false. One statement entails another if, given that the first is true, the second must, as a matter of logic, be true too, and, given that the second is false, the first must be false too. (Actually this begs some questions, but they are unimportant here; we will look at them in Chapter 4.) Therefore, to use some convenient symbols, where p, q, etc., stand for propositions or statements, if p entails q, then not-q entails not-p. Strawson, however, in the course of a famous attack on Russell, argued that it was artificial at best to say that 'The present King of France is bald' is false, since this suggests that he exists and has hair. Rather we should say that it is a perfectly meaningful sentence, but anyone uttering it now (as against, say, in the seventeenth century) would be making either a statement that was neither true nor false or no statement at all. What we have here, for Strawson, is a 'truth-value gap'. We saw earlier that truth and falsity are called truth-values. For most purposes they are the only truth-values, but other truth-values are possible. One might have three truth-values and classify statements as true, false and indeterminate. A system doing this is called a three-valued logic, and Aristotle may in effect have had such a system for dealing with statements about the future. One can even have infinitely many truth-values; for example, if one lets degrees of probability count. We should distinguish, however, between many-valued systems which replace the true/false dichotomy (e.g., by the three values: known to be true/known to be false/unknown) and those which add to it.

Strawson held that when not only the truth of p but also the falsity of p (and the truth of not-p) carries with it the truth of q, then p presupposes, rather than entails, q. If p presupposes q, then not-p also presupposes q. If the King of France is to be bald he must exist, but so he must if he is to fail to be bald, Strawson would say. Actually the notion of presupposition has not gone unchallenged. I will mention one such challenge due to L. Linsky. A relation is called transitive if, when it holds from a to b and from b to c, it must hold from a to c. 'Is an ancestor of' is transitive. 'Is father of' is not, and neither is 'likes'. 'Entails' is presumably transitive; some have challenged this, but surely implausibly. Let p presuppose q. Then not-q entails 'p has no truth value'. But 'p has no truth-value' entails 'not-(p is true)'. Therefore, because entailment is transitive, not-q entails 'not-(p is true)'. But then, as we saw earlier, 'non-not-(p is true)' must entail not-not-q. Dropping the double 'not' in each case, as standard logic lets us do, we conclude that 'p is true' entails q. But p seems to entail 'p is true'. So, by transitivity, p entails q. If this argument is sound, whenever p presupposes q, p will also entail q. But this leads to a contradiction, for when p entails q, not-q entails not-p; but when p presupposes q, not-q entails that p has no truth-value, in which case not-p too will have no truth-value. One might object that p does not entail 'p is true', because when 'p is true' is false p may be not false but lacking a truth-value. Whether or not we allow this (Linsky does not), p can hardly presuppose 'p is true', since then not-p would have to presuppose it too. (I have followed a common convention in the above by dropping quote-marks round short expressions like 'p' and 'not-p' where no misunderstanding will arise.)

I have written so far as though it were indifferent whether an opponent of Russell said that the sentence 'The present King of France is bald', considered as uttered now, made no statement, made a statement with no truth-value (as the phrase 'truth-value gap' suggests), or made a statement with a third truth-value, such as indeterminacy. For Russell, we remember, it makes a false statement. Strawson later soft-pedalled the question whether Russell was right on this, but there are other cases where a similar question arises. Consider a conditional statement with a false antecedent: 'If Antarctica is warm, London is French.' Note that this is different from 'If Antarctica *were* warm, London *would be* French'; conditionals of this second kind, which raise further problems of their own, are called subjunctive conditionals or counterfactuals; conditionals of the first kind can be called counterfactuals, but usually this name is limited to the second kind and the first kind have no special name.

In the King of France case we seem to vacillate between calling it false and giving it some sort of intermediate status, as the contrasting treatments of Russell and Strawson show. But what we do not want to do is call it true. If we must choose between true and false we would surely call it false. But in the conditional case rather the opposite holds. It would only be false if Antarctica were warm and London not French. Since the antecedent is false we probably feel that the conditional as a whole simply lapses. Its assertion would be out of place, much as the assertion of the sentence about the King of France would be. But if we were forced to choose between true and false we might this time call it true, simply to express our refusal to call it false. Logicians who took this line would say it was 'vacuously' true. Another example, from Strawson, is 'All John's children are asleep', where John is childless. Strawson himself puts this on a level with the King of France case and says it has no truth-value. But for Russell it would have a truth-value, like the King of France case, only this time it would be true, not false. This is because Russell would interpret it as saying the same thing as 'There is no-one who is both a child of John and not asleep', which is obviously true, if John is childless.

Cases of this kind where what is said seems neither true nor false differ among themselves. Some seem nearer to being true and others nearer to being false. This suggests that if there are more than two truth-values they can perhaps be grouped into two groups, those resembling truth and those resembling falsity. Logicians have in fact done this in a context where they were interested in valid arguments involving more than two truth-values. Initially a valid argument is one where, if the premises are all true, the conclusion must be true as well. Truth is transmitted, as it were, from the premises to the conclusion, and the argument is 'truth-preserving'. But a valid argument is not in general falsity-preserving, and neither is an invalid argument; in either case, if one or more premises are false, the conclusion may be either true or false. One can then divide truth-values into two groups, as above. Logicians call truth-values in the first group 'designated values' and those in the second group 'undesignated values'. Validity is then redefined so that a valid argument preserves not truth but designatedness. If each premise in a valid argument has a designated value (not necessarily the same one), the conclusion also has a designated value, while if one or more premises have an undesignated value, the conclusion may have any value. But the notion of preserving has itself been weakened now. For an argument is valid here if the corresponding conditional statement, i.e. the one with the form 'If (the premises), then (the conclusion)', merely has a designated value – it need not be true – whatever may be the values of its component parts (the sentences from which its premises and conclusion are formed).

It should be noted, incidentally, that an argument is not the same as a statement. Roughly, an argument can be regarded as what we present by two groups of statements joined by 'so' or some equivalent word, while the statements within each group (where a group has more than one statement) are joined by 'and' or 'or'. Only statements can be true and false. Arguments are valid or invalid. Any argument which is not valid is invalid; no question of a third value arises here.

One modern logician, M. A. E. Dummett, has argued that, since there is no temptation to insert a third term between 'designated' and 'undesignated', this parallel supports the view that basically there are only two truth-values anyway, even if each of them may have subdivisions. Most of our arguments about truth and falsity, he thinks, are really about designated and undesignated values, or, as we might say, about truth and falsity in an extended sense. Dummett insists that to understand what truth is we must understand the point of calling things true or false, and he sums up his view as follows (G. Pitcher (ed.), *Truth*, p. 104 (pp. 11–12 in his *Truth and Other Enigmas* (TOE) to which I shall be referring later)):

> We need to distinguish those states of affairs such that if the speaker envisaged them as possibilities he would be held to be either misusing the statement or misleading his hearers, and those of which this is not the case: and *one* way of using the words 'true' and 'false' would be to call states of affairs of the former kind those in which the statement was false and the others those in which the statement was true.

On this view the statements about the King of France and about John's children would be false, since they misleadingly suggest that the King and the children exist; while the Antarctica statement would be true, since it in no way suggests that Antarctica *is* warm. But did not Russell call the statement about John's children true, the reader may ask, and did not this seem plausible? It depends on how we interpret the statement. If we assimilate it to 'There is nothing that is both a child of John and not asleep', or to 'If anything is a child of John it is asleep', it will come out as true, but if, as perhaps seems natural, we assimilate it to 'John has some children but none of them is awake', it will come out as false.

But now we come to a further issue. Dummett thinks that basically there are only two truth-values. Yet he also thinks that there are some statements for which the law of excluded middle, which for our purposes here says that every statement is true or false, cannot be maintained. Dummett takes the example 'Jones was brave', where Jones died after a life where his courage was never tested. He then argues that 'Jones was brave' is true only if the following is true: 'Had Jones met danger, he would have acted bravely' (call this B_1). He adds that 'Jones was brave' is false, or 'Jones was not brave' is true, only if the following is true: 'Had Jones met danger, he would not have acted bravely' (call this B_2). But it might be that however many facts we dug up about Jones we would never be in a position either to assert B_1 or to assert B_2. Dummett accepts this much from the correspondence theory, that 'a statement is true only if there is something in the world *in virtue of which* it is true' (Pitcher, p. 106; TOE, p. 14). Since we have just supposed that there is nothing accessible to us in the world in virtue of which B_1 or B_2 is true, B_1 or B_2 could be true, if at all, only in virtue of something inaccessible to us, a sort of 'spiritual mechanism' which was Jones's character (*ibid.*, p. 107; TOE, p. 15). But he thinks that 'Jones was brave' could not be true in virtue of something in principle inaccessible to us, because if it were, it 'would not have the meaning that *we* have given it' (*ibid.*, p. 108; TOE, p. 16). The point is that if a statement has a meaning at all, it must have a meaning *to us*, and it is unintelligible how this meaning could involve reference to something totally inaccessible to us. This is an aspect of the verification theory of meaning, of which we shall see more later. Note incidentally that this sort of example of something that might lack a truth-value is more fundamental than the 'King of France' example: see TOE, pp. 23–4. The arguments we have just been through lead Dummett to reject what he calls realism, where this is the view that 'for any statement there must be something in virtue of which either it or its negation is true' (*ibid.*, p. 107; TOE, p. 14). The issue I referred to at the start of this paragraph is whether realism in this sense is true.

Here I can do no more than sketch the issue. On the one hand, surely truth should be something in reality itself, and independent of whether we can know it. Clearly there are many truths we can never know in practice, such as what Caesar dreamed about on the night before his murder. Why should there not also be truths we can never know in principle, because no method could ever lead us to them? Typical examples would be cases where we could discover the truth only by inspecting an infinite number of objects. Suppose, for instance, that the universe is infinite in space and time, as it could be, even if current theories suggest the opposite, and consider the statement 'Nowhere and at no time does there exist a purple cow'. We can never examine all times and places to settle the matter, but it could surely still be true that there is none. Yet on the other hand it seems plausible to say that if we could not say what would count as our finding out for certain that our statement was true, we would not know what we were talking about. Of course it might be impossible in fact to find out, because we are too spatially or temporally distant, or for some other reason, but we ought to know what would count as our finding out.

Here we must leave this issue, at least in its general form. We will return to it briefly in Chapter 6. But there are some particular cases of statements which at least seem to be neither true nor false which have raised fundamental issues in another branch of philosophy, namely ethics. Let us have a look at some of these issues.

3   Value judgments

'Abortion can never be right.' 'You were wrong to use that legacy for going abroad when your great-aunt was half-starving in her garret.' 'Inflicting pain for the fun of watching one's victim's writhing is worse than inflicting it to reform a man's character.' 'Even Hitler was a better man than Stalin.' 'The Romans ought to have risen in wrath against Nero's persecution of the Christians.' 'The practice of educating children is intrinsically evil.' All these are central examples of moral judgments. Some of them are pretty general (the first), while others are quite specific (the second). Some are non-controversial (the third, presumably), while others are highly controverted (the first), or would be generally rejected (the sixth). But can any of them be true or false? In the last chapter we did not come to any final conclusion about the nature of truth, nor even discuss all possible theories of it. But it did seem plausible to go along at least this far with a weak correspondence theory and call something true if it 'corresponds to the way things are' (p. 35). But in what sense could any of the above judgments express 'the way things are' – or aren't, for that matter? How can we find out how they are? And what really are we trying to find out? We can envisage the Romans rising in wrath against Nero, but can we envisage them 'oughting' to do so? Perhaps we are being too picturesque. Of course we cannot picture them 'oughting' to do so, but we might still find out definitely in some way that they ought. Perhaps God, at least, knows the answer, and may one day reveal it to us. But doubts remain. Assuming we know all the relevant historical facts, what else is there to know? Suppose God told us that the judgment about the Romans was true: could we accept this as a revelation? Could we regard God as reporting something to us, as He might report that the universe contains no purple cows, rather than as simply issuing a divine fiat?

Some people have taken this last idea seriously, and supposed that moral judgments are purported divine commands, and are true whenever it is true that God commands them. This does not seem very adequate as it stands. At least we should want to be assured that the God who gave the commands was a *good* God, and that it was *right* to obey Him, where this meant more than simply that (not surprisingly) He approved of Himself and commanded us to obey Him.

Many philosophers, however, especially in the present century, have held a view rather like this one. They have despaired of ever finding truth or falsity in spheres like ethics, and so they have suggested that moral judgments are not really statements at all, but are disguised commands or, more generally, expressions of attitude – the commands or attitudes being those not of God but of the speaker.

Views like this take many different forms; but they say in common that to pass a moral judgment is not to state any specifically or peculiarly moral facts, because there are none. After all, we say things like, 'These are the facts – the rest is a matter for judgment'; it would sound odd to include a 'moral fact' among the 'facts'. Moral judgments may state or imply other kinds of fact. For instance, our Nero example states or implies, or perhaps presupposes, that Nero did persecute the Christians, and possibly also that the Romans did not rise up in wrath, or at least that the speaker does not think they did. These various things may be implied, if at all, in different senses of 'imply', but that does not matter for the moment. The point is that they are all factual or historical matters, and don't cover the specifically moral aspect of the judgment. This moral aspect does not consist in stating any facts at all, but in doing something else, like expressing an attitude, or prescribing a norm. One who utters our Nero judgment, for instance, might be condemning the Romans for their apathy, or recommending his hearers to rise up against persecutors.

Another view is that the specifically moral aspect of a moral judgment does state a fact, but not a specifically or peculiarly moral one. It might, for instance, state that the speaker disapproved of something, or that most people in his society did so, or mankind in general did so. These would be psychological facts about people's attitudes, and this kind of view is a form of subjectivism. Alternatively, the fact stated in the moral part of the judgment might concern the nature or results of the act, or whatever was being judged. To call an action wrong, for instance, might be to say that it would produce more pain than pleasure on the whole. This kind of view, and the psychological view just mentioned, are often called naturalism, because they make moral judgments say something about the world of nature, as against some transcendent world of values or obligations. G. E. Moore (1873–1958) castigated all such views for committing what he called the 'naturalistic fallacy', something we will return to briefly later.

Let us now return to the views sketched in the paragraph before last.

One of the difficulties about supposing that there are specifically moral facts is that of deciding how we could get to know them. We could hardly perceive them with the senses. Do we know them by intuition, despite our apparent disagreements with each other? Could we deduce them by logic, without already having to know some moral facts to deduce them from? Is there some other way in which we could get to know them by the use of reason? Some of these problems we shall return to later; but they will all be by-passed if we say there are no moral facts, and so nothing, apart from ordinary 'natural' facts, to be known. One way of holding this, as we have seen, is to say that the moral aspect of moral judgments does not state any facts at all, and so nothing that needs to be known. This approach is therefore often called non-cognitivism. Until fairly recently much of ethics was dominated by a dispute between prescriptivists, who said that moral judgments prescribed norms or attitudes, and descriptivists, who said that they stated facts, or described states of affairs. This conveniently euphonious contrast is often treated as the same as that between non-cognitivists and naturalists. But they are not quite the same. Prescriptivism is one form of non-cognitivism (emotivism, saying that moral judgments express emotions, is another), while naturalism is one form of descriptivism (or cognitivism). Moore held that at least some moral judgments (or more strictly, in his case, some value judgments) expressed special *sui generis* facts about goodness; he was a descriptivist but not a naturalist.

Anyway, ought we to accept some form of non-cognitivism? So far we have seen two reasons for doing so. First, moral facts seem rather elusive things, too insubstantial to take their place along with the 'hard' facts of science or the world around us. Second, there are difficulties, at least, about how we could know such facts. Perhaps the first of these reasons itself seems rather elusive; but in a way it is more fundamental than the second. After all, if moral facts do exist, then they do; and if we cannot know them, or can only guess at them, that is just too bad. Some theologians, after all, have held the doctrine of Total Depravity, where only God can know moral facts, and men are not only incorrigible sinners but invincibly ignorant of values and duties as well.

The first reason is not an easy one to assess; but before looking further at it, how about the case against non-cognitivism? Actually we have come across part of this already. What the non-cognitivist says is that in passing a moral judgment we are not stating anything, but doing something else, such as commending something, or expressing disapproval of it. When we discussed the difficulties negative statements raise for the correspondence theory of truth (pp. 31–2) we considered the possibility of treating asserting and denying as two activities co-ordinate to each other, and noted an objection raised by Frege, that negative sentences often occurred when no denial was going on, as in the antecedent of a conditional statement. Now doesn't exactly the same thing happen with moral judgments? Don't we constantly say things like 'If he does anything wrong his conscience will find him out', or 'Many people doubt whether abortion really is wrong'? In neither case are we doing any condemning, or anything like that at all.

Perhaps we can get over some cases. The second example might be analysed as: 'Many people are in doubt about (cannot make up their minds) whether to condemn abortion.' But this still leaves the first example. The trouble here is that the only thing that can follow an 'if' seems to be a proposition; i.e., something that can be asserted or not asserted. There does not seem to be anything which, in the same sense, can be condemned or not condemned. It is true that there are cases where the expression of an attitude does seem to be governed by an 'if' in this way. To borrow an example discussed by Bernard Williams, we can say, 'If he's broken his blasted tricycle again, ...' where the exasperation is, as it were, held in reserve, to apply only if he *has* broken it. But this will not really get us very far. The bag that holds our exasperation in is rather thin; the exasperation is already peeping out. The mere idea that he might have broken the thing is enough for us. A slightly different case is that of the condemnation implied in a word like 'nigger'. To call someone a nigger is to call him a negro and condemn him for being one. Now suppose I say, 'If he's a nigger he certainly shan't marry my daughter.' Since I don't yet know that he *is* a nigger, I haven't yet condemned him. But any condemning that is hovering around is already being done; I am expressing my hostile attitude to negroes in general, an attitude I already hold. Incidentally, what about my own use of 'nigger' in the sentence just above beginning 'Since ...'? Could I not have made the point equally well by using 'negro' there, and if so, why didn't I? Yes, I could, but I hope I shall not be called prejudiced because I didn't! I wrote 'nigger' because I was playing along with the terminology I was discussing. This, I hope, illustrates some of the complexity surrounding the study of emotive or evaluative language.

Yet it does seem that the use of a word like 'wrong' necessarily involves some reference to condemnation. How could we call something wrong without condemning it, at least in one respect? And if 'wrong' is *necessarily* linked to condemnation ought not this feature to appear even when we use it after 'if'? Normally when we call something wrong we do so by reference to a standard. Abortion, for instance, might be said to violate the standard of not taking innocent life. Perhaps then our original example, 'If he does anything wrong, ...', means 'If he does anything which those applying the relevant standards would condemn, ...'. This has the advantage of getting in a reference to condemning without making us say we are actually doing some condemning whenever we apply the predicate 'wrong' to something, even after an 'if'. It also abandons non-cognitivism, for whether those who apply the relevant standards would condemn something is presumably a matter of psychological fact, or else logic (if ' would condemn' means 'would be committed to condemning'), and can be true or false. Clearly there are difficulties here. How do we decide which are 'relevant' standards, and what is involved in being a standard anyway? But let us go back to the difficulty we noted about the elusiveness of moral facts, for we now seem to be landed with them again.

It is often said that non-cognitivism cannot account for moral disputes. We *disagree* over whether, say, abortion is wrong; and though non-cognitivism does not make 'Abortion is wrong' an autobiographical statement *about* the speaker's attitudes, as one form of naturalistic subjectivism does, it still leaves it as a mere expression of the speaker's attitude, and so as unacceptably subjective. The non-cognitivist can reply to this in two stages. First he can say that a great deal of our disagreement really, though perhaps not obviously, concerns matters of non-moral fact. We disagree perhaps over the effects of abortion on the mother, or on whether a foetus is conscious. Second, he can say not only that commands and prescriptions can conflict with each other but also that there is such a thing as disagreement in attitude, and that this may be quite fundamental, and not the sort of triviality his opponents often pretend, as when I like rice pudding and you hate the stuff. The first stage, he may admit, is rather thin by itself; much moral disagreement no doubt does resolve eventually into disagreement about non-moral facts, but it is far from obvious that it all does. But with the second stage he may go over to the offensive. Consider a Conservative and a Socialist, he will say. The Conservative makes it a fundamental pillar of his philosophy that liberty is better than equality or security, where they clash. The Socialist holds exactly the opposite. (We are not concerned, of course, with the accuracy or adequacy of this.) But do we seriously want to say, the non-cognitivist asks, that of the two statements 'Liberty is better than equality and security' and 'Equality and security are better than liberty' one is true and the other is false, regardless of who may hold or reject them, that there is a neutral, dispassionate and objective answer laid up in heaven? The true/false dichotomy is the wrong measure for this kind of case. Rather we have two fundamental, but clashing, ideologies. And if 'true' and 'false' do not apply here, why should they apply any more in cases where we are all on the same side, as we presumably are in the third of the examples at the beginning of this chapter?

By now it may have occurred to the reader to ask whether the predicament facing the Conservative and Socialist does not apply just as pressingly to the cognitivist and non-cognitivist themselves. (If this has occurred to him, without benefit of a philosophical training, he has the makings of a good philosopher.) Is there really a true answer to the issue between them, or are they too engaged in an ideological conflict? One thing this question suggests is that the problem we are facing applies far more widely than to the narrow field of morality to which we have almost confined ourselves so far – 'almost', because the political example already begins to go beyond it. But let us spend just a few more minutes with the issue as we have conceived it so far.

Really there seem to be two questions underlying our discussion. First, do moral questions admit of unique unambiguously correct answers? And second, can we justify rationally a stance we adopt on a moral question? It is the difficulty in saying Yes to the first question that makes us hesitate, if we do, to say that 'true' and 'false' have a proper place in morals. A realist, in the sense we discussed at the end of the last chapter, will say that a correct answer to a moral question could exist, even if we could never discover it, even in principle. But his opponent may reply that if the alleged answer is in principle inaccessible to us, then not only can we, naturally, not say what it is, but it will be purely arbitrary and without content to insist that an answer does exist. The case in morals is even worse for the realist than the cases we considered earlier, he will insist. For suppose we have no way, even in principle, of discovering for ourselves that the universe contains no purple cows. We might be persuaded to concede to the realist that we know what it would be like for there to be none. If God revealed to us that there were none we could *understand* this revelation. But could we understand the analogous revelation in morals? Could we understand what was being revealed? The point is this. We know what existence is from other cases. And we know what a cow is and what purple is. But if we know what existence is we must also know what non-existence is. We do know it, because we know that there does not exist, say, a purple cow in our back garden. But we also *must* know it, because we could not know what it is for a concept to apply to a thing without also knowing what it is for it not to apply. We could not recognise anything as being a cow unless we could recognise at least some things as not being cows. So we have the equipment for knowing what it is for there to exist no purple cows. But this kind of argument will not work in the moral case. We have been given no grounds for saying we have the equipment for knowing what it is for something to be, or not to be, wrong.

So much then for what the non-cognitivist will say, basing himself on an anti-realist position. The cognitivist might be tempted to reply as follows: 'Your case in effect amounts to saying we do not understand words like "wrong". But plainly we do. You are just flying in the face of common sense.' But his opponent has an easy answer to this: 'No, I am simply saying we don't understand "wrong" as a predicate or descriptive word. Gramatically it certainly behaves like one. But my case is that grammar is misleading, and really we understand it in some other way, e.g., as expressing condemnation.'

The cognitivist's real case lies in turning to the second of the two questions we raised two paragraphs ago, and the implausibility of answering No to it. Surely moral judgments can be rationally justified, at least in principle – and this not merely by reaching agreement on the non-moral facts of the situation. Morality is objective. It is this perhaps that we want to insist on, rather than some point about the use of the word 'true'. For sometimes perhaps 'true' *can* be used to express mere agreement in attitude: 'She's a wow, isn't she?' 'That's true!' It hardly seems necessary to regard her wowity as an objective timeless truth laid up in heaven and contemplated by God.

The real issue seems to be emerging as this: It seems implausible to say anything but Yes to the second question. But must we then say Yes to the first? If we insist that moral positions can be rationally justified, must we agree that moral questions can have unique and unambiguously correct answers? There seem to be two lines of thought that make us unwilling to say they can. One is that it is not clear that to say this is ultimately intelligible. This is the line we have mainly been discussing. The other is that even if to say that moral questions have such answers is intelligible, it seems to run up against the facts of moral relativism. The Eskimoes abandon their parents in the snow; the British don't. The medieval Church condemned usury; modern capitalism is founded on it, with the Church's blessing. What is the significance of these and a host of similar facts? Do they reflect fundamental differences in moral outlook? Or is this an illusion, which arises because we have too superficial a conception of what the contrasting positions really amount to? Is there real moral change, and if so, is it random in direction or does it represent a progressive enlightenment – or indeed a progressive decline?

There are two questions then which now invite us to explore them. How much must we give to the relativist? And how can moral judgments be rationally justified? I must leave the reader to explore them on his own. I shall end this chapter with some general considerations aimed mainly at broadening the field we are looking at, though I will return briefly to the second question right at the end. A short while ago I said we were confining ourselves too narrowly in looking only at moral judgments, interesting and important though these are. Actually there is a problem about deciding how moral judgments differ from judgments of aesthetics, prudence, etiquette, technical efficiency, political and social philosophy, and value judgments in general. In fact our discussion so far has been narrowly conceived on two scores. First, most of the words we have considered (words like 'good', 'bad', 'right', 'wrong', 'ought') apply just as readily outside morality as inside it. Cars, cricketers and cabarets can be 'good', as well as saints and self-sacrifice. One can give 'right' answers to 'wrong' questions, and some may think this book 'ought' never to have been written. In fact very few terms are confined to morals, apart from 'moral' and 'immoral' themselves. Even 'wicked' is not a moral term when applied to spin-bowlers or dust-storms. Second, though words like 'good', 'wrong' and 'ought' are central terms of evaluation, and in some sense *the* central terms, they are only a tiny selection, and in some ways are untypical. This is just because they are so general, and therefore rather colourless. Most of our value judgments, both in morals and out of it, are far richer and more specific. A man is 'heroic' or 'uncouth', a dress 'divine'. An argument may be 'novel' or 'unheard of', and we should be 'well advised' to treat it with 'caution'. Compare how rarely we use 'beautiful' in a real-life judgment of a picture.

It is tempting for the philosopher to limit himself to the central terms. Surely with them we can isolate what is really important about value judgments, without irrelevant complexities. There is some truth in this, and I took advantage of it myself when introducing the problems in the early part of this chapter. But it is easy to push it too far. It assumes the complexities *are* irrelevant, which is only sometimes true. It tempts us to exaggerate how sharp the distinction is between 'ordinary' facts and values, whether moral or otherwise. It helps the non-cognitivist, because if we purge our descriptive words of all value elements and keep our value words free of all descriptive elements, then surely we can apply any value word to anything we like. Give a dog a bad name and hang it; but give it a neutral name and we are free to hang it or give it a bone, as we please. To adapt the old rhyme:

> Treason hath never approval. What's the reason?
> Well, those who approve it will hardly call it treason!

Often a neutral term is easy to find. We call our black friends negroes and not niggers, if we want to keep them. But what do we call the treason we approve of? Is there a simple value-free synonym for 'treason'? Suppose nearly everyone hated black men, including even black men themselves, if they had been conned into feeling ashamed of their colour. Then if I want to secure approval for my black friend, my best policy will be to say he is not really black; just dark brown, perhaps, if you look closely. As things are this move is not needed in most milieus. But if I want to introduce my treasonable friend to polite society, what shall I say? 'No, he didn't give away his country's secrets, only those of its ruling class,' or 'Treason, you know, is not just giving away one's country's secrets, it's doing so for financial gain.' In either case what I am striving to do is to show that the purely descriptive content of 'treasonable', if there is such, does not apply to my friend. But, in present society, I feel no need to insist that my foreign friend is not really black. 'Probably everyone disapproves of treason; but it's perfectly *possible* to approve of it.' So says the non-cognitivist. Perhaps he is right. But I have been arguing that the matter is not all that simple. It is not so obvious what the 'it' is.

We can hate or not hate a man for being black. Can we approve of a man *because* (not although) he acted in a way in which he (not we) thought he ought not to act, and did so purely to gain pleasure? Here it seems fairly clear what the 'it' is we are being asked to approve of. But if we cannot approve of it, is this a mere psychological fact? Or is there something incoherent in the idea of approving of this? Can a man *like* pain, or feeling sick, or terrified? The fact of masochism suggests Yes. But we are approaching the edge of intelligibility. At least we feel impelled to ask what it is masochists really like about them, while it scarcely makes sense to ask what it is that most of us dislike about them.

The fact/value distinction, as it has come to be known, is more problematic then than we might have thought. This conclusion is reinforced if we consider the general notion of assessment. When we assess someone's motives we might be deciding how good or bad they are. But we might equally be deciding *what* they are, and, as I have suggested, it may not be easy to separate these two. And we often need to assess things even when applying ordinary predicates. 'My garden is large.' Is it? How large? Larger than gardens in general? Than my neighbours' gardens? Than the gardens of philosophers? Larger than can easily be kept in order? We have to decide what standard to apply. 'The sky today is blue – well, bluish anyway; there's all that tufty cumulus, of course, and it's very hazy round the horizon.' 'France has the shape of a regular hexagon.' True or false? 'Wellington won at Waterloo.' Not in the German history books, he didn't.

It is not only in morals then, or even in what we are ordinarily inclined to call value judgments, that unique and unambiguous applications of 'true' and 'false' are hard to come by. This is not to say there are no differences between assessments of this kind and those of value judgments as normally understood, or those involving words like 'right', 'wrong' or 'ought'. (Strictly these are not value judgments, but the problems they raise have much in common with those of value judgments proper, and so it is convenient to include them there. Hence the title of this chapter.) What we have done is erode the sharpness of the distinction, not abolish it. There are central cases of things being blue or hexagonal — gentians and certain geometrical figures, for instance — and they differ from central cases of the other kind, like 'Inflicting pain for fun is wrong' or 'Handel is greater than Humperdinck'. There are, for instance, the sort of difficulties we saw about the possibility of revelation.

I have tried to show that the fact/value distinction, though not exactly illusory, is more complex than its name would suggest. It is not the case that assessment and psychological attitudes lie all on one side, and truth, falsity and objectivity all on the other, with a sharp division down the middle. Nor is there necessarily just one division to be drawn through this whole area. The bracket in the last paragraph hinted at some of the complexity on the value side, for instance, and we noted the difference between calling gentians blue and calling the sky blue on a certain type of fine day. Another distinction, which I have not discussed, is between what have been called 'brute' facts and facts involving a reference to institutions or rules, like 'Fred scored a goal'.

Let us leave the fact/value distinction along a path it has created through the tropic of justifying value judgments. Some writers have held that one way of justifying a value judgment is to derive it logically from ordinary factual premises. A famous example of this is J. R. Searle's claim that if one has made a promise it can be shown as a matter of logic that, special circumstances apart, one ought to keep it. Here it is claimed that a factual premise (that one has made a promise) logically entails an evaluative conclusion (that one ought to keep it). This example is complicated because the premise is of the 'instititional' sort (promising is an institution), but Searle claims that we can start further back with the 'brute' fact that one uttered certain words, like 'I promise to do so-and-so'. Given certain presuppositions, for example, that one is not acting in a play, this fact itself entails that one has promised, Searle claims, and so entails that one ought to do the so-and-so. This kind of case, where it is claimed that a premise or premises purely about what is the case can entail a conclusion about what ought to be the case, has given rise to what is called the is/ought question, which is usually traced back to a famous paragraph in Hume. To put it snappily, can an 'is' entail an 'ought'? Or more generally, can factual premises entail an evaluative conclusion? The 'ought', incidentally, need not be a moral 'ought'.

People who emphasise the fact/value distinction say that such an entailment can never be valid, because the conclusion contains something (a value, to speak roughly) which is quite different from anything in the premises, and an argument can only be logically valid if the conclusion contains no more than the premises do. Pure logic cannot help us to get from one kind of statement to a fundamentally different kind, and only some logical sleight-of-hand can make us think it can. In fact such an argument commits one form of the 'naturalistic fallacy', they claim, a notion I mentioned before and said I would briefly return to. Actually, many who support the sort of thing I have been saying about the fact/value distinction would join its supporters in rejecting this particular use of logic. Searle's position represents rather an extreme form of opposition to the fact/value distinction.

I am not going to discuss this particular argument any further, but one thing can be said about it. It relies on the logical notion of entailment, so let us examine this notion, and how it relates to other notions in the general field of implication to which it belongs.

4 Implication

In the most general sense, one thing implies another when it somehow
enfolds the other within itself. But there are many different kinds of
implication. We have already looked briefly at two of them, when we
discussed the relations between entailment and presupposition towards
the end of Chapter 2. But let us now consider at least some of them a bit
more systematically.

We must start, because of its importance, with a notion that will
probably strike the lay reader as rather odd. It is called material
implication, though it is hardly a kind of implication at all except in
name. There are two symbols in common use for it, ' $\supset$ ' and ' $\rightarrow$ '. The
hook or horse-shoe (' $\supset$ '), introduced by Russell, is specific to material
implication, so I will use it. The arrow is a general symbol for several
different kinds of implication; the context normally shows which kind is
intended. One proposition materially implies another, or in symbols,
$p \supset q$, iff (if and only if) it is not the case that p is true and q is false. We
are assuming that an ordinary two-valued logic is being used (see
Chapter 2) and that p and q both have truth-values. The point is that we
are concerned only with the relation between propositions in virtue of
their truth values. Given that p is true (or false) we are not interested in
whether what it says has any relevance to what q says. The propositions
p and q may be related in four ways in respect of their truth values: both
true; p true, q false; p false, q true; both false. '$p \supset q$' says simply that the
second of these does not hold; it leaves open which of the other three
does.

Two consequences in particular follow from this definition. A false
proposition materially implies any proposition, and any proposition
materially implies a true proposition; for if p is false, or if q is true, then
whatever the other one is it cannot be the case that p is true and q false.
'The pope is a woman' materially implies 'Snow is white' – or 'Snow is
black', for that matter. These consequences are often called the
paradoxes of material implication. But they are only paradoxical in so far
as material implication is taken to be a genuine kind of implication, with

the suggestion of some connection, logical, causal or other, between what it relates. We have not got a paradox in the meaty sense of the Liar paradox which we met in Chapter 2. Incidentally, this notion is called material implication by contrast with formal implication, a notion used by Russell, but little referred to now, so we will leave it aside.

But there is a real connection between material implication and ordinary implication, because if p implies q in the ordinary sense, then p materially implies q. The same thing holds when we compare material implication with the if/then relation. Whenever 'If p then q' holds, 'p ⊃ q' must hold; for 'If p then q' could not possibly be true if p were true and q false, i.e. if 'p ⊃ q' were false. Material implication gives the bare minimum that must hold when apparently stronger relations hold like ordinary implication or the if/then relation.

What is controversial, however, is whether these apparently stronger relations are really stronger, or if so, in what sense. Let us start with the if/then relation. In Chapter 2 (p. 44) we considered the sentence 'If Antarctica is warm, London is French'. We saw that, though it perhaps seemed most natural to say it had no truth-value, some people preferred to call it (vacuously) true, to express the fact that whatever else it is it is not false. They feel that at least it is harmless to call it true. Whichever view we take, incidentally, we should take account of conditional questions and commands, etc. ('If it rains, what shall I do?', 'If it rains, take a bus.') These I must leave to the reader. One important feature of conditionals might be thought to be this: their *point* is not primarily to inform us about the world, but to enable us to find out about it for ourselves, by inferring that the consequent is true when we find that the antecedent is. But they can do this if we regard them as true or false just when the corresponding material implication is true or false. This is because the conditional will then never lead us astray. If we regard its antecedent as false, we shall never be in a position to use it to infer the truth of the consequent. If we regard it as true, we shall need some further justification for asserting the conditional anyway. Similarly we shall not be led astray by a conditional whose consequent is true.

There is then at least some reason to say that 'If p then q' and 'p ⊃ q' have the same truth conditions, i.e., that 'If p then q' is true in just those conditions in which 'p ⊃ q' is. 'If Antarctica is warm, London is French', or, to give an example where the antecedent is true, 'If snow is white, grass is green', sounds odd. But let us remember the example we discussed in the last chapter: 'He's a nigger'. This seems to say the same as 'He's a negro', but in a polite society there is something wrong with it, and we hesitate at first to call it true. But the trouble is not that it is false, or fails to be true (when said of a negro), but that it reveals, and not only reveals but gives expression to, an attitude on the speaker's part. Perhaps then what is wrong with our 'if/then' sentences, which resemble true material implication sentences, is not that they fail to be true. It is rather that they carry a suggestion that the antecedent is somehow relevant to the consequent. The reason they carry this would presumably be that only when there is such a connection is there any point in our asserting the conditional. At least this is normally so. There are a few cases, which Strawson draws attention to for purposes of his own, where no such connection holds, such as, 'If that's so, then I'm a Dutchman'. The point of this utterance is to take an obviously false consequent and then rely on the fact that the conditional will only be true if either its consequent is true or its antecedent is false; since the consequent is not true, the antecedent must be false. These cases are exceptional, and Strawson thinks they have their rhetorical force just because we see they are exceptional. To spell it out: normally we first know the conditional is true and then use this knowledge to find that the consequent must be true (because the antecedent is true), or that the antecedent must be false (because the consequent is false). But in the Dutchman case we only pretend to argue like that; really we only say the conditional is true at all because we already know the antecedent is false.

Strawson's point is this: it is only in cases like the Dutchman example that if/then sentences work like material implication sentences; but the Dutchman example only works because we realise it is exceptional; so normally if/then sentences do not work like material implication sentences.

This is fair enough so far. It suggests there must be some difference between if/then sentences and material implication sentences. But it does not show that they must have different truth conditions, and so does not show that the if/then relation is a different relation from material implication. What distinguishes them may be the use to which we put conditionals, and the point of uttering them. And this may in turn be that they carry a suggestion, not, as with 'nigger', of an attitude, but a different kind of suggestion: namely, of a connection between their parts. This would be suggested, not stated, and so would not affect the truth conditions of what was said.

Possibly one more example might be useful. 'If there are only ten of them, then they can't be an eights crew.' This sounds odd. 'Only' is clearly out of place. But is it false, or even not true? On the line we have been pursuing it will be true, since without 'only' it would be uncontroversially true. What does 'only' mean? Roughly, 'not more than'. Roughly, but not exactly. 'Not more than ten', unlike 'only ten', is compatible with 'less than ten'. Adding 'only' in our example doesn't tell us there are not more than ten, since we know this without 'only'. 'Only', I suggest, does not give us any more information, but invites us to make one contrast rather than another, to contrast there being ten with there being more than ten, not with there being less than ten. But the ensuing 'then' clause shows that this invitation is inapposite.

We might notice that the 'suggesting' we have been talking about is itself one kind – or perhaps several kinds – of implication. I say 'several kinds' because what is suggested may be that something is the case (that the antecedent is relevant to the consequent of the conditional), or that one should do something (make one contrast rather than another), or an attitude (prejudice against negroes). These differences are perhaps not very important. What is more important is that even when what is implied is that something is the case, they do not themselves involve material implication as a minimum content. The sentence stating the implication can still be true, even if what is implied is false. 'If Antarctica is warm, London is French' implies a connection between its parts, but on this view may be still true even if that connection does not exist. The implication is in this sense of a weak kind. A notion rather like this has been called 'contextual implication'. Here the implying is done by the speaker rather than by what he says. I. Hungerland says of it in *Inquiry* (1960, p. 255): 'a speaker in making a statement contextually implies whatever one is entitled to infer on the basis of the presumption that his act of stating is normal' (i.e., he is not acting in a play, etc.). A similar notion has been called (by H. P. Grice) 'conversational implicature'. Again it is the speaker, or perhaps the act of uttering – but not what is uttered – that does the implying. Perhaps this is why Grice uses 'implicature' for 'implication'. But this time we are concerned with certain conversational maxims governing what is normally implied by speakers generally rather than with what is implied on a specific occasion.

We can single out two such maxims in particular, that normally one has reasons for what one asserts, and that one's assertions are not arbitrarily weaker than they might be. Of course we often deliberately withhold information, or only hint, but the point is that *normally* if I tell you something I don't say less than I think is true and relevant. The way this affects 'If p then q' is as follows. Suppose I say 'If p then q', but know of no connection between p and q. Then if I am to satisfy the condition of having a reason for what I say, I must presumably think either that p is false or that q is true. But all I have told you, in saying 'If p then q', is that either p is false or q is true; I have not told you which. But since I think I know which, I have not told you as much as I might; it would after all have been easy enough for me to say just 'p is false' or 'q is true', as the case may be. So if you assume the situation is normal, and that I *am* telling you as much as I can, you can assume, when I say 'If p then q', that I do have in mind some connection between p and q, and so that probably there is some connection. But since you can assume it like this, there is no reason to make the connection part of *what* I am saying. 'If p then q' can be safely allowed to *mean* no more than 'p ⊃ q'.

Before going on, three words of caution. What a sentence means is not always the same as what is said by it. The reader knows perfectly well what 'I am hot' means, but he cannot know what is said by it until he knows who said it and when. Words like pronouns and tensed verbs, which render a sentence variable in this way, are called 'token-reflexives'. I am assuming that 'If p then q' does not contain any token-reflexives, or not in relevant positions, and so I shall ignore any differences between meaning and what is said. The second caution is that a distinction may be needed here which I have not mentioned. R. C. S. Walker, for instance, thinks it absurd to say the truth-value of 'If p then q' depends on the truth-values of its parts in the way I have been suggesting. He thinks the Gricean would, or should, say that its meaning (Walker uses Frege's term 'sense') does indeed depend on the truth-values of its parts, but that its truth-value depends on its implicatures as well. He thinks it absurd to call 'If I stop writing now the Queen will abdicate' true merely because I shan't stop. As a description of what common sense would say this is fair enough. One might reply, however, that common sense need not have the last word on these matters, and that the example rather suggests the stronger type of conditional, like 'If Antarctica were (not: is) warm ...'. His point seems to apply more cogently to 'If I were to stop writing now the Queen would abdicate'. We shall return to this stronger type later. Walker's article as a whole is a tentative defence of a Gricean approach. Third, I am ignoring certain complications and qualifications, in particular concerning a notion Grice calls 'non-detachability'.

So far I have taken the line that 'If p then q' means no more than 'p ⊃ q', and that the apparent differences between them can be accounted for in other ways, along Grice's lines. But this might be objected to. Suppose the following were the case: I am born blind, but in childhood learned many facts about colours: snow is white, grass is green, etc. Unfortunately I have forgotten most of these, but I do remember that 'If snow is white, grass is green' was true. Perhaps I used it in childhood games. I therefore say this now to you, who are also blind. Here I have a reason for what I say (that I remember it), and say as much as I can, but you cannot assume I have in mind any connection between the colour of snow and of grass.

We might try replying that this is an exceptional kind of case, and that it is enough that normally our reasons for asserting if/then sentences are that we have in mind a connection between their parts. This is enough, perhaps, to account for why we feel that 'if/then' goes beyond '⊃' in the way we do. Note that this appeal to normality is different from our previous one. There we said that normally people have reasons for what they say. Here we are saying that the reason people have, in certain cases, is normally of a certain kind.

But now take this example. You are preparing a sherry party and I say, 'Jim either hates chips or likes cheese – I forget which; so if he likes chips he likes cheese'. Again I have a reason for what I say (what he told me) and say as much as I can. But I am not suggesting any link between a taste for chips and a taste for cheese. What I have done, presumably, is give you information which, if you find that he likes chips, will let you infer that he likes cheese, which you couldn't infer from his liking chips, by itself. There is no Gricean implicature here. Now suppose he in fact hates chips, whatever he may feel about cheese. Is the second part of what I said true? Yes, if 'if/then' has the same truth conditions as '⊃', for it is true that 'He likes chips' materially implies 'He likes cheese' (since 'He likes chips' is false). And even if we feel some tendency to call it neither true nor false in this case, calling it true seems harmless. But what about the absence of the implicature? If the Gricean still wants to say that the implicature is present in 'normal' cases he will have to allow the abnormal ones to cover a very large range. Perhaps he might talk of primary and derivative cases, rather than normal and abnormal ones, and include among the derivative those like the present example where the 'if/then' sentence is embedded in a wider context. Certainly if someone just said out of the blue, 'If Jim likes chips he likes cheese', we should be much more likely to assume that the speaker saw a link between these likings.

A second objection is raised by Strawson and involves 'so'. 'Snow is white, so grass is green'. Is that true? The conjunction 'Snow is white and grass is green' is certainly true. Is this enough to make 'Snow is white, so grass is green' true, in the same way I have suggested that the truth of '$p \supset q$' is enough to make 'If p then q' true? This seems harder to swallow. In fact, with 'so' we seem to have not a statement at all, but an argument which involves two statements, both of which are asserted. Arguments cannot strictly be true or false; they are rather sound or unsound, or valid or invalid. 'Valid' raises certain other problems, so let us stick to 'sound', and call an argument sound if and only if its premises and conclusion are all true and the conclusion is in some sense a consequence of its premises. 'Snow is white, so grass is green' is then presumably an unsound argument, if the colours of snow and grass are irrelevant to each other, as I assume. 'So' seems to add to the meaning of the sentence, since it raises the question, if not of the truth, at any rate of the soundness, of what is said. In 'p, so q' both p and q are asserted. We cannot say 'p, so q' and deny p or deny q. Strawson's point is that there ought to be some conjunction that links p and q in the same way that 'so' does, but leaves p and q unasserted. And he suggests that 'if/then' plays just this role. On this view 'so' presents an argument as sound – which incidentally is not the same as saying that it is sound; 'if/then' presents an argument as one that is sound provided its premises are true, which is left open. So 'if/then' contributes to the meaning of the whole sentence, just as 'so' does, and the Gricean account will not fit. Furthermore, if 'so' does not introduce a statement, i.e. something with a truth-value, then on Strawson's view the same should hold of 'if/then'.

The Gricean might perhaps answer this by saying that what Strawson is looking for does exist, but is supplied not by 'if/then' alone but by a more complex device, namely the use of 'if/then' with the subjunctive or with a word like 'must' or 'cannot'. 'Snow is yellow, so grass is blue': this is wrong, not just because of the 'so', but because its component parts are false. Should we take account of this by substituting 'If snow is yellow, grass is blue'? This is what Strawson suggests. But we have another device, which will express the connection more strongly. We can say, 'If snow were yellow, grass would be blue', or, if we want to leave open what colour snow is, 'If snow is yellow, grass must be blue'; though I should add that the indicative followed by 'must be' does not only have this use. At any rate these stronger sentences, whether or not they represent statements, have got to be accounted for somehow, and they suggest that our account in terms of suggestion, implicature, etc. won't cover all cases, even if it does cover the ordinary if/then with the indicative, as I am tentatively assuming it does; but the reader should be warned that this is very controversial.

Russell once argued that material implication was the only relation between propositions that was needed for logic. He thought this for the reason we saw earlier, that however paradoxical it might sound to say that p implies q whenever p is false or q is true, we could only use the relation to make an inference when we believed p was true, and if the relation held and p *was* true, q would also be true, and so we should not be led astray. To put it otherwise, to infer q from p we must believe that p implies q and that p is true. The paradoxes are harmless, because if our belief that p implies q comes from our believing that p is false, we cannot use it as a principle of inference, while if it comes from believing that q is true, we do not need to use it, since we already believe that q. The only time we can use our belief that p implies q to infer q from p is when we believe that p implies q in a way that does not depend on knowing whether p and q themselves are true, and this is as it should be.

Maybe it is. But if we lack any belief about the truth-values of p and q themselves, how can we believe that p materially implies q, if not by believing that some stronger relation holds between them? We might, admittedly, just accept it on the authority of someone who told us so. But again if we are to use it we must come to believe also that p is true, so how, we must ask, did the authority know that p materially implies q? Not by knowing that p is false, since (we believe) it is not. So, if the stronger relation is not to creep in again as being what the authority knew, we must regard the authority as knowing that q is true. But in that case we are relying after all, for our inference, on knowledge that q is true, even if not *our* knowledge. The point really concerns how we justify our inference of q. To justify our belief that p materially implies q we must assume that our authority either knows that a stronger relation holds between p and q, or knows that q. But in the latter case we are really inferring q from p because our authority knows that q, and not because p materially implies q at all. We have used a premise that our authority said that p materially implies q, but not a premise that p does materially imply q.

It looks then as if we need at least one relation of implication that is stronger than material implication, one that corresponds to a phrase like 'logically implies'. We had better leave aside the question whether any further relations are needed, such as one corresponding to 'causally' or 'scientifically implies'.

Such a relation was introduced into logic early in this century by the American logician C. I. Lewis (1883–1964). He called it strict implication, and defined it like this: p strictly implies q iff it is logically impossible that p be true and q false. He symbolised it by the fish-hook or anchor, '–3', which is now its standard symbol.

Clearly this is a stronger relation than material implication, but in a significant way they are parallel. For the above definition is exactly the same as that for material implication except that 'logically impossible' appears in the main clause here where the definition of material implication has 'false' (or 'not the case'). The effect of this is that strict implication has its own pair of 'paradoxes', parallel to those of material implication. These are that a logically impossible proposition strictly implies any proposition, and any proposition strictly implies a logically necessary proposition. For if p is itself logically impossible, or inconsistent, then plainly it is logically impossible that p be true and q false – it doesn't matter what q is. The same holds if q is itself a logically necessary proposition, or a tautology, in which case it won't matter what p is. The point is this. With both strict and material implication we find that 'p implies q' can hold in virtue of something about p by itself, or something about q by itself, without there being any relevant connection between p and q.

This has led to a dispute about whether Lewis has found what at this point we are really looking for: namely, that relation which holds between two propositions when, in informal language, one logically implies the other, or the second can be deduced from the first as a matter of logic. G. E. Moore gave the name 'entailment' to this relation. He says p entails q if and only if q follows from or is deducible from p.

Words like 'entail' and 'deduce', when used by philosophers in this century, always refer to logical relations or processes, and not to the looser ones for which they are often used in ordinary life. 'From the footprints on the flower bed I deduce that the murderer entered from the garden,' says the detective. 'A life devoted to drink entails misery for all concerned,' proclaims the preacher. But they do not mean, as a logician would, that there is a logical inconsistency in the idea that there could be those footprints in the flower bed while the murderer entered from the street, or in the idea that a life of inebriation should produce continuous happiness until one slipped peacefully under the table for the last time at the age of ninety. As far as logic is concerned those footprints could have been made by a freak pattern of raindrops, or indeed could have appeared spontaneously from nowhere. (It is controversial how such terms should be interpreted when they appear in philosophers of earlier centuries.)

The issue, then, is whether Lewis has captured, with his technical notion of strict implication, the relation we intuitively feel should link two propositions when one entails, or logically implies, the other. The dispute is about the nature of entailment. Everyone agrees in using 'strictly implies' in accordance with Lewis's definition; and everyone agrees that if p entails q, then p strictly implies q. But if p strictly implies q, does it follow that p entails q? Or must there be some further connection between p and q to exclude the paradoxes? For it sounds odd, at least initially, to say that 'The Pope is both a woman and not a woman' entails 'The moon is made of green cheese', or that the latter is deducible from, or follows logically from, the former; and similarly it sounds odd to say that 'The moon is made of green cheese' entails 'The Pope is either a woman or not a woman'.

Clearly there is an analogy between this dispute about entailment, arising out of the strict implication paradoxes, and the dispute we discussed earlier about the if/then relation, arising out of the material implication paradoxes. In each case the technically defined relations, material and strict implication, seem to some too thin and artificial to form the substance of the if/then relation and entailment respectively. They seem to ignore unduly the content or meaning of the propositions they link and the relevance of one to the other. And in each case one side says a different and stronger relation must be substituted, while the other says the relation itself is simply that of material or strict implication, respectively, and the extra factor lies in some sort of suggestion or conversational implicature.

But the analogy is not complete. Whenever 'p ⊃' is true, either p is false or q is true. But it is not the case that whenever 'p–3q' is true, either p is logically impossible (contradictory) or q is logically necessary (tautological). 'Poppies are scarlet' strictly implies 'Poppies are red', but 'Poppies are scarlet' is not impossible, and 'Poppies are red' is not necessary. In this sense material, but not strict, implication might be said to be exhausted by its paradoxes. We saw above that there seem to be three ways of discovering that 'p ⊃ q' is true. We can find that p is false, or find that q is true, or find that p and q are joined by some stronger relation such as strict implication – for obviously if p strictly implies q, p materially implies q. There are three ways too of discovering that 'p–3q' is true. We may find that p is impossible, or find that q is necessary, or find it in some other way. This third way will be needed when both p and q are contingent, i.e. neither impossible nor necessary. For instance, how can we find that it is impossible for 'Poppies are scarlet' to be true and 'Poppies are red' false? Evidently we must look for some connection between them, in this case a connection of meaning.

Everyone now agrees that some such connection is needed for p to entail q when p and q are both contingent, because in that case only when it is present will p strictly imply q. But those who think that entailment is something beyond strict implication insist that even when p and q are necessary or impossible propositions p only entails q when such a connection between them exists. They would allow that an impossible proposition like 'Twice two is five' might entail 'Twice two is greater than four', but not that it entails just anything.

Lewis, who thought that entailment was the same as strict implication, claimed to prove that any proposition could in fact be deduced from an impossible proposition. Consider these five propositions:

(1) p and not-p
(2) p.
(3) Not-p.

(4) p or q.
(5) q.

(1) is an impossible proposition. Each of (2) and (3) is deducible from (1). (4) is deducible from (2). (5) is deducible from (3) and (4), and so from (1). But q represents any arbitrary proposition, so any such can be deduced from an impossible proposition. By a similar proof Lewis claimed that a necessary proposition could be deduced from any proposition. Those who want to distinguish entailment from strict implication usually devote themselves to blocking these proofs. They also face the task of giving some definition or reasonably precise account of entailment. The issue remains open.

I will end this discussion with four remarks. First, we have met two questions: should one identify the if/then relation with material implication? Should one identify entailment with strict implication? An identifier on one issue may naturally tend to be an identifier on the other; but we have seen that there are enough disanalogies between the issues for this not to be inevitable. Second, the 'identifying' view of entailment often plays a substantial part in philosophical arguments. It is often argued, for instance, that if a certain proposition is impossible, any other proposition can be deduced from it. Third, and connected with the second point, conversational implicatures of the Gricean kind have less of a role with entailment. Perhaps because 'entailment' is more of a term of art than 'if' and 'then', and more likely to be used in technical arguments, 'identifiers' are more likely to use it with a good conscience even in cases where there is no connection of meaning, etc. between the terms it relates; they don't wait for a conversational implicature. Fourth, it seems intuitively that when p entails q, p in some sense already says everything that q says. It can only imply q, in a logical sense, if q does not go beyond it. This itself raises problems, which I cannot discuss. But I will mention one problem in particular. If we do think that value judgments involve some element that goes beyond mere assertion, can we frame a notion of entailment that will apply to value judgments? Could we sketch a relevant sense in which one judgment could say (or do?) everything that another does, when either or both is a value judgment?

From time to time we have noted a distinction, without saying much about it, between 'If Antarctica is warm, London is French' and 'If Antarctica were warm, London would be French'. Conditionals of this second kind, often called counterfactuals, have played an important role in recent philosophy of science, in connection with laws of nature and scientific necessity. We might now go on to say something about that area by having a closer look at them.

5   Laws of nature

A scientist is a person who discovers laws of nature. That is how a layman might begin to define one, though few scientists find it given to them to do anything so glorious. Still, laws of nature do seem in a way to be what science is all about. But what are they? That copper conducts electricity, that unsupported bodies near a massive body move towards it, that temperature varies inversely with pressure, that cats are carnivorous: all these might reasonably be called laws of nature. One thing about them is that they seem to be general. They say something about all copper and all cats, etc. This might be doubted. Maybe in some conditions copper does not conduct electricity, and maybe there is the odd cat somewhere that will not touch meat. But if there are exceptions like this, they cannot just be dismissed as of no account. Perhaps the law is too crudely formulated, and we ought to say all copper in condition C conducts electricity. Or at any rate some special explanation must be given for the deviant case: perhaps the cat had had some nasty experience with meat as a tiny kitten. In that case we could still say that cats *normally* eat meat; it would not be a mere accident that so many of them happen to, as it is presumably an accident that many of them happen to be black.

Actually there is a certain tension between these ways of dealing with the exceptions. The first way represents our feeling that a law of nature ought to be in some sense necessary, and how can a thing be necessary if sometimes it doesn't happen, however good a reason there is for its not happening? But the second way represents our experience that it is very hard to find generalisations that are absolutely always true; we usually find we need what is called a *ceteris paribus* clause: 'other things being equal'. Also when we do succeed in specifying the conditions in which the thing in question always happens we may find that nothing is ever in those conditions. All bodies unacted on by forces move with constant velocity in a straight line, said Newton. But who ever met such a body?

Can this tension be resolved? In a way it looks as if Newton's law has nothing but exceptions, its force being that deviations from constant

70

motion in a straight line call out for explanation, and we have to provide suitable forces to explain them. This is indeed the way the law works in science, but the 'exceptions' to it are not exceptions in the same way that the vegetarian cat is to the law about cats. This animal after all, defective though it may be, is still a cat. But in the Newton case it is not that we have bodies unacted on by forces and failing to move constantly in straight lines. It is rather that, as the law is stated, nothing seems to fall under it.

We could admittedly ensure it had instances, indeed that everything was an instance of it, by formulating it like this: All bodies are either acted on by forces or else move constantly in straight lines. Alternatively, we could replace it by its contrapositive, where the contrapositive of 'All As are Bs' is 'All non-Bs are non-As'. This would give 'All bodies not moving at constant velocity in a straight line are acted on by forces'. But these moves do not get to the real issue. They do not distinguish Newton's law from generalisations like 'All the coins in my pocket are silver', or 'All ruminants are cloven-hoofed'. And also what about the cat case? This does have exceptions, so is it perhaps not really a law at all? Or not one of the same kind?

Let us return to conditionals. If there were another coin in my pocket it would not necessarily be silver, and if there were another species of ruminant it would not necessarily be cloven-hoofed, since being ruminant and being cloved-hoofed only accidentally go together (at least, so I assume). But if there were another moving object around it would obey Newton's law, and if there were (as there is not) a cat on my knee as I write, it would be a meat-eater – though in this last case we ought perhaps to add some qualifier like 'very probably'. The reader may object that we can very easily conceive of an object not obeying Newton's law. Indeed we can. The law is not logically necessary; it is not that nothing would *count* as a violation of it, at least as I have described it so far. But to the extent that we allow the real possibility of a violation of it, to that extent we are not really treating it as a law in the strictest sense; even in the cat case any violations must be both explainable and abnormal.

Laws are often said to 'sustain' counterfactuals, conditionals like our previous example 'If Antarctica were warm, London would be French', which might be sustained if there were a law which implied that the Gallic spirit flourished on warm planets. Certain other statements too might be thought to sustain counterfactuals. 'John always acts like that, so he'd have done the same if he'd been here tonight.' Statements about John's ways of acting are perhaps not very naturally called laws. But the implication of the remark about John is that it is no accident that he acts

71

like that. It is not just that he does, or always has, but he can be expected to go on doing so; it is his nature to do so. Perhaps we ought to distinguish different grades of law statement: top-grade ones like Newton's law, those of lower grade like the one about cats, and those of lower grade still about individuals. But what they have in common is that they are regarded as in some sense necessary rather than accidental even if to some extent they may have exceptions, and this is what their connection with counterfactuals shows.

Necessity is a very puzzling thing. If I let my pen go, it will fall to the ground. And not only will it, but it must. 'Gravity says so.' But what is meant by saying that it must? What, if anything, is added to saying simply that it will? Can we throw any light on this by examining counterfactuals?

First of all, what are counterfactuals? Speaking very roughly, the point of a counterfactual has something to do with the falsity of its antecedent. They are sometimes said to be conditionals which entail or presuppose that their antecedents are false. On these views it follows that, if the antecedent is in fact true, the counterfactual as a whole will be false (on the entailment view) or lack a truth-value (on the presupposition view). But consider the following soliloquy: 'If he had entered by the window he would have left footprints, so let's see if there are any. Yes, there are. So (probably) he did enter by the window.' If the detective concluded from all this that his initial counterfactual was to be rejected as false or lacking a truth-value he would undermine his own argument. The detective might instead have said, 'If he did enter by the window he did leave footprints, ...' But now suppose the murderer did not enter that way. On the view I tentatively suggested in the last chapter, the detective's remark will now be true but vacuously true. On the main alternative views it will either lack a truth-value, or its truth-value will depend on whether there is a connection between entering by the window and leaving footprints. The first of these alternatives, that it lacks a truth-value, we have already discussed, albeit rather inconclusively (pp. 44, 60). The second gives the same truth conditions to 'If he entered by the window he left footprints' and 'If he had entered by the window he would have left footprints', in which case we might wonder why the two forms (let us call them the indicative and subjunctive forms) both exist.

The subjunctive form seems more closely linked than the indicative with a connection between the antecedent and the consequent. It seems plausible to say that the existence of such a connection affects both the meaning and the truth-value of a subjunctive conditional. If so, one would expect it to be harder for a subjunctive conditional to be true than for its corresponding indicative form to be true. One would not expect to find the subjunctive form true and the indicative form false. But let us take an often-used example.

(a) If Oswald did not shoot Kennedy, someone else did.
(b) If Oswald had not shot Kennedy, someone else would have.
(c) If Oswald did not shoot Kennedy, Kennedy wasn't killed.
(d) If Oswald had not shot Kennedy, Kennedy wouldn't have been killed.

W. A. Davis claims that these pairs are related in opposite ways. (a) is true and (b) presumably false, as we might expect. But (c) is false while (d) is presumably true. Shall we accept this? Suppose that Oswald did shoot Kennedy. Then the Gricean will say that (c) is true, and nothing has been said yet to refute him. What is no doubt true is that (c) would not be accepted by anyone who had doubts about who shot Kennedy; but that is beside the point. Now suppose that Oswald did not shoot him. Then (c) is false, since Kennedy was killed. But for the same reason (d) is presumably false also; at any rate it is hardly clear that it is true. It is worth noting, however, that there are some problems about just when an indicative and a subjunctive form do correspond to each other.

Let me clear up a few loose ends before going on. I left undecided a page or two back the question of how a counterfactual involves the falsity of its antecedent. There were objections to saying it entailed or presupposed this. Here I think we might bring in conversational implicatures again. Usually it would be misleading to say 'If snow were white, grass would be green' if one thinks snow *is* white. One should say rather 'If (or since) snow is white, grass must be green', or something like that. As I suggested earlier, this gets in the linkage without the suggestion that the antecedent is false. However, as we saw with the detective example, the implicature is rather a weak one and does not always apply. The wider term 'subjunctive conditional', which I have been using, caters for this fact. In fact 'counterfactual conditional' and 'subjunctive conditional' are often used almost interchangeably. Incidentally, 'since' seems to have as part of its meaning that the clause it introduces is true; but it does not introduce a conditional. One can say, though perhaps a little awkwardly, 'If snow is white (though in fact it is not), ...' but it seems plainly contradictory to say, 'Since snow is white (though in fact it is not), ...'.

One more example of the relations between conditionals: At noon I say, 'If he caught the 11.15 he'll arrive by one; if he didn't, he won't arrive till two.' When he arrives at two, having missed it, I can go on saying 'If he caught the 11.15 he arrived by one', altering the tense, of course, to suit the time of utterance, since 1.00 is now past. On the view I have suggested, this will be true, but vacuously true. To say anything interesting I must substitute the counterfactual, 'If he had caught it he would have arrived by one.'

This example can take us to our next point. We have talked of a link between the antecedent and consequent of a counterfactual. But *what* actually does 'If p were so, q would be so' say? We are now at the heart of a very difficult problem, and I have no very convincing solution to offer. But let us explore a few avenues. I have assumed so far that the link I mentioned is somehow part of the meaning of the counterfactual, and that the counterfactual can be true or false. One approach is to deny this last point, and say that counterfactuals do not state facts but represent instructions or principles, so that 'If p were so, q would be so' means something like, 'From p infer q', or 'From p, to infer q'. This is rather a defeatist policy, though we might have to settle for it eventually. It raises the question why we should obey any such instruction, or what lies behind such a principle. 'If I hadn't jammed on the brakes then, we'd have crashed.' It seems a bit tame to interpret this as saying simply, 'From "I didn't jam on the brake" infer "We crashed", and do so irrespective of the truth-values of those sentences themselves.' Since we assume the first sentence was false, it is hard to see what is the point of such an instruction; we should have no occasion for making the inference.

A second approach makes the counterfactual state a link in some such way as this: 'There is a true proposition which, taken with the antecedent, but not without it, entails the consequent.' Here of course the question is, what true proposition? If we are not careful we shall run into triviality, for q is entailed by 'p ⊃ q' together with p, though not by p alone, and whenever p is false (and the point of a counterfactual is that it normally is false), 'p ⊃ q' is true, and so will serve as the true proposition we are looking for. The difficulties of this approach have been explored particularly by F. L. Will. What the spirit of this approach really wants is a complex proposition describing (in our example) the traffic situation, or in general the initial conditions, and adding in some laws of physics. This seems a reasonably hopeful line, but it deprives us of the chance of using counterfactuals to help us analyse laws of nature, if we have already to include a reference to laws of nature in analysing counterfactuals themselves.

Another form of this second approach makes the counterfactual say that it is rational to infer the consequent from the antecedent. But here we must beware of a regress. For who is to do the inferring? Presumably someone who already believes the antecedent, which the person uttering the counterfactual normally implies that he does not.

Furthermore the person uttering it presumably does not wish to imply that there is someone who does believe it. So the analysis is in danger of coming to this: 'If anyone were to believe the antecedent, he would be justified in inferring the consequent.' But this is simply another counterfactual, or anyway a subjunctive conditional calling for the same sort of analysis.

A third approach appeals to our feeling that counterfactuals ought to say something about the world, not just about rational inferences. They ought to tell us what makes them rational. After all, in the braking example what we escaped was a nasty accident, not some bloodless situation where certain inferences might be made. They do not describe the actual world perhaps, because I did jam the brake on, but they describe a possible world.

The idea of possible worlds effectively starts with Leibniz (1646–1716), who, notoriously, called this world the best of all possible worlds, to the considerable disgust of Voltaire. Possible worlds have come back into fashion recently in connection with necessity, the necessary being that which is 'true in all possible worlds', an idea again stemming from Leibniz. One trouble with possible worlds is that there are so many of them, and this leads to a distinction we need to make among counterfactuals, if they are to be of any use to us. A famous example which illustrates this goes as follows: 'If Bizet and Verdi had been compatriots, Bizet would have been Italian.' But would he? Why shouldn't Verdi have been French? Or both of them have been Russian? All these conclusions represent possible worlds, and there seems to be no reason to choose one rather than another. At first sight this applies to other cases too. Take the braking case. Someone might reply to my remark, 'No, you wouldn't have crashed. You'd have swerved, or the other chap would, or you both would; or you'd have had a blow-out, or there'd have been an earthquake, or your patron saint would have intervened.' Some of the possible worlds here described look more far-fetched than others. But what makes us say this? Once we leave the narrow path of the actual and stray into the lush pastures of the possible, what is to guide our steps and stop us from running riot? Well, one thing that might guide us is the narrow path itself. Even if we are not on it, we might try to stay as near to it as we can. If the antecedent of our counterfactual, being false, represents an object off the path and in the pasture, we might represent the consequent as a track we must follow to reach the antecedent, and then try to choose that track which keeps as near to the path as possible. All this implies that we can arrange possible worlds into an order according as they are more or less remote from the real world. An attempt to treat counterfactuals in this way has been

75

elaborated by D. K. Lewis in his book *Counterfactuals* (1973).

To pursue this a little further, why do we prefer 'If I hadn't jammed on the brake then, we'd have crashed' to '... the car would have stopped spontaneously before we hit'? After all, neither of these things happened. But the second is different from the first. Cars do crash, but they don't stop spontaneously. The second alternative would seem to represent not a possible world at all, so it is not surprising that we prefer the first. Let us compare a third possibility, that of the earthquake. Earthquakes are not impossible, but there were none of the usual accompaniments of earthquakes in the offing on this occasion (let us assume). No pressure build-ups were detectable, or anything like that. So to assume an earthquake would have occurred would involve us in assuming too that a whole lot of other things were different from what they actually were, things apparently quite unrelated to my behaviour with the brake; otherwise we must assume that earthquake would have occurred without its proper causes, which would again take us outside the possible worlds.

How does the Bizet/Verdi case fare in all this? If they had both been Russian they would both have had different nationalities from their real ones, while in the other two possibilities I mentioned only one of them need have been different. This perhaps gives us some reason for rejecting the 'both Russian' alternative in favour of the 'Bizet Italian' and 'Verdi French' ones. But how could we choose between these two? Like Buridan's ass, who starved to death because he was just half-way between two equally tempting bales of straw, we seem quite unable to justify preferring one alternative to the other.

Perhaps then we should distinguish between what we might call spurious counterfactuals of the Bizet/Verdi type and those where we at least have some hope of making a rational choice for what to put in the consequent.

Appeal to possible worlds might help us with counterfactuals. But there are some more difficulties with possible worlds themselves. One is that they have a misleadingly geographical sound about them. One is tempted to picture them as rather like Mars and Venus, only a bit shadowy – perhaps in black and white rather than the rich colours of the real world. But if they are alongside the real world in this way, how can they contain the same objects? We can call this a silly confusion due to a misleading picture, no doubt, but there are still problems. In this world I have fair hair. Are there possible worlds in which I have dark hair? And ones in which I am born in the eighteenth century, or am a world-famous ichthyologist? How far can we go? This problem is known as that of 'trans-world identity'.

Some, such as D. K. Lewis, try to solve this problem by saying that what appear in the other worlds are not me, or this pen, but 'counterparts' of me and the pen. But this seems to go to the opposite extreme. It may be hard to conceive that I, remaining myself, should be an eighteenth century ichthyologist; but it seems equally implausible that I could not be different by so much as a hair's breadth from what I now am without being a different person. After all, many of our counterfactuals begin, 'If I (not someone else) were in such-and-such a position ...'. In fact one might ask of possible worlds themselves: Is a world that differs ever so slightly from the real world to be called a different world? Couldn't this world be different from what it is? And if variation can be continuous and not discrete in nature, how many possible worlds are there? A non-denumerable infinity, corresponding to the continuum of real numbers? Maybe quantum physics could rescue us on this last point; but I have neither space nor qualifications to discuss that.

The defender of possible worlds can claim that the trans-world identity problem is with us in one form or another on any view. How different can I be without ceasing to be me? But why, we might ask, must there on other views be any answer to this question, at any rate with most objects (personal identity raises special problems)? The possible worlds view, on the other hand, presumably must insist on an answer being possible: either one has one possible world or another. Possible worlds have their allure, and evidently we must live with them, for the present anyway. But they constantly tempt us into the misleading 'Mars and Venus' picture, and we must be careful.

Alluring or otherwise, however, possible worlds have not yet solved the problem of scientific necessity for us. The necessary may be what is true in all possible worlds, but how do we distinguish possible from impossible ones? Clearly this is a vast question: and I can make no serious attempt to solve it here. But let me mention briefly one approach.

As I have said already, scientific necessity is a puzzling notion because it seems to make us admit of things that not only are the case but must be the case, and what does this strange addition come to? When a stone is released it falls. What is added by saying that it must fall? To bring this problem vividly before us is one of the most striking achievements of Hume in the eighteenth century. He put it in the form: if we have an idea of necessity, as we seem to, where in our experience can we possibly have got it from, for surely it must come from our experience somehow? Other philosophers, such as Kant, disagreed, and the issue is still open. But to return to the approach I started on:

One kind of necessity that seems at any rate easier to grasp is logical or conceptual necessity – these are near enough together not to need distinguishing here. A proposition is logically necessary if its denial is a contradiction, or if nothing would *count* as its being false. This idea itself has problems. Would anything count as my roses being in C minor? If not, does it follow that they are necessarily not in C minor? Or is this senseless too, with its suggestion that they are in some other key? Still, be that as it may, logical necessity seems a good deal clearer than scientific necessity, and it is tempting to think it is really the only necessity, and that scientific necessity is somehow a disguised form of it – *pace* Hume, who would sharply distinguish them.

We cannot straightforwardly equate the two. It is not contradictory, or inconceivable, that a law of nature should be broken. We can imagine water flowing uphill, in a way we cannot imagine, say, twice two being five, or a square being round. Or can we? Might it not be said that anything that flowed uphill certainly wasn't water? Maybe it was liquid helium, or some stuff hitherto unknown. Or perhaps it only appeared to flow uphill; it was an optical illusion. Or perhaps some of the tacitly presupposed conditions didn't apply; after all, water does flow uphill when there's a vacuum at the top, or suction wouldn't work.

This last example brings us back to the difficulty of stating laws of nature that are strictly universal. If we try something very general like 'Matter obeys the inverse square law of gravity', we may feel happier about dismissing apparent exceptions as not really matter at all. If there are fundamental particles that do not obey that law, common sense would probably be happy enough to say they were not material.

There is in fact a tendency for laws of nature to become fossilised into logical truths in this way. When a law becomes so well confirmed that a lot of science is built on it, we tend more and more not to *allow* anything to overthrow it, and thereby we treat it as a logical truth. In fact this is sometimes taken further. Some say that quite ordinary terms like 'cat' or 'chair' embody in their very meanings a reference to ways in which they will behave. They are 'theory-laden', as it is expressed. To call a term 'theory-laden' means in the first place that it would not make sense outside a certain theory. 'Electron' for instance would hardly make sense outside certain theories of physics. If someone suggested that an electron, though invisible and tiny at the moment, might grow, become visible, sprout arms and legs, and start reciting Shakespeare, we might well think of replying that whatever else it was that behaved like that, it certainly was not an electron. If someone suggested that the chair I am sitting on might suddenly dissolve beneath me or fly out of the window, I might reply, following this line, that if it did that, it was never a chair in the first place. The reader may feel that this treatment applies more plausibly in the electron case than in the chair case. Here I shall only remark that the cases are indeed less alike than I have so far suggested; one of the features of electrons is that there is a difficulty in principle about picking out *an* electron, which can be identified and re-identified as a single object lasting over time.

However things may stand with chairs and electrons, this approach is part of a wider approach which holds that in classifying things, in saying what they are, we are committing ourselves to saying a great deal about them. We are treating them as members of a 'natural kind', whose members are united to form that kind by having in common a certain set of properties. Common sense might think some of these properties more central than others to the objects in question. For instance, cats may have in common that they are animals and also that they have whiskers, where common sense would call the former more central than the latter. But the nub of this approach is that it is part of the meaning of the word 'cat' that either all these properties, or perhaps a loosely defined 'cluster' of them, must belong to anything that is to be a cat.

However, this whole approach has recently been attacked, from at least two different points of view. Some writers, led by the American logician W. V. Quine, have disputed the view which holds that, whatever we say about scientific necessity, logical necessity at least is sacrosanct. Quine would agree with the view that scientific and logical laws are not sharply distinct, but for a quite different reason: not because scientific ones are to be grounded in the security of logical ones, but because even truths of logic are open to revision, and their security is greater only in degree. Other writers, notably two other Americans, H. Putnam and S. Kripke, have attacked the idea that the meaning of a word like 'cat' is given by a set of properties that cats, to be cats, must have in common. These two movements by no means always agree with each other, but they have in common the view that even such an apparently rock-solid statement as 'All cats are animals' could come to be doubted. This suggests that our next line of enquiry should be about the notion of meaning.

6 Meaning

Meaning is a vast subject, as we can see from a few almost random examples: 'What do you mean?' 'What does this word mean?' 'What does that funny ticking in the engine mean?' 'He gave her meaningful glances as she read him her meaningless poetry.' 'Beans means Heinz.' Still, it is no doubt fairly clear that some kinds of meaning are more central than others. In general meaning has something to do with communication. It is that in virtue of which we communicate with each other. Basically we communicate in language, and language consists of sentences, which are made up of words. At least, most languages are like this. I have heard it said that some Eskimo languages do not distinguish between words and sentences. Since I know singularly little about Eskimo languages, I cannot assess this claim. But perhaps we can assume, at least tentatively, that if we come to any conclusions about the vast mass of languages, they will hold of Eskimo languages too, even if in a disguised form. There are indeed certain difficulties in saying just what counts as a word; but I think we can ignore these for our purposes. Meaning then, in its most central sense, should be something belonging to words or sentences or both, in virtue of which we use them to communicate. It need not belong to them first. They may acquire it in being used to communicate, just as possession of a wife is that in virtue of which a man is a husband, but he only acquires it in becoming a husband. This point can seem rather confusing, because each of us learns a language which is already a going concern; we communicate by using words that already have a meaning. But this is only generally true. We can sometimes invent a word and so use it that the audience catches on, or, as more commonly happens, use an old word in a new or extended sense.

We live with each other in a world; and for much of our talking we are talking about the world, in some sense or other. If we use words and sentences to talk about the world, and do so in virtue of their having meaning, then surely meaning must be something that relates those words and sentences to the world. Let us start with words, since a word, being smaller than a sentence, could surely exist without sentences, while a sentence could certainly not exist without words. If a word is part of a sentence, and a sentence is what we use to talk about the world, then surely the meaning of a word must be part of the world; or at least this must be so of some words, even if other words act like glue, as it were, to bind these words together in the right way.

This sounds like a correspondence view of meaning, and we may feel a bit suspicious in view of what happened to the correspondence theory of truth in an earlier chapter. As with that theory, we may feel there must be some grain of truth in it. After all, the meaning of 'table' must surely have something to do with tables. But the question is, how big is the grain?

One trouble with 'table' is that there is one word 'table' but indefinitely many tables – or else, as with 'unicorn', none at all. But some words seem to avoid this difficulty, by being attached to one particular object, which they are proper to, so that we call them proper names. 'Aristotle' names Aristotle, and there was only one of him, so surely he is the meaning of the name. True, there is also Onassis; but Onassis and the Stagirite are not two Aristotles in the way that the thing I lunch at and the thing you lunch at are two tables. That the same sound, 'Aristotle', applies to both is an irrelevant accident, rather as it is that 'table' applies to things made by carpenters and things made by statisticians. And if it turned out that Onassis and the Stagirite, and everyone else called Aristotle, had never really existed, we might well feel that somehow the name was meaningless or deficient as a name, that its use embodied some sort of illusion; though the fact that there are no unicorns does not in the least affect the meaning of 'unicorn' (at least if it means 'horse with a horn', or whatever. But see section III below, on Putnam.) This last point is not, I think, seriously affected by the fact that some names are avowedly fictional, like 'Pickwick'; it could well be said that 'Pickwick' is not really a full-blooded name, but only a word we use rather like a name, and are able to do so only because we know what real names are like, and how they behave, and then pretend that 'Pickwick' is a name. But if it turned out that none of the Aristotles, i.e. the people called 'Aristotle', ever existed, this would be worse, because we were not pretending in our use of that name. It would be rather as though we discovered that even the novel attributed to Dickens had never really been written at all, by him or anyone else.

One small caution before going on: Surely it is not an accident that a man and his son have the same name? No; but the reason depends on a social convention, and is *ad hoc* in a way that the reason for calling two (carpenter's) tables tables is not. A man does not change the language when he changes his name by deed poll. Also a word like 'Smith' is often used to abbreviate 'person called Smith', or 'person related in certain ways to someone called Smith', and these phrases are perfectly ordinary descriptive phrases like 'table'; cf. my use of 'the Aristotles' above.

Here then we seem to have a kernel from which we can develop a theory of meaning, at any rate for many words. Other words perhaps work in more complex ways than proper names, but in ways derived from them. As 'Aristotle' stands for Aristotle, so 'table' perhaps stands for tablehood, or for an idea or concept in the mind, or maybe each time anyone uses the word 'table' that particular utterance stands for some table or other, or some idea in his mind. Similarly 'red' or 'run' may stand for the colour red or the notion of running, or each utterance of them may stand for some red thing or some instance of running.

Theories of virtually all these kinds have been held, and as a matter of history so-called 'naming' theories of meaning have been among the earliest to be developed, going back at least to Plato. But there are difficulties. One perhaps the reader may already have noticed, in what I said about deed polls. For if I change my name and this does not count as a change in the English language, proper names hardly seem to be a typical part of that language. I should certainly be changing the language if I decided to use 'chair' for those flat-topped four-legged things I have lunch off.

But a more fundamental attack on the whole idea that the meaning of a name could be its bearer, the thing we use the name to talk about, was launched by Ludwig Wittgenstein (1889–1951) in the first forty-three sections or so of his *Philosophical Investigations*. First let us look at a not very plausible form of the objection. It is sometimes said that the meaning of a phrase like 'a glass of beer' cannot be what it is used to talk about, namely a glass of beer, because then we should have to say that I could drink the meaning of 'a glass of beer', which is absurd. But how absurd is it? Of course I would not normally call the glass that, because in ordinary social contexts I don't talk semantics, but it might *be* that, if the meaning is indeed the object, I would not normally say that in drinking my beer I was drinking my health away, but I could be doing just that, all the same. This form of the objection just begs the question against the theory under discussion.

One point Wittgenstein makes is that if Aristotle is the meaning of 'Aristotle' then, since Aristotle is dead, that meaning no longer exists, so how can we know it? Yet we can use the name just as sensibly as when he was alive, so evidently we do know its meaning. This seems a stronger point. At first it might seem a mere trick. Of course I am not acquainted with Aristotle. Neither have I ever been to Tokyo. But if I am asked, 'Do you know the capital of Japan?' I reply, 'Of course; Tokyo.' Why can I not similarly know the meaning of 'Aristotle'; i.e., by knowing that 'Aristotle' means Aristotle, as I know that the capital of Japan is Tokyo? But this 'i.e.' is a bit precipitate. 'Knowing the capital of Japan' is ambiguous. I know what city is the capital, but I don't know that city itself which is the capital. Similarly, on the view that 'Aristotle' means Aristotle, I may know what the meaning of 'Aristotle' is, but not know that thing (Aristotle) which is the meaning. So I may know facts about the meaning, without knowing the meaning itself.

Does this matter? I have been using a distinction between acquaintance with something and merely knowing facts about it. But what does this distinction amount to? How does my knowledge of Bromsgrove, where I live, differ from my knowledge of Tokyo? Isn't it just that I know many more facts about Bromsgrove? Not necessarily; I may not. I have been to Marseilles (once, briefly, at midnight), but I probably know more facts about Dublin, where I have never been. Why we say I am *acquainted* with Bromsgrove (and marginally with Marseilles) is because at least some of my knowledge of it has come by a certain route, by my seeing it and being present in it. Knowledge acquired by this route has perhaps a certain richness and fullness, even when it is confined to a small part of the thing known (Marseilles station, in my case). But why should this be at all relevant to our knowing the meaning of 'Aristotle'? What matters is that we know it well enough to use it, and why must we have acquaintance, in particular, for that? So it looks as if Wittgenstein's argument is a trick after all.

Wittgenstein has not proved that the meaning is not the object. But there is an important truth in what he says. If to know the meaning is to know the object, then in knowing the object I ought to be fully equipped for understanding and using the word. For whether or not it is *necessary* that I should be acquainted with the meaning, if I am acquainted with it, especially if I know it well, as I know Bromsgrove but not Marseilles, that should be enough, and I should be able to understand and use the word. But it is not enough. However well I know Aristotle, this will not help me to understand 'Aristotle' unless I know that Aristotle *is* the meaning of 'Aristotle', and I might not know this, just as I might spend a lifetime in Tokyo without realising that it was the capital of Japan.

To use a word, then, what I must know is not an object but a fact, whether it is the fact that the meaning is the object, or some other fact. Perhaps the meaning is not the object itself, but a relation between the word and the object. But what relation? Presumably that of naming, i.e.

being a name of. But now Wittgenstein has another shot to fire. What sort of a relation is this? Something like tagging or labelling perhaps. But suppose we tie a label on a piece of luggage: what might it say? Any of the following, at least: 'Smith' (its owner), 'Edinburgh' (its destination), 'books', 'express', 'fragile', and so on. Clearly, to understand any of these requires a knowledge of a whole set of conventions about transport services. A mere word tacked on to an object tells us no more by itself than, say, a red cross on it would.

If a word's meaning is a relation between it and an object, it must evidently be a much more complicated one than a sort of mental or abstract juxtaposition of the two. Certainly one would think that the meaning of 'Aristotle' should have *something* to do with Aristotle, and the meaning of 'table' something to do with tables – and the meaning of 'unicorn' something to do with unicorns if there were any, though also it should not be that 'unicorn' has a different meaning according as there are or aren't any. The fact that there are many tables and no unicorns tempts us to think that if meaning involves a relation at all it ought to be to that of which there is just one, namely the concept or universal *table* or *unicorn*, or something like that. Philosophers have long used the word 'universal' (as a noun) for an abstract entity supposed to link together all the members of a class (all tables, all unicorns, all red things, all acts of running, etc.); 'universal' does not, like 'concept', suggest something in the mind, though some philosophers identify them. But if we appeal to universals here, we lose the neat connection with proper names; for 'table' is used to talk about tables, if anything, not (normally) about tablehood or the concept *table*, whereas 'Aristotle' is used to talk about Aristotle.

Perhaps we have been taking too simple a view of meanings in thinking that the meaning of a word must be an entity or a relation to an entity. Perhaps indeed, as often happens in both philosophy and science, we are asking the wrong question, and instead of asking what meanings are, should ask first what it is for a word to have meaning, or under what conditions it has meaning. The question of what some particular word's meaning is will then become the question of what results when the conditions are satisfied in the case of the word in question. It would be rather like asking a biologist what is the function of the liver. We would not expect to be given an entity, the function, but to be told how the liver contributes to the well-being of the body, etc. We saw some chapters ago, when discussing statements, that for some words, like 'amends', it is misleading to ask what amends are, and we should instead consider the whole phrase 'make amends'. Perhaps 'meaning' is rather like 'amends', and we should take the phrase 'have meaning' as a whole. Of course we can still ask 'What is the meaning of ...?' as we can ask 'What amends did you make him?'

This approach recalls a famous remark of Frege, who said that a word only has meaning in the context of a proposition. It will be better for us to replace 'proposition' by 'sentence' here. Frege's German has the same word (*Satz*) for both, but in English there are often important differences between sentences and propositions. In fact in an analogue of the type of theory we have just been considering, where something's meaning is treated as an entity, propositions have sometimes been treated as the meanings of sentences. Let us, however, leave that aside, and ask instead when a sentence is meaningful and when it is not. If the way a word means depends on its contribution to a sentence, we might as well know something about how sentences mean.

Sentences achieve more than single words do. This rather epigrammatic remark is basically true, but we must take it with a pinch of salt all the same. Neither words nor sentences achieve anything. Only we achieve things by uttering them. But what the remark amounts to is this. If I utter a word, like 'table' or 'run' or 'if', I present you with a tool which could be used for various purposes. But (with a qualification coming in a minute) if I just utter it by itself I have only presented a tool. I have not presented a job as having been done, or even a make-believe picture of a job done. But now suppose I say, to return to our old friend from Chapter 2, 'The cat is on the mat'. If I utter it as I have just written it, as a mere example, I have not done the job of informing you of anything; I have not even specified any particular cat. But I have, as it were, presented you with a picture of a job done, in a way I have not if I merely utter the word 'table'. To put it another way, the sentence has a certain completeness that the isolated word has not. The sentence can be used to inform you of something, to ask a question, give an order, congratulate you, insult you, or just express my feelings. These acts one can perform by speaking are among those nowadays called speech acts. Some of them are called illocutions and others perlocutions. We have in fact already met some of them when discussing assertion and denial in Chapter 2 (p. 32), and also in Chapter 3. But one cannot perform illocutions and perlocutions by just uttering isolated words. Actually this is not quite true, as the reader may already have objected. There are plenty of one-word sentences, usually followed by an exclamation mark, like 'Fire!', 'Golly!', 'Diamonds!', 'Never!'. However, these are a special case. They are pretty clearly equivalent to sentences like 'Fire your rifles!' (or: 'There is a fire here!'), 'What has happened is surprising!', 'Here, surprisingly (or: at last), are diamonds!', 'I shall never do it!'. There is no sentence that is similarly equivalent to 'table', uttered in an ordinary tone of voice, and not in a special context, like answering a question. (This is the qualification I referred to earlier in this paragraph.)

An important claim about meaning is that assertion is somehow prior to other speech acts. A question is a request to know whether a certain possible assertion would be true. A command is a command to make one true. Things like thanking or congratulating are less straightforward, but still seem to presuppose asserting. If we keep the distinction between phrastics and neustics (p. 31), phrastics seem to be related to assertions more closely than to any other speech acts: could one understand 'The cat being on the mat' without first understanding 'The cat is on the mat'?

This claim has not gone entirely undisputed. R. G. Collingwood (1889–1943), for instance, seems to have thought questions were more basic than assertions. But it has been, and is, very widely accepted, and underlies many theories of meaning.

If assertion is basic in this way, we may expect to find that truth too is basic to an adequate theory of meaning. For to assert something is to present it as being true.

There is a difference, at any rate at first sight, between truth and meaning: truth belongs to the world; meaning belongs to us. Whether something is true is, so to speak, for the world to say; but what something means is for us to say. This at any rate has been the view of many philosophers, typified by Moritz Schlick, a leading logical positivist, who was murdered by a disgruntled student on the steps of Vienna University in 1936. Shortly before suffering this he wrote: 'If we utter a sentence without meaning it is always *our own fault*'. It is for us to give meaning to what we say. I will say a bit more about logical positivists later, but for the moment I want to introduce their theory of meaning, which has been extremely influential.

If it is because our words and sentences have meaning that we can communicate with each other about the world, and if truth underlies assertion, and therefore communication is general, in the way I have sketched, then it seems natural to say that at bottom whether something is meaningful is a matter of whether we can decide whether it is true or false. This is the main point of the so-called verification theory of meaning, which is now largely associated, in the first instance, with the logical positivists, though it goes back behind them at least as far as Hume, and has survived their downfall as a school, as we shall see.

Sometimes verificationists, as they are called, tell us what the meaning of any (indicative) sentence is: it is the method of verifying it, i.e. the method we should have to apply to find that it was true, if it *were* true. Take the sentence 'My pen is red'. Actually this is false, but that does not matter. The way of finding that it was true, if it were, would presumably be to look, and as a result of looking to get a certain experience: the one we would call 'seeing a red pen here'. For these verificationists the meaning of 'My pen is red' will be this procedure, including the experience that would result if the pen were red. One objection to this is that often, especially with more complex examples, there will be many methods of verifying a sentence, and none that is obviously preferable to the others; yet we don't want to say the sentence has correspondingly many meanings.

Before going on, two brief cautions. First, a historical one: Schlick talked of propositions rather than sentences as what have meaning. I have already mentioned the German conflation of 'sentence' and 'proposition' (though Schlick was writing in English), but to go further into this point would take a lot of space, so let us forget it. Second, 'verify' normally means 'find to be true', so how can something false be verifiable? The answer is that 'verifiable' is ambiguous. For us, as I have tried to show, a sentence is verifiable if we know a method that would reveal its truth if it *were* true.

Let us go on then to the more modest claim of the verificationists that, whatever meaning may be, a sentence is meaningful if and only if it is verifiable, or if and only if what it states is verifiable. To avoid bogging us down in a long discussion of sentences, statements and propositions it will be convenient for most of the time to talk of statements and say they are meaningful, on the theory, if and only if they are verifiable. This is, of course, only one use of 'statement' (borrowed from A. J. Ayer); cf. p. 29 above.

Now, when is a statement verifiable? The most obvious case is when we can tell that it is true, if it is, by using our five senses. In fact if we are considering statements about the world, what other methods have we for getting in contact with the world except our five senses? We might perhaps add introspection or kinaesthetic sensations (sensations of movement within the body) for telling us certain facts about ourselves, but with these exceptions it seems plausible to say that all our knowledge about the world must come somehow through our senses. Some perhaps would like to add extrasensory perception and other so-called 'paranormal' devices; but these are at best controversial, and a theory of meaning which looks for acceptance would do well to avoid them, at any rate at first.

There are indeed a whole lot of other statements, notably in logic and mathematics, which we do not seem to use the senses to tell us about. But these statements do not, in themselves, seem to tell us anything about the world. In fact many of them do not seem to tell us anything about anything at all. Take a statement like 'All red roses are red', or 'Either it is raining or it isn't'. We feel like calling these true, but they hardly tell us much. Because of the form of the first example, where the predicate 'red' seems to be analysable out of the subject 'red roses', such statements are usually called analytic, even if, like the second example, they are not obviously of that form. More interesting examples are where the analytic nature of what is said is concealed. Suppose I tell you that the sun rises in the east. Have I really told you anything? It depends on what I mean by 'east'. If I define 'east' as the direction to your right when you face the pole star, yes, I have. But if I define it as the direction in which the sun rises, then my statement is analytic, since it boils down to 'The sun rises where the sun rises'. This sort of ambiguity is an extremely common source of fallacy. A speaker says something which can be interpreted either as analytic (and so undoubtedly true, even if not very interesting) or as not analytic (and so interesting, even if rather dubiously true). He may then look as if he has said something both true and interesting, a highly desirable state for him to be in. Statements that are not analytic are called synthetic, because, in the basic cases, the predicate is added to the subject and not analysed out of it. The negation of an analytic statement, as so far defined, is of course false ('Red roses are not red'), but it is convenient to call it analytic rather than synthetic, when we need to call it anything. 'Analytic' itself is therefore ambiguous, and can mean 'analytic and true' or 'analytic, whether true or false'. But in practice the ambiguity is harmless, and it is pretty clear which sense is meant.

However, the whole analytic/synthetic distinction bristles with difficulties. I started the last paragraph with two examples, about roses and rain, and pointed to the form of the first example. I then cheerfully added that 'such statements' are called analytic. But such as what? Even the second example does not on the face of it have the same form; and are we to say that all the statements of logic and mathematics are equally uninformative? In recent years the whole distinction has been hotly attacked, notably by Quine, and equally hotly defended. But for the moment I want to return to the verification theory, so let us just follow the logical positivists and say that statements of logic and mathematics can ultimately be analysed in this way, and can be called true or false in virtue of something about their form.

We got as far as seeing that the most obviously verifiable statements are those we can verify by using the senses. But how far will this get us? I could verify that my pen was red, if it were, by looking at it. But how about the statement, 'There are rational fish in the methane seas of Jupiter' (as some astronomers, I think, have held there could be)? I can hardly go and look, and even NASA is not very well equipped to do so at the moment. But in principle we could go and look, and probably one day we shall. Let us assume we should have no trouble in recognising a rational fish if we saw one. But it would seem unfortunate that our views on which statements were meaningful should have to wait on technological developments. And how could we try to look for the Jovian fish if the statement that there were any was still meaningless because still unverifiable? Also, how about statements about the past, like 'Caesar crossed the Rubicon'? Technology will not provide us with time-machines. One way out, which has been taken before today, is to say that we can verify it by, say, going to the British Museum and getting certain experiences from looking at certain manuscripts, and so that is what makes it meaningful. But suppose we cannot: suppose the statement is that on the night before he died Caesar dreamed he was chased by a lion – but never had time to tell anyone. No rummaging in the BM will help us this time. But isn't this statement just as meaningful as the other one?

Maybe we are paying too much attention to mere practicality. Isn't it enough if we can in principle verify the statement? If one day we shall go to Jupiter in real earnest, we can go there in principle today. We have no time-machine, but in principle we could have the experience of verifying that Caesar crossed the Rubicon; namely, by standing on the bank watching him. Similarly we could in principle listen to him recounting his dream, or even perhaps be him and dream it ourselves. Compare these with statements like, "Twas brillig and the slithy toves did gyre and gimble in the wabe', or 'My pen is in C minor': what possible experiences could count as verifying these? These are just the sort of statements we would want to call meaningless (at least in any straightforward sense; all sorts of complications arise when we turn to metaphor and poetic licence, but we are not concerned with them here).

Most verificationists in fact have taken this line, so let us follow them. But I cannot refrain from another quick kick at that sleeping dog, the view that the method of verification *is* the meaning. Maybe 'Caesar crossed the Rubicon' is verifiable in principle because in principle we could watch him do so. But in the absence of a time-machine what sort of *method* is this? All we seem to have is a picture, not a method which will take us even in principle from where we are to a situation where we can watch Caesar's activities.

But there is a worse objection. How do I verify that a pen is red? Just by looking at it? But maybe I am colour blind, or the pen is reflecting a red light, or I am looking at it under a sodium light, so it will not look red anyway, even if it is red. How in fact can I be sure that my experience is a reliable guide to the outer world? Perhaps there are a few statements where it is absolutely reliable: namely, those about experience itself. To take a time-honoured example, 'I am now seeming to see a red patch' is surely a statement I can hardly go wrong about, since it could be true even if I am merely having a hallucination. Such statements are sometimes called incorrigible, on the grounds that someone who sincerely asserts them cannot be corrected or shown to be wrong. Actually 'infallible' would be a better term, meaning that one could not be deceived about them. For suppose I sincerely report having had a certain dream: I could hardly be corrected – who could correct me? – but I might be misremembering all the same, and so be being deceived. But anyway let us stick to 'incorrigible'. It is not obvious, and is in fact disputed, whether any statements are in fact incorrigible. Even when reporting my experiences might I not choose the wrong words, and this not just through linguistic ignorance? Perhaps this is unlikely in a case like seeing a red patch, but how about if the patch is puce or beige: is this, which I am now experiencing, really what counts as beige? Or is it rather fawn? Or if purely linguistic error is more likely here, can I not doubt whether something, straight ahead of me in a good light, is blue or green? Remember the old advertisement for Persil soap: 'I always thought my Johnny's shirt was white until I saw little Bobby's from next door, washed in Persil.' The lady was not ignorant of the English language.

Anyway, suppose there are some incorrigible statements. They will be a pretty small selection of statements generally. We do not usually go around telling each other about our immediate experiences. So it looks as if not many statements will really be verifiable. One response to this predicament (not the only one, as we shall see later) is to say we have been insisting on too high a standard for what counts as verifiability. Perhaps something can be meaningful if we know what would make it more probable, what would be relevant to its truth, without needing to know what would verify it conclusively. The most famous attempt to develop this idea was made by the main English representative of logical positivism, A. J. Ayer. As we have been doing, Ayer takes the five senses as our primary source of knowledge, and so calls a statement meaningful if observation by the senses is relevant to its verification. But the word 'relevant' is impossibly vague. Experience by the senses could be 'relevant' to almost anything. But Ayer, like the other positivists, had a motive. He wanted to show that many statements commonly accepted as meaningful, especially metaphysical ones, were in fact meaningless. So he wanted to tighten up the notion of relevance and give definite criteria for when something was meaningful and when it was not. To do this he used the notion of entailment, which we met earlier. Statements that one statement entailed another were dealt with by calling them analytic.

The idea is to give a *recursive* account of meaningful statements. This means that we start with a set of statements we call meaningful straight off. Then we add in any statements that stand in a certain relation to these first ones. Then we add in those that stand in the same relation to the second set, and so on. We generate more and more meaningful statements by adding in those that have the given relation to those we have already. Similarly, we might give a recursive account of Smith's ancestors by starting with his parents, then adding his grandparents, then his great-grandparents, and so on, to infinity if need be. In the end all we need say is this: Smith's ancestors include his parents, and the parents of each of his ancestors. Recursive definitions or accounts are very important in philosophy, as in mathematics and elsewhere.

We start with observation statements, as Ayer called them, i.e., statements describing a possible experience, like 'I am now seeming to see a red patch'. These may be true or false, but will count as meaningful. We also allow analytic statements. The relation we need is that of contributing to an entailment. To insist on entailment itself as our relation would make it too hard ever to get beyond observation statements, so we allow that, if p is an observation statement, q will be meaningful if it contributes to the entailment of p; i.e., if there is some statement r such that 'q-and-r' entails p, though r does not by itself entail p, q has, as it were, to do some work towards the entailment, and is not just a passive partner; and q will also be meaningful of course if it does all the work and does entail p. The general account will then read: A statement is meaningful iff it is either analytic or an observation statement or contributes to the entailment of a statement already accepted as meaningful. (I have slightly amended Ayer's view here.) As an example, let p be 'I am now experiencing red', let q be 'My pen is red', and let r be 'My eyes are in good order, and whenever I look at something red I experience red, and the only thing I'm now looking at is my pen'; it does not matter how complicated r is. p is meaningful (it is an observation statement), and r does not entail p, but 'r-and-q' does; so q is meaningful.

We saw in Chapter 4 that some people think one statement can entail another only if there is a connection of meaning between them. We can call this a semantic view of entailment. The rival view that entailment need not involve this we can call a syntactic view. Roughly, 'semantic' means concerning or involving meaning, and 'syntactic' means concerning or involving grammatical or logical form. One feature of the verification theory we are considering is that it takes a semantic view of entailment. For surely 'My pen is in C minor and not in C minor' ought not to be meaningful; yet it will be for a verification theory which takes entailment as syntactic; for, being a contradiction, it will on the syntactic view entail any statement, including all observation statements.

Isaiah Berlin pointed out, however, that the theory will have to count something like 'This problem is green' as meaningful; for together with 'I dislike all green things' it entails the presumably meaningful 'I dislike this problem', which is not entailed by 'I dislike all green things' alone.

In answering another objection Ayer had modified his criterion by insisting that the added premise, which I called 'r' three paragraphs ago, must itself be meaningful; i.e., we must know that it is so, independently of the argument we are now using it in. On the face of it this does not stop the 'green problem' case slipping through the net, because the added premise there was 'I dislike all green things', and surely that is meaningful enough. So it looks as if the criterion will not do the work we want of it, which is to reveal as meaningful all those statements, but only those, which we are in fact prepared to accept as meaningful; for surely 'This problem is green' is not among these.

Ayer himself seems to have ignored the 'green problem' objection completely (it appeared before the 'Introduction' I referred to), but to have abandoned for other reasons the attempt to find an adequate criterion of meaningfulness. At any rate he said on TV in, I think, 1960: 'Logical positivism is dead', apparently meaning mainly that no such criterion could be found.

However, perhaps Ayer's criterion could be defended from this particular objection, by following a hint from D. Makinson in *Mind*, 1965 (who does not mention this 'green problem' objection specifically). I said that the added premise, 'I dislike all green things', is surely meaningful enough. But what actually does it mean? What does 'all green things' cover? In particular, does it cover green problems, or not? If it does not, but only covers things like chairs and tables, and perhaps flashes and rainbows, it will not serve Berlin's purpose. For 'This problem is green, and I dislike all green chairs and tables, etc.' does *not* entail 'I dislike this problem', and so Berlin's counterexample to Ayer's criterion is broken-backed. But if it does, then we can deal with it by tightening the restriction Ayer placed on the added premise. A modern logician would analyse 'I dislike all green things' as 'Whatever x may be, if x is green, I dislike x'. Now consider the whole set of sentences we get by taking the last two clauses of this and systematically replacing 'x' by everything we allow it to cover: sentences like 'If grass is green, I dislike grass', 'If snow is green, I dislike snow', 'If your tie is green, I dislike your tie', and so on. Add in too the component parts of these sentences,

'Grass is green', 'I dislike grass', etc. Let us call all the sentences we get in this way *implicit parts* of the original sentence, 'I dislike all green things'. We now tighten Ayer's restriction as follows: not only must the added premise (in this case, 'I dislike all green things') be known independently to be meaningful, but so must each of its implicit parts. Now if, as we are now assuming, 'all green things' does cover this problem, then the implict parts of 'I dislike all green things' will include 'If this problem is green, I dislike this problem', and so will include 'This problem is green' – but this is the very statement under test, and obviously cannot be assumed independently to be meaningful. So Berlin's counterexample is again blocked.

I said some time ago (p. 9) that Ayer's theory was not the only response to the predicament that so few statements seem to be conclusively verifiable. It is worth looking, more briefly, at one other response. This is simply to say that the number of such statements is more than might be thought. I said that 'My pen is red' is not incorrigible, because even if I sincerely assert it after looking at the pen, I always might be suffering a hallucination. Clearly this is true, in the sense that the mere fact that 'My pen is red' is sincerely asserted by someone does not guarantee that it is true. But does this mean it can never be conclusively verified? Suppose I examine the pen carefully over a long period: it behaves just as a red pen should. A photometer registers 'red' when applied to it; all my friends and neighbours agree in calling it a red pen; the best oculists in the country declare us all free from colour-blindness; and so on. Will there not come a time when I shall be justified in saying: 'Well, it is red; I don't care what happens now – nothing will make me withdraw the claim that it is, or anyway has been up till now, a red pen (of course it could change later, but never mind)'? Will there not, in other words, be a cut-off point when we refuse to test the statement any longer, but just decide to accept it?

One word of caution here: to accept a statement is not necessarily to think it true, or even to think it very probable. I am bitten by a snake in the jungle, and shall certainly die if I take no remedy. This jungle has just three kinds of snake, and I have remedies for all of them, but unfortunately the remedy for any one will be useless as a remedy for the other two, and indeed will cancel the effects of the proper remedies for them. Judging from the brief glimpse I caught of the snake before it wriggled off, I conclude there is a 40 per cent chance it was of type A, 30 per cent it was of type B, and 30 per cent it was of type C. Presumably it is rational for me to *accept* that it was of type A, and take remedy A, even though I believe it 60 per cent probable that the snake was not of type A and that the remedy will be useless. This distinction between acceptance and belief has been of importance in the philosophy of science.

However, in the pen case our acceptance will surely carry belief as well. Isn't 'My pen is red' then conclusively verifiable? It does not matter if I can't carry out all these tests. I need only know what tests, and what results of them, *would* lead me to this state of acceptance.

On this view conclusive verifiability is not the clear-cut business it seemed to be in the case of incorrigible statements. It would be hard to point to a definite moment after which nothing would count as falsifying a statement. More important, however, is that it still leaves a good many statements unaccounted for, such as general statements like 'All ravens are black' — all of them, at all times and places. How could any finite amount of experience persuade us to regard this as conclusively verified, and not merely to accept it for practical purposes?

Shall we then return to Ayer's version of the theory? As I have said, Ayer himself has abandoned it, and in fact little is heard of it nowadays. Perhaps five reasons for this might be briefly mentioned.

First, it was often thought to have succumbed to objections like the 'green problem' one, especially to one due to the American logician Alonzo Church. For a brief account and criticism of it see P. Nidditch's note in *Mind*, 1961, and also Makinson (above).

Second, it relies on the analytic/synthetic distinction, and on the view that logical and mathematical statements, and in general all statements not ultimately based on the five senses, can somehow be treated as not really saying anything. Both these points have proved controversial.

Third, and related to the second point, the whole idea of basing our knowledge of the world on observation statements has been questioned. Ayer's position is closely linked with a doctrine called *phenomenalism* (literally, 'appearance-ism'), which says that the meaning of ordinary statements about chairs and tables is to be given by regarding them as abbreviations for very complex statements about appearances, i.e. about the experiences one would get if one looked or stretched one's hand out in certain directions, etc. (This is one of a family of doctrines which can all be called phenomenalism, which, incidentally, is not the same as phenomenology; but that I must leave.) This kind of phenomenalism has proved impossible to work out in detail, and has now been generally abandoned. Ayer's theory is not quite the same as phenomenalism, since he does not reckon to *give* the meaning of statements, but only to say under what conditions they are meaningful. But his programme is open to various objections to treating what he calls observation statements as the basis of all our knowledge. For instance, it is not obvious that the meaning of the phrase 'seems red' could be understood unless we already understood 'is red'. 'Seems what?' one might ask. 'Red.' But can we understand 'red' without understanding 'is red'?

Fourth, the theory is associated with the full-blooded programme of logical positivism, of which I will say more later. Here I will only say that it involved either rejecting completely, or giving what now seems an inadequate account of, whole spheres of discourse like metaphysics, ethics, and religion, which later writers have been unwilling to abandon so cavalierly.

Fifth, as I said under the third point, Ayer does not even offer an account of what meaning is, but only an account of the conditions under which something is meaningful. The other form of the theory that we considered (Schlick's) did say what meaning was; namely, the method of verification. But neither of these positions will be very congenial to someone who thinks it a mistake to regard meanings (whether of words or sentences) as entities, but who does want to have some account of the notion of meaning itself. To repeat the title of a book published as early as 1923, what is the meaning of 'meaning'? (Cf. C. K. Ogden and I. A. Richards, *The Meaning of 'Meaning'*, 1923).

II

One way of looking at the verification theory is to see it as a development – some would say a distortion – of an earlier theory held by Frege, and also in his early days by Wittgenstein. Frege's general idea is that the meaning of a sentence is given by its truth conditions, the conditions under which it would be true. Under what conditions would the sentence 'La neige est blanche' be true? Clearly under the condition that snow is white. So we can say that 'La neige est blanche' means that snow is white. Wittgenstein put the thought succinctly in his *Tractatus*: 'To understand a proposition means to know what is the case if it is true.' The verificationists can be regarded as seeing the meaning of a sentence not in the conditions under which it would be true but in those under which it would be verifiable. We have seen some of the disadvantages of this, and recently an attempt has been made to go back to the Frege/Wittgenstein view. This attempt is associated primarily with an American philosopher, Donald Davidson. His seminal article appeared in 1967 ('Truth and meaning'), though he has written much else, and in particular made an important modification to his theory in 1973 ('Radical interpretation'). I will refer to these two articles as TM and RI respectively. The final section of RI sketches briefly the difference between the modified version and the original version, but we shall naturally be more concerned with the modified version.

Let us start by changing the emphasis of our discussion so far. We started by discussing the meaning of words and then went on to that of sentences. But now let us emphasise that the latter depends on the former. A fundamental distinction between words and sentences is that the number of words in a language at a given time is finite, and in the great majority of cases we learn them one by one, but the number of sentences is potentially infinite, or at least indefinite. Descriptive phrases belong with sentences in this respect. If the human race is finite in its numbers and life-spans, the total number of sentences uttered will be finite; but more could always have been constructed and it is plain that we do not learn sentences one by one in the way we learn words. There are a few idiomatic exceptions, but the whole point of language as a tool for communication would be lost if we could not normally both construct and understand sentences we had never met before. True, we can always invent as many new words as we like; but then we are adding to the language in a way we are not when we construct new phrases or sentences. We saw earlier how Frege insisted that a word had meaning only in the context of a sentence or proposition. But clearly it is also true that the meaning of a sentence must somehow depend on the meanings of the words it contains, again with the exception of a few idioms – but these, like words, are essentially limited in number.

Davidson starts by agreeing with most other writers that a theory of meaning must explain how sentence-meaning can thus depend on word-meaning. It must show *how* words contribute to sentences. He than makes two further points, one negative and one positive. The negative one, which is not original to Davidson, is that we should not think of meanings, of either words or sentences, as entities. I touched on this point earlier, when discussing names: to know the meaning of a word is not to be acquainted with an object, whether concrete or abstract, even if in some cases (names) an object enters in somewhere. We have to know how to use the word, and what we can do with it. By itself this is not conclusive. But I think Davidson's point is this: if the meaning of a word is an entity, how can it do the explaining I mentioned at the start of this paragraph? If a word has meaning only because of its role in a sentence, and if this meaning is an entity, how can we pick it out except by calling it 'that entity which enables a word to make such-and-such a contribution to the meaning of a sentence'? If we then try to use this to explain the meaning of a sentence we risk being like a scientist who exclaims: 'I have a splendid explanation of cancer: it's caused by the cause of cancer!' The cause of cancer might be an entity – say, a virus.

But in the meaning case we seem to have no independent way of describing the entity, as though we could *only* describe the virus as 'the cause of cancer'. This at any rate, i.e. to find an independent description, is the challenge anyone must meet who wants to go on saying meanings are entities. (The challenge has in fact since been taken up.)

Davidson's positive point is more novel. If a sentence only has meaning because of what the words in it mean, and the words only have meaning in virtue of the contribution they make to all the sentences in which they can occur, it seems to follow that we cannot give the meaning of anything, word or sentence, except by giving the meaning of everything. As he puts it at TM, p. 308, 'Frege said that only in the context of a sentence does a word have meaning; in the same vein he might have added that only in the context of the language does a sentence (and therefore a word) have meaning.' In this respect Davidson's outlook is holistic. 'Holistic' means viewing the parts in the light of the whole, or insisting that a certain phenomenon or subject-matter must be interpreted as a whole and not piecemeal.

Now for Davidson's main proposal, the core of which comes at MT, pp. 309–10. The idea is not easy, and I will try to explain it in stages, using another of his writings ('On Saying That'). What is the meaning of 'Snow is white'? Put like this the question suggests we are looking for an entity, as the answer to 'What is the capital of France?' would be an entity, Paris. So let us approach the problem instead by asking what account we can give of what we are saying when we say things like, 'The sentence "Snow is white" means that snow is white', or ' "La neige est blanche" means that snow is white'.

At first sight this does not get us very far, for many philosophers have held that things beginning with 'that', like 'that snow is white', are propositions, which are a kind of abstract entity, so that we are back with the idea that 'Snow is white' does mean an entity, namely the proposition: that snow is white. But let us now use the fact, for which there is historical evidence, that in English at any rate the conjunction 'that' is a development of the demonstrative 'that'. We can make the point here most clearly by replacing 'that' by its sister demonstrative 'this'. We then get, ' "Snow is white" means this: snow is white'. This avoids the suggestion of a special entity, while remaining something we might naturally say. (It is this paragraph that uses 'On Saying That'.)

Now what about the word 'means'? First, we must avoid a possible misunderstanding. What we have got is ' "Snow is white" means this: snow is white.' This is not the same as ' "Snow is white" means the same as this sentence: "Snow is white".' This latter might be informative if the two sentences were in different languages, but will not give us

97

what we want. To say that two sentences mean the same as each other throws no light on what it is to mean something.

So what about 'means'? Whatever meaning is, it somehow connects our words and sentences with the world, and enables us to use them to communicate facts about the world. The primary use of 'Snow is white' is to say that snow is white, and it is correct to say this when snow *is* white, provided we are trying sincerely to describe the world. There are other occasions for saying the words 'snow is white', such as to raise the possibility that snow is white, which we can do by prefixing 'if' to 'snow is white'; but these uses are presumably secondary. Suppose now that there is some property – call it T – which the sentence 'Snow is white' has just when it is suitable for using in this primary way; i.e., just when snow is white: we might then give the meaning of 'Snow is white' by saying it has T if and only if snow is white. So ' "Snow is white" means this: snow is white', could be replaced by ' "Snow is white" has T if and only if snow is white'. We are not appealing to any entities like propositions in all this.

Is there then such a property T? We might think simply of the property *being suitable for use in communicating a fact*. But this does not go quite far enough. It does not tell us in virtue of what the sentence is so suitable, let alone telling us how the meaning of the sentence depends on the meanings of the words in it. But another eminently suitable property lies to hand, namely truth. (It was with this in mind that the letter 'T' was chosen.) We can use 'Snow is white' as we do because it is true if and only if snow is white. The term 'T-sentence' is now generally applied to sentences of the form ' "Snow is white" is true iff snow is white', or ' "La neige est blanche" is true iff snow is white', or for that matter ' "Snow is white" is true iff snow is black'; i.e., sentences of the general form 'The sentence s is true iff p', where p purports, whether correctly or not, to be a translation of s. Of those just mentioned the first two are true T-sentences and the third is a false T-sentence. When, as in the first example, the quoted sentence is the same as what follows the 'iff' the T-sentence is called homophonic (literally, 'same-sounding'). Incidentally, we shall assume throughout that in homophonic cases the object language, or language we are talking about, is part of the metalanguage, or language we talk about it in. Otherwise there is a slight complication about these cases; the same sentence might occur in different languages with different meanings, as the same word often does. The old schoolboy quip, 'Caesar adsum jam forte; passus sum sed Antoni' in Latin means (charitably) 'I Caesar happen to be here already; but I have suffered, Anthony.' Read aloud as an English sentence it means something quite different.

So far so good – but so far not very far. We have replaced 'means that' by 'is true iff', but our labours are not over. 'Iff' is used here in its material implication sense, as it normally is in logic, and so if we simply said that the meaning of a sentence was given by a true T-sentence involving it, we should have no way of barring appeal to a T-sentence like ' "Snow is white" is true iff grass is green', which is a true T-sentence, since 'Snow is white' *is* true and grass *is* green. But we do not want to end up saying that 'Snow is white' means that grass is green.

What we want is a way of getting just the right T-sentences; namely, those which are either homophonic or else are such that what follows the words 'is true iff' is a translation of what precedes them; an example of this latter would be the T-sentence ' "La neige est blanche" is true iff snow is white'.

One way of getting these desired T-sentences would be to have an axiomatic theory, rather like Euclid's geometry, where we start with a finite number of axioms and rules of inference and derive indefinitely many theorems. In the Euclid case the theorems will include all the truths of Euclidean geometry (including the axioms, which count as theorems too). In our case the axioms will be about what individual words contribute and also about such things as the effect words like 'and' and 'not' have when applied to sentences, and the theorems will mainly consist of T-sentences.

Let me give a very simple example, which may be easier if I make it non-homophonic, though nothing here hangs on this. Suppose we have the following axioms:

(i) 'Jean' names the man we know as John.
(ii) 'Chauve' is the word for the property *bald*; in Tarski's terms, 'x is chauve' is satisfied by just those sequences beginning with a bald object.
(iii) 'Est' is the present tense copula.

From these we might derive the T-sentence: ' "Jean est chauve" is true iff John is bald'. This is very crude. We assume, for instance, that we know all about copulas, and about what naming is. But it may give a rough idea to start from.

This whole approach is founded on Tarski's theory of truth, which we discussed in Chapter 2. Tarski is interested in truth, and looks for a way of expressing what might be expressed in longhand, as it were, by the totality of the right T-sentences for a given language. Following Tarski, it is now usual to say that a theory which entails all the right T-sentences for a given language is a theory which satisfies Convention T, or Criterion T. The device whereby, in homophonic cases, the truth conditions of a sentence can be expressed by repeating it, first with and then without quote-marks, on either side of 'is true iff' is sometimes called a device of disquotation. What Davidson does is to take Convention T, and Tarski's theory of truth that goes with it, and make them the foundation of a theory of meaning. He claims that this brings out the philosophical importance of Tarski's theory, whether or not we regard that theory as throwing light on our ordinary notion of truth (TM, p. 310).

However, there is an important difference between the positions of Tarski and Davidson. Tarski is concerned with truth, not meaning. In formulating Convention T he happily uses the term 'translation', which can only be explained in terms of meaning: a translation, at least of the kind that concerns us here, might be defined as a sentence in one language designed to have the same meaning as some sentence in another language. Since meaning is the very thing Davidson is trying to analyse, he plainly cannot just cheerfully use the notion of translation in this way.

Suppose for a moment that Davidson could ignore this difficulty. Then what he would seek would be a theory that generated true T-sentences as theorems, subject to a certain constraint: namely, that the theory should satisfy Convention T. It would do this by delivering for every sentence of the object language a T-sentence linking it to its translation into the metalanguage, or else, where the object language is part of the metalanguage, to a repetition of the sentence itself, as in ' "Snow is white" is true iff snow is white'. As things are, however, Davidson must seek some other constraint instead – or at least, as he puts it elsewhere, he must 'read it [Convention T] in a new way' (see his 'Reply to Foster', p. 35; this 'Reply' is a useful supplement to the articles I am mainly using).

I said earlier that Davidson's theory was holistic, in that it involved appeal to a theory covering the whole of a language; i.e., generating T-sentences for *each* sentence in the language. The constraint which he puts on a theory which is to be adequate for his purpose is also holistic, and at the same time brings out the sense in which the theory is, as Davidson claims it is, empirical, i.e. to be tested by observation. The constraint, though reasonably straightforward once one grasps it, is not easy to state briefly, and so it must have a few paragraphs to itself.

Suppose I hear someone speaking in a language I do not know. For convenience let it be French. He says 'La neige est blanche', and I wonder what he means. Assuming I have no dictionaries, etc., my best plan will be to try to find out what he is most likely to be saying in the circumstances. It will also help if I collect as many other utterances as I can by him and others of his community and try to interpret them as a whole. I shall then be engaged in what Davidson calls 'radical interpretation', an idea that stems from a similar idea called 'radical translation' made famous by W. V. Quine (see RI, notes 1 and 14). What we are looking for is a theory – what Davidson calls a theory of truth for the language in question – which entails certain T-sentences. French being what it is, the theory the radical interpreter accepts should be one that entails as a T-sentence ' "La neige est blanche" is true iff snow is white', though of course he will not know at the outset that it should. Because of the role that truth plays in T-sentences the radical interpreter will be primarily concerned with sentences that look as if they are being used to assert truths, and he will therefore use as much information as he can get about the sort of things the speakers of the object language hold true. He will assume that the speakers are reasonably rational, sincere, and well-informed, and that they desire the sort of things that people in general desire. This assumption is sometimes called the principle of charity, though as Davidson points out it is not really a contingent principle that might turn out to be false, for, 'If we cannot find a way to interpret the utterances and other behaviour of a creature as revealing a set of beliefs largely consistent and true by our own standards, we have no reason to count that creature as rational, as having beliefs, or as saying anything' (RI, p. 324). But the principle of charity as so far stated must be widened a little, for we have other information we can use about the people we are interpreting. We may, for instance, have reason to think they hold false beliefs on certain topics, as the medievals did on astronomy. The name 'principle of humanity' has been proposed for what results when the principle of charity is widened in this and similar ways.

Let us try a very simplified example of how this principle might work. Suppose we have got far enough in our attempt to interpret French to suppose that our Frenchman – call him Pierre – is engaged in a conversation about mountaineering, and has just said that a mountaineer should always take goggles, whereupon someone asks him why. Pierre then says, 'La neige est blanche'. Suppose also that for some reason we are trying to choose between two theories, A and B, where A entails as a T-sentence ' "La neige est blanche" is true iff snow is white', while B entails instead ' "La neige est blanche" is true iff grass is green'. Would anything tempt us to prefer A to B as a theory of truth for French that would serve to give us the meanings of French sentences? If what Pierre said was that snow is white we might assume he had in mind some point about snow-blindness, whereas if he said that grass is green we could only assume he was dotty, or not listening, or both. The principle of humanity therefore suggests that we choose theory A.

The constraint we are looking for can now be put in Davidson's own words. It is 'that the totality of T-sentences [generated by the theory in question] should ... optimally fit evidence about sentences held true by native speakers' (RI, p. 326). Of course theory A in the above example does not tell us directly that 'La neige est blanche' means that snow is white. All it tells us directly is that it is true if and only if snow is white. It is also true if and only if grass is green, but *this* is not something told to us by theory A. As Davidson says in the sentence following the one just quoted, 'The present idea is that what Tarski assumed outright for each T-sentence can be indirectly elicited by a holistic constraint. If that constraint is adequate, each T-sentence will in fact yield interpretations.'

So our T-sentence does in the end tell us that 'La neige est blanche' means that snow is white, but only because the T-sentence is derivable from a theory satisfying the above constraint and we know that it is so derivable. This last bit is important. We do not need to know (as Davidson originally thought, in TM and elsewhere) what the theory is in its totality, nor how the T-sentence is derived in it, but we do need to know *that* the T-sentence is derivable in some theory which satisfies the empirical and holistic constraint we have been discussing, if we are to understand what Pierre means. Of course ordinary chaps who understand French know nothing about T-sentences and truth theories as such. But on Davidson's view what they know is something equivalent to what we have just said.

We must mention one modification Davidson makes to his theory at the end of the first paper (TM). For Tarski truth is a property of sentences. But Tarski deals only with formalised languages. The truth of an ordinary language sentence like 'I am tired' obviously depends on who says it when. Davidson therefore makes truth a relation between a sentence, a person, and a time. Our T-sentences will therefore include ones like ' "I am tired" is true as (potentially) spoken by Smith at noon iff Smith is tired at noon'. But this modification is often ignored when not relevant.

A further feature of Davidson's view, and one which in fact links him closely to Quine, is that he does not think that if we apply the constraint I have discussed we shall find exactly one theory of truth for a given language that satisfies it. Any acceptable theory must generate only true T-sentences, but it may prove to be a matter of judgment which of indefinitely many theories gives the best fit for our evidence about what the speakers hold true. No-one after all is perfectly rational or knowledgeable, and we may have to decide between, say, attributing to a speaker a rather unlikely belief and attributing to him, or perhaps to someone else, a rather unlikely reaction to something said.

A few final comments may make clearer the nature of Davidson's enterprise and tie up one or two loose ends.

First, the theory as I have stated it looks like a theory of sentence-meaning. But it shows how this depends on word-meaning. The axioms are largely about the words, and the meaning of a word can be thought of as the way in which it contributes to the deduction of the theorems. As Davidson puts it at TM, p. 311:

> The theory reveals nothing about the conditions under which an individual sentence is true; it does not make those conditions any clearer than the sentence itself does. The work of the theory is in relating the known truth conditions of each sentence to those aspects ('words') of the sentence that recur in other sentences, and can be assigned identical roles in other sentences.

Second, as we saw in Chapter 3, some sentences which look grammatically like assertions or statements have been thought not to be so really, but to need some other kind of analysis. Value judgments were our main example. The present theory stays neutral on this point. To take Davidson's example at TM, pp. 316–17, ' "Bardot is good" is true iff Bardot is good' is a perfectly good T-sentence for our purposes. This problem associated with 'is good' simply travels with it from the object language to the metalanguage; i.e., from its appearance in the inner quote-marks to its appearance after the 'iff'. The T-sentence does not reckon to tell us anything about the metalanguage in which it is itself expressed. This is one aspect of a certain 'thinness' of the theory, which I will come back to.

Third, as I said above, Tarski limits himself to formalised languages, while Davidson caters for natural languages. But Davidson is under no illusions about the magnitude of his task. His approach is programmatic. His claim is not to have provided a complete theory covering all different types of sentence, but to have shown what such a theory would consist in. For instance, one might need a special rule to transform sentences with active verbs into sentences with passive verbs, so that we could derive T-sentences like, ' "Caesar was killed by Brutus" is true iff Brutus killed Caesar'. Even our old friend 'Snow is white' gives trouble. What does 'Snow' stand for? All snow? Any bit of snow? All possible bits of snow? Davidson ends TM with a whole battery of problems still to be solved, though in RI, written some years later, he is able to report some progress (p. 320). Problems of this kind, however, will arise for any theory of meaning.

Fourth, the theory remains firmly in the tradition that gives primacy to assertion over other speech acts. Most of the problems listed in TM concern sentences that at least purport to have truth-values. That of 'all the sentences that seem not to have truth-values at all: the imperatives, optatives, interrogatives, and a host more' (p. 321) brings up the tail.

Fifth, we must distinguish what is empirical and what is not empirical in what Davidson is doing. To construct for any given language a Davidsonian theory of truth, i.e. a theory of the kind we have been discussing, and to ensure that it satisfies the holistic constraint, is an empirical enterprise. But to claim that this is the correct approach to analysing the notion of meaning is to make a philosophical and non-empirical claim.

I said a few paragraphs back that Davidson's theory has a certain thinness about it. It is 'reductionist', in the sense that it reduces a theory of meaning to a theory of truth, or anyway tells us that the notion of truth conditions is all we need to analyse the notion of meaning. This is its main claim, and it is not surprising that this has been the main target for attacks on it. The main question is, can it give us as much as we really want? One writer who doubts if it can is Dummett, whom we met briefly at the end of Chapter 2 as one who rejected realism in favour of what is now called anti-realism.

Apart from the article on 'Truth' I mentioned previously Dummett has written two articles that are especially relevant. The second is intended as a sequel to the first, but can be read independently. Both have the title 'What is a theory of meaning?', which highlights the question of how much we ought to expect from such a theory. I will refer to the second of them as WTM2. Both sides agree that a theory of meaning for a given language must be a theory of understanding, a theory which enabled anyone who knew it to understand the language. But should it also explain what that understanding consists in? In particular should it explain either how the understanding is acquired by speakers of the language or how it is manifested by them; for if it cannot be manifested by them, then what counts as their having it? Dummett thinks it should explain both of these and that Davidson's theory cannot. Contrasting his own approach with Davidson's he says (WTM2, p. 130):

> I have been concerned ... not with the upward process of
> constructing a theory of reference [a theory generating T-sentences, as
> I explained above] from the records of initially uninterpreted
> utterances, but with the downward process of deriving, from the
> theory of reference, the practice of using the language; if the claim
> that a given theory of reference is the correct one ... is to be

substantiated, such a downward process of derivation must be possible.

Both Dummett and his critics concentrate more on the manifestation strand than on the acquisition strand of these questions, and I will do so too.

The issue is an intricate one and not very easy to grasp. But it represents the deep philosophical cleavage between realists and anti-realists. Dummett's position is strongly influenced by two connected sources, the later philosophy of Wittgenstein, represented in his *Philosophical Investigations* especially, and the 'intuitionist' school of L. E. J. Brouwer and others in the philosophy of mathematics.

Wittgenstein's views, which differ from his earlier views in the *Tractactus* that I mentioned earlier, will meet us again from another point of view in Chapter 8. For our present purpose they can be summed up in the slogan that 'meaning is use', a slogan that also heavily influenced post-war linguistic philosophy. Roughly, the point of the slogan is this: how can our language have any meaning to us except in so far as we can use it? Language has developed as what expresses our thought, so how could it express a thought we could never have? And how could we ever have a thought, or understand it, if there was no way in which we could manifest our understanding of it? Here we want to ask what would count as manifesting this. Dummett replies that we must be able to verify it, or at least to recognise a verification of it if one is offered to us; he does not insist that we must be able to construct one for ourselves. Let us take our previous example, that the (infinite) universe contains no purple cows. What, Dummett would ask, could count as our ever being in a position to recognise that this had been verified, and so to assert it? But if in *no* circumstances could we assert it, how could it mean anything to us? Yet for Davidson its meaning would be given by the T-sentence ' "There are no purple cows" is true iff there are no purple cows', provided one knew that this T-sentence was derivable in a suitable theory, and there seems no obvious reason why it should not be. Dummett might indeed ask how we understood the T-sentence itself; but if he pressed this line of argument he would risk falling to an objection of J. McDowell: if we insist, with Dummett, that a theory of meaning must be something that guides our ability to talk, and then insist that we must first understand a statement of the theory itself, we shall be dangerously near to demanding 'the impossible ideal of a theory we could state to a person in order to teach him to talk'.

The other influence on Dummett, mathematical intuitionism, is similar in its concern to avoid giving meaning to statements that transcend our capacities to intuit what it would be for them to be true. Intuitionists think it makes no sense to call a mathematical statement true unless one has, or at least thinks that someone has, a proof of it. Correspondingly they think it makes no sense to call such a statement false, or its negation true, unless one has a proof of this negation, a disproof of the original statement. But this leads them to the famous, or infamous, 'intuitionistic logic'. One principle of classical logic is that of double negation, that any proposition is equivalent to the negation of its negation; p implies not-not-p, and not-not-p implies p. The intuitionist accepts the first half of this but not the second half. In his eyes to say 'not-p' is to say you have a disproof of p, and to say 'not-not-p' is to say you have a disproof of the idea that one could have a disproof of p, and he refuses to allow that this amounts to having a proof of p. Note that he is not saying merely that absence of a disproof of p does not amount to a proof of p, as anyone might agree. He says that even the known impossibility of a disproof of p does not amount to a proof of p. A consequential casualty on the intuitionist's system is the law of excluded middle. Classical logic would formulate this as '(p)(p or not-p)'. (Remember from Chapter 2 that '(p)' means 'for all p' or 'whatever proposition p may be'.) But for the intuitionist this becomes '(p)(p is provable or p is disprovable)', and this he refuses to accept.

Dummett extends these ideas from mathematics to discourse in general. He combines them with the 'meaning is use' doctrine, and concludes that the notion that underlies meaning is not truth but assertibility. A statement has meaning for us if we can understand it, and to do this we must be able to manifest our understanding; we must be able to react in some relevant way, such as expressing agreement, when we are confronted with a verification of the statement. Since we are not confined to mathematics now, the verification may consist in other things than proof: we may, for instance, observe something which we take to verify the statement, or we may infer something from what we observe and take what we infer to verify the statement. The point is that a statement can have no meaning for us unless there are conditions under which we could manifest our understanding of it by asserting it, or else asserting its negation. If there is a purple cow, we might come across it, and then we could reject 'There are no purple cows' and assert that there is at least one. If there are none, then obviously we could never be in a position to reject 'There are no purple cows'; but neither could we ever be in a position to assert it, by verifying that there are none. So we cannot guarantee in all circumstances that 'There are no purple cows' is true or false, and we cannot understand it in its full generality. We can only understand it in so far as we take it as short for something like 'There are no purple cows today in Bromsgrove', which we could show to be either true or false. The same applies to our Chapter 2 example, 'Jones was brave'. Jones being dead, we may not be able to produce any situation that would show, even with some probability, how he would have reacted in the face of danger.

But neither have we any guarantee that we shall never be able to decide the question about purple cows, or Jones's bravery. This brings out Dummett's attitude to the principle, or family of principles, called the law of excluded middle. (For the relations between some members of the family see the Preface to Dummett's *Truth and Other Enigmas* (TOE), p. xix.) Dummett refuses to accept the principle that every statement is either true or false, usually called the principle of bivalence. But he accepts its double negation, that no statement is neither true nor false (*ibid.*, p. xix); for he thinks we could never actually disprove of any statement that it was either true or false. True to his intuitionist logic, he refuses to infer the principle of bivalence from its double negation. Similarly in the sense of 'correct' in which it is correct to assert true statements and incorrect to assert false ones he refuses to call any assertion neither correct nor incorrect, but also refuses to infer that every assertion must be either correct or incorrect (see especially WTM 2, pp. 121–4). We saw in Chapter 2 that he refuses to admit any third alternative to designated and undesignated truth-values.

Two final subsidiary points about Dummett's position: First, I have spoken mainly in terms of verification and correctness. But actually he thinks a proper account should treat falsification and incorrectness as prior to these. (Cf. WTM 2, pp. 123–6, and also the quotation in Chapter 2, p. 46, from the 'Truth' article.) Second, he normally speaks as though verifiability meant conclusive verifiability. But sometimes he does allow a role to a weaker form of verifiability. (See p. xxxviii of the Preface to TOE.)

Because of his emphasis on verification Dummett's reaction to Davidson represents something like a return to logical positivism, or rather an attempt to preserve an insight that Dummett attributes to logical positivism. I cannot stop to explore just how close to the logical positivists he is, but for his own view on this see WTM 2, p. 111. The most fundamental philosophical issue arising here is that of realism versus anti-realism, which is reflected in the question of how truth is related to assertibility. As so often happens in philosophy, part of the difficulty turns out to lie in saying just what is meant by realism and anti-realism, and it is interesting that in his later writings Dummett soft-pedals his adherence to anti-realism, though without specifying very explicitly why: see the 'Postscript (1972)' to the 'Truth' article in TOE,

p. 24, and also pp. xxxi and xxxix of the Preface to that volume. But we might say in general that the realism/anti-realism issue as Dummett conceives it amounts to this: whether we use truth to analyse meaning or, as Dummett prefers, substitute for truth some notion like assertibility, can the notion which we use for analysing meaning transcend what is accessible to our minds? Does it make sense to suppose that something could be true, assertible, or whatever, even though it was in principle impossible for us to find out that it was so? If we think the answer must be negative for whatever notion we use in analysing meaning, we may well feel inclined to call the notion in question assertibility rather than truth. We could then, so far as that goes, go on being realists about truth while giving some Dummett-style analysis of meaning in terms of assertibility.

III

Before leaving meaning we ought to look, however briefly, at one more theory in this area, a theory which has wide ramifications, and is associated especially with Kripke and Putnam. This takes us back to the meaning of terms, and names in particular. We have already seen some reason to doubt the view that a name's meaning is its bearer. But a name can have, and many would say must have, a bearer, so we might well ask how a name is related to its bearer. What conditions must be satisfied for 'Aristotle' to be the name of Aristotle? Since we last discussed names we have examined theories which make names, like other words, have meaning only in the context of a sentence, if not in that of a whole language. The question we are now coming to can be viewed within that framework. It asks for a bit more detail about how certain words contribute what they do to our communications. For instance, on a Davidsonian view what does the axiom governing 'Aristotle' amount to, and what conditions must be satisfied for it rather than some other axiom to belong to the relevant system? Suppose an axiom says that 'Aristotle' designates Aristotle. 'Designates' is a semantical term, i.e., one belonging to the general sphere of meaning. One might expect a pure axiom system to contain only syntactical terms, i.e., those not concerned with relating symbols to the world. But if we want our system to contain semantical terms – and it might be hard to avoid this in a useful system – we should be prepared to explain them: under what conditions, for instance, does 'Aristotle' designate Aristotle?

Historically two conflicting views about names have held the stage, stemming from John Stuart Mill and Frege. Mill thought names were 'meaningless marks' attached to objects merely to identify them. Most names after all sound pretty meaningless and arbitrary, and even though a name like 'Dartmouth' suggests that the town bearing it stands at the mouth of the Dart, this is a mere suggestion and quite inessential. The Black Sea is no blacker than any other. Frege, however, thought that names were really no different from descriptive phrases, which apply to objects in virtue of some meaning they have, which Frege called *Sinn*, usually, though not always, translated 'sense'. A proper name might not wear its sense on its face, as it were, but it must have one, for otherwise how could it get, and stay, attached to its object? Russell, incidentally, is sometimes coupled with Mill and sometimes with Frege. This is because he agreed with Mill about real names, which he called 'logically proper names', but thought, for reasons I cannot go into, that there were few if any of them. (Russell talks of 'a name ... in the proper strict logical sense of the word'; but 'logically proper name' is now standardly used in discussions of Russell.) He agreed with Frege that ordinary proper names should be treated as descriptions in disguise; actually he rejected Frege's notion of 'sense' and substituted for it his own so-called 'theory of descriptions' – but that is another story.

Mill's view taught one to regard a name as meaning its bearer, a view we have seen some reason to reject, I think. It also makes it hard to see how a sentence like 'Tully is Cicero' can be informative, as sometimes it can: but only some of the rival views take this problem into account. The obvious way of avoiding Mill's view seems to be to supply a Fregean 'sense' to be the name's meaning and to link it to its bearer. But what sense? What does 'Aristotle' mean (we will assume we are using it of the Stagirite, not Onassis)? Aristotle had vastly, indeed infinitely, many properties, some known to us and some not, some important and some not. How many and which are to appear in the sense of 'Aristotle'? Does 'Aristotle' mean, say, 'the man who was born in Stagira in 384 BC and wrote the *Metaphysics* and tutored Alexander the Great'? But suppose he did not: historians may have his dates and birthplace wrong, and maybe Theophrastus wrote the *Metaphysics*. Anyway does not any such selection of properties look rather arbitrary? Perhaps we should look for essential properties, properties Aristotle must have had on pain of not being Aristotle at all. Being human might be one of these, for it seems plausible to say that nothing non-human could have been Aristotle. In fairy tales princesses turn into frogs, but not very froggy ones. They tend to spend their time wishing some handsome prince would come and rescue them, which ordinary frogs don't. But if we stick to essential properties, can we distinguish Aristotle from anyone else? Should we try 'the man who was called

"Aristotle" '? But he was not (he was called 'Aristoteles'), and anyway he could easily have had another name. Nor will 'the man *we* call "Aristotle" ' do. Like the previous suggestion it gives us a neat way of providing a different sense for different names, and so solving the Tully/Cicero problem. But it is circular. 'By "Aristotle" I mean the man I call "Aristotle" ' does not really get us very far.

A sophisticated version of this approach is one associated in particular with J. R. Searle ('Proper names', *Mind*, 1958, and also his book *Speech Acts*), and sometimes called a 'cluster' theory. It derives from a similar view of universals taken by Wittgenstein and now called the 'family resemblance' view; but let us stick to names. Here we take a large set of properties, like being born in Stagira, writing the *Metaphysics*, etc., and weight them according to their importance. We then say 'Aristotle' means 'the man who has sufficiently many of these properties'. There is no particular property, and no definite number of them, that he must have, though important ones count for more than less important ones.

This view has many advantages. We can take any single property and still say something informative by saying Aristotle had it. Similarly we do not contradict ourselves by saying he did not have it. The property of having sufficiently many of certain other properties is a second-order property, because defined in terms of ordinary, first-order, properties. This second-order property seems to be essential to Aristotle, and also to distinguish him from other people.

Kripke, however, disagrees. He advocates a quite different approach. Suppose that all we know or believe about Homer is that he wrote the *Iliad*. Might we discover that actually we were wrong and the *Iliad* was written by another man with the same name? Kripke thinks we might. The Fregean must disagree, since for him 'Homer' just means 'the author of the *Iliad*'. He could agree that Homer might not have written the *Iliad*, if this means that that man, whoever he was, who in fact wrote the *Iliad* might not have done so. But he cannot agree that Homer may not have written the *Iliad*, if this means that perhaps that man, whoever he was, who in fact wrote the *Iliad* did not write it – a plain contradiction.

First, let us distinguish between saying that a description is synonymous with a name and saying that it fixes the reference for the name. 'Metre' is the name of a length, defined as that of a certain stick of platinum in Paris (call it stick S; incidentally, as we shall see, Kripke does not limit his theory to proper names). Since sticks can grow and shrink, let us define a metre as the length of S at a certain time t. (This oversimplifies, but never mind.) Now 'metre' does not *mean* 'the length of S at t'. It is the name of a certain definite length, in fact about 39 inches. S had that length at t, and that is why we chose that particular length to call a metre. We used the length of S to fix the reference of 'metre'. But it is the length we are calling a metre, and the length – *that* length: about 39 inches – could not have been any other length than it was. But S could easily have had some other length instead. So 'metre' cannot be synonymous with 'the length of S at t'. We could, of course, have used the word 'metre' for that other length instead, but then 'metre' would not have meant what it now does mean. We could, even now, decide by fiat to use 'metre' synonymously with 'the length of S at t, whatever that might be', so that when we said Smith was two metres high we should be saying he was twice the height of S. In that case we should have to admit that, had S been longer or shorter at t, while Smith stayed the same height, Smith would not have been two metres high. But this is not in fact how we use 'metre'.

Once a metre, always a metre. Something a metre long could have been any length instead, and the word 'metre' could have meant 'fishcake'. But a metre itself could not have been any length but what it is, and so, as long as 'metre' means what it does, it must apply to just that length. Kripke uses 'designator' to cover both proper names and descriptions like 'the length of S' or the 'length of S at t'. He then divides designators into rigid and non-rigid. A rigid designator designates the same thing in any possible situation (or any in which the thing exists). 'Metre' is a rigid designator, and so is 'square of three', since in no situation could it designate anything but nine. But 'the number of planets' is non-rigid, since there could easily have been some other number than nine. It is essential to remember that we are considering possible situations, including those in which the English language was different from what it is; but the language we are using to talk about these situations is ordinary English.

Kripke next claims that proper names are always rigid designators. If they are, they cannot be synonymous with any descriptions that are not. Also, identity statements linking proper names, like 'Tully is Cicero', will be necessarily true, if true at all. Yet surely it is a significant discovery, not just something obvious, that Tully is Cicero? Maybe, replies Kripke. But it is still necessary that that man who is in fact Tully should be identical with that man who is in fact Cicero: namely, himself; for how can a man fail to be identical with himself?

Proper names could still, so far as this goes, be synonymous with rigidly designating descriptions. But Kripke thinks they are not, and that often when we use a name we may have no such description in mind, nor any description which applies uniquely to the thing we are talking about. Perhaps sometimes we do fix the reference by means of a description; an example might be when we use 'Jack the Ripper' as a name for whoever may turn out to have committed certain murders. But normally, he thinks, what happens is that we take a name over from the society we live in, complete with its reference but without any particular descriptions attached. Therefore we might find that Aristotle did *none* of the things we previously thought he did, provided these did not include any properties essential to him, as they well might not.

Kripke's theory of names is a causal theory. The point is that Aristotle stands in some causal relation with those who first call him 'Aristotle' (or 'Aristoteles' or anything else; the name can change). They see him, for instance. These people then cause their children or pupils to use the name in the same way; i.e., to talk about the same person. (There is a bit of a problem about just what counts as doing this.) These pupils may decide to call him 'Smith' instead, but they transmit the name, or its replacement, to their own pupils, and so on down to ourselves, so that there is a causal chain linking Aristotle himself with our own use of the name we call him by. The chain can include writing books, and any other way we might have of transmitting uses of words.

Now for that Homer example: Suppose a man called Homer by his contemporaries wrote the *Iliad*. But he then died, and another man, also called Homer, pinched the manuscript and successfully passed it off as his own. His contemporaries told their children about this Homer (the second one) and how he wrote the *Iliad*. The first Homer got forgotten. Succeeding generations passed on the tradition, but it got thinner as time went on, and by the time it reached ourselves the only fact associated with Homer was that he wrote the *Iliad*. Then the truth would be that Homer – the chap we call Homer, the second one – never wrote the *Iliad* at all, but someone else of the same name did, now totally unknown.

Not everyone accepts all this, but rather than discuss it further I want to mention three of the wider ramifications of Kripke's theory, two in this chapter and one in the next.

First we need two distinctions. One we have met already. This is between necessary and contingent statements, between statements which say what must be so and those which say what happens to be so or not so but might have been otherwise. (Like 'analytic', 'necessary' may or may not include 'necessarily false'. It is often convenient to limit it to 'necessarily true'.) The other distinction is between the *a priori* and the empirical. This is an epistemological distinction, concerning how something is known or knowable. Etymologically 'empirical' means 'by trial and error', but in fact it now means 'by observation'. We know something empirically if we know it through our senses, though these may be supplemented by calculation, inference, and interpretation.

(Interpretation involves difficulties, but let us pass them by.) We know something *a priori* if we know it without using our senses. A statement is called *a priori* if it can be known *a priori*. Some people insist that what can be known *a priori* must be known *a priori*, if at all. But this, as Kripke shows, is surely mistaken. I can know that there are infinitely many prime numbers in the same way I know that Tokyo is the capital of Japan: because I have been reliably told so.

Many people, and especially logical positivists, have held that the necessary and the *a priori* go together: whatever is necessary can be known *a priori*, and what can be known *a priori* must be necessary. Both these positions are plausible. If something is necessary, why should we be beholden to observation before we can know it? Surely it must be true anyway, whatever observation tells us? But if something is not necessary, if it could be otherwise, then what other means can we possibly use to tell us of its truth except observation?

Kripke, however, denies both these positions. Take Goldbach's famous conjecture, so far unproved and unrefuted, that every even number is the sum of two primes. Presumably if it is true, it is necessarily true. And might it not be that it is indeed true, but that no proof of it will ever be known, because none exists? (If we say yes, we are diametrically opposing Dummett's 'intuitionist' outlook.) But more germane to Kripke's purpose is our old example, 'Tully is Cicero'. If 'Tully' and 'Cicero' are both rigid designators, as he thinks, then 'Tully' designates the same thing in any possible situation (i.e., the name 'Tully' in actual English does; the *sound* 'Tully' could of course be used differently in other possible worlds). So does 'Cicero'. So 'Tully is Cicero' is either necessarily true or necessarily false. But only observation can tell us which. The observation will take the form of a historical investigation of how we come to use the names as we do.

More striking perhaps, at first anyway, is Kripke's denial of the other position, that what can be known *a priori* must be necessary. Let us go back to the case of the metre, defined as the length of stick S at t. How do we know that S is one metre long? We need not measure it, and measuring it would give us no help, for we have simply defined a metre as whatever length S was at t. We know *a priori* therefore that S was one metre long at t. But as we said before, S could have been any length instead: we never defined a metre as whatever length S *might* have been at t. 'S was one metre long at t' is therefore contingent.

Shall we accept this? Can I be said to *know* that S is one metre long if I have just defined it as being so? What is there for me to know? Well, it will be true that S is one metre long, however it came to be true, and I can answer questions about its length, just as I can about things whose length I do know. In all this we assume it is I that did the defining; if someone else did, my knowledge that S is one metre long is empirical, since I can only know it by hearing it, etc. Anyway Kripke's separation of the *a priori* from the necessary is clearly important for epistemologists and metaphysicians not immediately concerned with the topic of meaning.

The second ramification of Kripke's theory I must treat far more briefly than it deserves. It is here that Putnam comes into the foreground, and we come back to the end of Chapter 5. How could we ever doubt that all cats are animals? Surely 'cat' just means 'animal of such-and-such a kind'? No, it does not, says the theory. Its meaning is no more to be given in terms of an equivalent description, or set of descriptions, than that of a proper name is. Perhaps some terms do have that sort of meaning, as 'bachelor' is simply an abbreviation for something like 'unmarried adult male'. But terms denoting natural kinds, like 'cat', do not behave like that. Cats have been around for some time and we have got to know them. But how well? Do they purr, for instance? Well, most of them do, it seems. But suppose, fancifully but not inconceivably, that we woke up one morning to find all our cats barking. Suppose, however, we found on investigation that this was only true of cats in advanced countries. Elsewhere they still purred. Further investigation reveals that cats have been subject through the ages to a hitherto unobserved virus, which attacked the vocal chords and reduced an original healthy bark to the present miserable purring noises. When the virus is removed the vocal chords quickly recover. Moreover, the virus turns out to be vulnerable to certain chemicals released into the atmosphere by modern industrialisation; purring cats born in New Guinea promptly start barking when brought to Europe. If all this happened, might we not say that cats do not purr at all, normally? They do under certain conditions, of course, just as men continually wheeze under certain bronchitic conditions, but cats are no more a purring species than men are a wheezing species.

Now take the statement 'Water is H_2O'. Does this give the meaning of 'water'? Hardly. We used the word 'water' long before H_2O came into the picture. But now suppose we go to Mars and find there a liquid that looks just like water and behaves like it in all ordinary situations, including hydrolysis and other common processes. But refined examination shows that actually it is not H_2O at all, but has a complicated structure – call it XYZ – which mimics the effects of water in all but the most subtle experiments. Would we call it water? We could, thereby using 'water' as a name for two different natural kinds; but we probably would not, Putnam thinks. Water has to be H_2O. But it has to only if it *is* H₂O. If our refined experiments showed that the stuff on Earth was XYZ, while that on Mars really was H_2O, we should keep 'water' for the stuff on Earth and deny it to the stuff on Mars.

The point of these examples (in essence Putnam's, though the details are partly mine) is to dispel the idea that a word like 'cat' or 'water' is synonymous with a group of properties, and that we decide its extension (what it applies to) by seeing what things have the relevant properties. We do indeed decide part of the extension in something like this way, as with the water case above, but only part of it. The point is that the rest of the extension is what we start with, and what fixes our use of the term. Cats are *these* things, and water is *this* stuff, and here we indicate standard cases by certain properties they have. But the point is that once we have picked them out – once we have decided that a certain group of objects are what we primarily count as cats – then it does not matter whether cats go on having those properties, or even whether they really had them in the first place. What does matter is certain *essential* properties they have, such as genetic constitution or chemical composition; but we may not know at the beginning what these essential properties are, and so they cannot enter into the meaning of the word. Once we have fixed the reference in this way, cats and water will be whatever things turn out to have the same essential properties, whatever they may be, of the cats and water we started from. (There is a slight puzzle in the case of cats: must they be genetically related to our cats? Would Martian beasts that not only looked the same but had the same essence be cats, or not? Suppose all natives south of the Wallace line turned out not to come from Adam, or the Olduvai Gorge, or wherever: would we exclude them from the human race? If not, why exclude Martians, if otherwise suitably qualified?)

But if we are concerned with essential properties in this way, how might cats fail to be animals, for surely being an animal is essential to a cat, if anything is? Yes, if cats *are* animals. But suppose, says Putnam, that all the cats we know turn out to be specially programmed robots radio-controlled from Mars and sent to spy on us? In that case, since these objects are robots, and they are also what fix the reference of 'cat' for us, cats are robots, and necessarily robots, and not animals at all. 'Cats are animals', if true, will be necessarily true, but, as we saw earlier, it does not follow that we can know it *a priori*. If cats are animals, they cannot be anything else; but they might *turn out* to be (and to have always been) something else, just as Goldbach's conjecture might turn out to be false.

Let me mention just one objection to all this. Suppose cats were what they seem to be, and the word 'cat' entered our language in the normal way, whatever that might be, but that one night the Martians came down and secretly killed all the cats and substituted for each of them a robot programmed to carry on, to all appearances, from where that cat had left off. The change being undetectable to us, we go on talking about cats, and the situation continues for years or even generations. (The cats are programmed to have kittens, which are also radio-controlled robots.) Our word 'cat' refers to these familiar things we have known for so long. But which of them? Only the animal ones, which gave us the word originally? Or the robots too, which are what now sustain our use of the word, except perhaps when we make certain historical remarks? Or did the word change its meaning that fateful night, even though our experiences remained quite unchanged, and language is *our* device for communicating about a world mediated to us through our experiences? The view under attack, where 'cat' means something like 'furry animal that purrs, etc.' and 'animal' means 'thing of such-and-such appearance and behaviour', would not face this particular difficulty. It would say there were two radically different kinds of cat, all of which were animals, but some of them, and therefore some animals, were not animate. Descartes managed to think that no non-human animals were conscious: they squeaked like dolls when you trod on them; his view probably strikes us as absurd, but not as unintelligible.

It is ironic perhaps that proper names, those fringe elements of our linguistic equipment, should once again take the centre of the stage in a theory of meaning. But whether or not this new doctrine is accepted, of its importance there is no doubt. The first ramification of the doctrine, concerning the *a priori* and the necessary, led us into the sphere of epistemology and metaphysics. This second one belongs largely in the sphere of philosophy of science. A third ramification springs from the idea that identity statements whose terms are rigid designators, like 'Tully is Cicero' or 'A metre is 39 inches', are necessarily true or necessarily false. This has important repercussions on a certain theory in the philosophy of mind. But that deserves a chapter to itself.

7 Mind and body

I

How many things am I? I am a man, to start with. I am also an Englishman, an adult, a don, a house-owner, and a dog-hater. I manage to combine being all of these quite happily for most of the time. But can I combine all my attributes quite as easily as this? I weight nine stone odd, and I often think about philosophy. But is it the same me that does both these things? My body weighs nine stone, and would go on doing so, for a bit anyway, if I died. But it sounds a bit odd to say my body thinks about philosophy.

I have answered the question 'How many things am I?' by saying I am several sorts of things. But am I also several things in another sense, as my suit is two things, a coat and trousers? My body, as I have said, can survive my death – for quite some time if I happen to be a mammoth frozen in the tundra. But doesn't it at least make sense to suppose that I too might survive my death, and go on thinking or having experiences, quite irrespective of what happened to my body? Do I need a body to dream with? Or anyway, do I need this body? So perhaps I am something quite separate from my body; or at least (since it is I, after all, that weigh nine stone) perhaps I am a body but something else as well. Perhaps I am two things, somehow bound up into one, a body plus a mind or soul. I once saw a letter in a newspaper from a perhaps rather unorthodox vicar claiming that he was five things: body, mind, soul, spirit and psyche. His reason, as far as I could make out, seemed to be that if you were five things, it was surely a fair bet that at least one of them would turn out to be immortal.

I know of no quintalists among philosophers; but dualism has had quite a respectable run, peaking at least twice, with Plato and Descartes. Both of these thought that the essential 'I' was something quite independent of the body, at least in certain circumstances, such as after death; a person was a pair of things, but one of the pair was very much the dominant partner. As one might expect, since he had nearly two thousand years more of philosophy behind him, Descartes took much more seriously than Plato did the problem of saying how this 'I' is related to the body it temporarily occupies; and clearly this is a problem we must take very seriously if we hold this view. We can hardly *just* say I am two things in one, and leave it at that.

If I am indeed two things, then one of them is much more obvious than the other. It is pretty clear that I have a body. This would only be denied by idealists of one sort or another, who deny the reality of anything physical or material at all. To discuss that position would take us beyond our present muttons, so I will only say one thing about it. Idealists do not escape the mind/body problem; they still have to explain why we say that we think, but not that our bodies think, and how the ideas we call people differ from those we call chairs and tables. But the other thing I might be, the mind or soul, is more problematic. Perhaps part of the reason for this is that, if there are such things, they seem to be the only denizens in their own realm. There are lots of material things that are not bodies (in the present sense of 'body', where it is connected with 'mind'). But there are less obviously any spiritual things that are not minds or souls. Such things might be called spirits, but they would seem to be just like souls except for the purely historical feature of never being tied to bodies. They are therefore less different from souls than chairs and tables are from human bodies, and there is minimal evidence for their existence (at any rate if we except God), or for variations among their kinds and species that might make them interesting for us to study, as we study the material world.

Many philosophers, it is true, believe in the existence of a whole lot of non-material things, abstract things like the universals we have met already, or numbers, or propositions. But these are generally felt not to be fellow denizens of souls and spirits in the spiritual realm, but to belong, if they exist at all, to a further realm alongside the material and the spiritual. Frege and Karl Popper (1902–) have both referred to this realm simply as the 'third realm', or 'third world', and it will not concern us further in this chapter. Finally, how about things like neutrinos and fields of force? These again are hardly in the same realm as souls. They are postulated by a theory aimed at explaining the material world, and differ from ordinary material things mainly by lacking mass. They might be called quasi-material.

Effectively then we are left with material or quasi-material objects and souls or minds. From now on I will normally talk of 'minds'. 'Mind' has a more intellectual sound, while 'soul' carries greater suggestions of a separate entity, but is now perhaps uncommon except in theology and pop music, and as the stock translation for the Greek word *psyche*.

Have I a mind? I like to think so. Maybe I also have a happy disposition. But if I have, it isn't something I take from the cupboard when the sun shines. My tendency to catch colds, my admiration for mathematicians, and my ability to get totally tied up in knots whenever I do any mathematics, are all things I 'have', but we feel little tempted to think of them as entities separate from the rest of me.

But *am* I a mind, either at the same time as being a body, so that I am two things, or else as a mind basically on its own which happens to be attached to a body at the moment? Am I, to use a simile as old as Aristotle, like a pilot in a vessel, or like a ghost in a machine, as Descartes has been (not altogether justly) accused of holding? Both these views are called dualist, for they both think of mind and body as two entities, whether they think that 'I' am somehow both at once, or am only mind, with body, as it were, trailing along behind. We will discuss later a view that I am both a body and a mind, but that these are one thing, not two.

I am not sure whether the reader who is new to the subject will think dualism so obvious as hardly to need stating, or so extraordinary that only a philosopher could have thought it up. It is certainly embedded in much of popular talk. We have already rehearsed some of the reasons in its favour. It seems that my mind and my body could each exist without the other, and there seem to be properties which can apply to one but cannot apply to the other (weighing nine stone, thinking about philosophy). Surely I cannot be just a body, because bodies, like other material things, are essentially extended in space. Their properties therefore should essentially involve extension, in the way that, say, weight and colour do; or at the very least should involve location, in case we think points could be coloured or weight regarded as acting at the centre of gravity. The involvement might be indirect; a physical object might have the property of being, say, useful or beautiful, which does not directly involve extension; but on the view we are considering the object will be useful, etc. only because of certain spatial properties it has. This is a feature of physical objects that philosophers like Descartes used to express by saying that physical objects only had one attribute, extension; their other properties were 'modes' of this attribute; i.e., ways in which it manifested itself. But thinking does not seem to involve space essentially at all. Why do I need to be extended, or even located, to think about mathematics?

I have divided dualism (suitably enough) into two kinds, one saying I am a pair of things, a mind plus a body, and the other saying I am a mind, which occupies a body, whether or not it always will do so. That there is no third kind, saying I am a body which has or is occupied by a

119

mind, is not surprising. For in talking about this subject at all I am doing philosophy, and if there are two things there at all, body and mind, it is hardly likely to be the body *as opposed to* the mind that philosophises and refers to itself as 'I', indeed refers to anything as anything. However, we can assimilate the two kinds for most purposes while discussing them, for an objection to one of them can normally be re-expressed as a corresponding objection to the other.

The most obvious objection to any view saying that I am two things is simply to ask how I, one person who refers to himself by one word, 'I', can possibly be two things: not just one thing seen from different points of view, as I can be both a don and a house-owner, but two substantively different objects, where one is not the other; the don, after all, *is* the house-owner, even though to be a don is not the same thing as to be a house-owner. Are the two things *parts* of a single thing? But how are the parts put together if one is extended and the other is not? Verbally we could answer all this by switching to the other form of dualism, and saying that I am a mind and possess a body. But then the objection will turn into a request to explain what we mean by 'possess' here. On either view, how is the mind related to the body?

Descartes for all his insistence on dualism was well aware of this problem. I am not in my body, he said, as a pilot is in a ship. (This is why I suggested earlier that it is a little unjust to saddle him with the 'ghost in a machine' view without further ado.) His reason concerned the way I know about what is happening in my body. If a ship is damaged the pilot may observe this, just as he may observe that another ship alongside is damaged. But if my foot is damaged I do not just observe this; I feel it. If I am something separate from my body I might receive messages from my foot telling me of the damage. But I do not just receive messages; I feel a pain and also, as he might add (and does say elsewhere), I feel it in the foot.

What does this show? Descartes thought that if it showed anything it was in danger of showing too much. For sometimes we feel a pain 'in the foot' when the damage is elsewhere, or even when there is no foot there to feel it in, because the foot has been amputated (the 'phantom limb' phenomenon). Could we not in principle, we might add, feel a pain 'in the tail', even though we have never had a tail? I am not sure how far such thought experiments could be extended. Could I feel a pain in the book lying on the table beside me? Or in the moon?

Descartes concluded that, though the damage, if there was any, might be in the foot, the pain was not in the foot, but only in (in another sense) the mind. The foot might not even be there. The mind has a single attribute, consciousness; Descartes called it 'thinking', in a wide sense.

Feeling a pain in the foot was a mode of this attribute, a form which our conscious experience took. We can give Descartes credit for being aware of the problem and not glossing over it. It is not so obvious that he solved it. We are still left to wonder *how* something going on in the foot, or in the brain for that matter, could cause such a feeling, and we still have no explanation of the 'footiness' of the feeling itself.

A similar difficulty arises when we consider actions. For Descartes the mind controlled the actions of the body by setting in motion the 'animal spirits' at a certain point in the brain. (The animal spirits were a sort of animal whisky flowing along the nerves. We might substitute: by firing certain neurones). Everything then followed mechanically. But do we act in that way? We fire a gun by pulling the trigger, and pull the trigger by flexing our finger, but we do not flex our finger *by* doing anything – we just flex it. Actions like flexing our finger are often called basic actions. No doubt when we do flex our finger certain neurones fire. But firing them is not a basic action in this sense. In fact, if you tell me to fire certain neurones, the only way I can obey is probably *by*, say, flexing my finger, which will bring it about that they *have* fired. Are we to attribute to our Cartesian minds a knowledge of physiology that few of us overtly possess? Or are we to posit an unconscious mind alongside, or as part of, the conscious mind, despite Descartes's insistence that the attribute of the mind is consciousness? But apart from anything else, what would be the point of the conscious mind in this case, and how would it relate to the unconscious one?

Perhaps anyway it is time we counter-attacked and questioned Descartes's assumption that thinking is something we can conceive ourselves doing without any reference to the body or to anything extended.

Can we think without language or some kind of symbols, and what follows if we cannot? We are on the edge of a deep and bubbling volcano, and we shall only be able to take a brief walk along the rim of the crater. To borrow an example from an article published some years ago by W. J. Ginnane, suppose it suddenly occurs to you that Peter might drop in for a drink. What actually happens? Perhaps a vague image of Peter standing at the door flashes across your mind, mixed up with one of yourself taking a bottle and glasses from the cupboard. Perhaps you inwardly half-hear the word 'Peter', and have a sensation of pleasure or annoyance. The possibilities are endless, but what in any case do they add up to? How can such bits and pieces possibly constitute a coherent thought? How, for instance, can they make the difference between thinking that he might drop in and merely imagining him doing

121

so while knowing that he won't? Yet how can *all* such bits and pieces be dispensable from such thoughts? This is the problem of imageless thought, a problem which occupied psychologists and philosophers more some fifty years ago than it does today – but more, I think, because it has been given up than because it has been solved. I cannot pursue it further now. But suppose the bits and pieces are not only not sufficient for a thought to occur but not necessary either. Suppose that thinking is what Ginnane calls 'pure intentionality', which just means that the bits and pieces are quite superfluous. The question then arises whether, in the case of any given individual, this could always have been so. Could relatively complicated thoughts, such as that Peter *might* drop in *for a drink*, occur to anyone who had never learned a language? Or could they only occur without any words or images, etc. in the way that habitual processes can take quick short cuts after they have been learned slowly? One might ask this question even more pressingly concerning abstract thoughts about mathematics or philosophy: could such thoughts occur, however wordlessly or imagelessly, to someone who had never learned a language?

If the correct answer is no, as I suspect, the next question is: what is involved in learning a language? In particular, how far must the world of spatial extension be involved? A language presumably involves symbols, and it seems reasonable to think that these must be drawn from the worlds of sight, touch or hearing. Maybe one day dogs will invent a language of smells, but let's forget about that until they do.

Symbols drawn from sight or touch, like letters or braille pins, must occupy space. Does this imply that a mind which is to receive and understand them must itself occupy space? Perhaps not in any strict sense. But such a mind must be connected to extension in a fairly intimate way. The different parts of an extended object must be able to represent themselves to the mind as separate. It is not just that the mind must be able to imagine an extended world for itself, but that it must be able to be differentially affected by different parts of the world. This connection of the mind with space is reinforced if the mind is not only to receive and understand symbols but also to produce them, even if only in soliloquy. Of course, it is obvious that our minds are connected with space to this extent anyway. What the present consideration suggests is that anything we should call a mind at the human level – anything that can use a language or engage in abstract thought – *must* be so connected with space.

Actually this is a little too strong. I have said nothing of symbols drawn from the world of hearing. Sounds do not obviously involve space, at any rate in the literal sense; they may be said to occupy a 'space' of their own, but this, which could be said of things like numbers too, simply means that they can be distinguished from each other and ordered in various ways. Language could be, as of course it mainly is, based on sounds. So a mind need not, so far as having a language goes, be connected with space. Furthermore, it need not even appeal to space to provide the objects it talks about, for these too could be sounds. But if we use all this to escape from the considerations of the last paragraph, we must remember two things. First, how would a mind produce sounds? It is not in principle impossible that sounds should be produced without the use of any extended objects; but such production of them would be something quite outside our actual experience. Second, even if a mind does not have to be directly connected with space in order to have language, and everything that depends on language, it does seem that it must be connected with the material (light, sound, etc.) that we receive through the senses. Many philosophers, from Plato onwards or even earlier, have tried to discount the senses and have treated them as providing mere subsidiary, if not downright misleading, material to the independent activity of a pure mind. Such philosophers may be accused, I think, of underestimating the need for language if any worthwhile mental activity is to occur.

There are at least two further problems that confront us when we try to think what it would be like for a spirit to exist quite independently of any body. They may not necessarily be insurmountable, but they must at least be faced. One of them is connected again with language, and is this: how could such a spirit distinguish between thoughts that were communicated to it by another spirit and thoughts which arose spontaneously within itself? It will not do to say that its own thoughts are at its beck and call and under its control, because this is often not so. Thoughts arise in us quite unbidden, and most people are familiar with the obsessive thought that one cannot get rid of. We might add that difficulties of this nature also arise for some forms of telepathy.

If the spirit were able to perceive the world of the senses (colours, sounds, etc.) one might suppose it could identify thoughts coming to it from outside as we do at the moment, for example, by hearing them as opposed to merely imagining that we hear them. But this brings us to the second problem: how would such a spirit be able to distinguish these two, perceiving and imagining? How, for instance, would it distinguish being in Piccadilly Circus and imagining the Place de la Concorde from being in the Place de la Concorde and imagining Piccadilly Circus?

II

Traditional dualism, then, has its difficulties. But if we reject it, what shall we put in its place? Philosophers through the ages have come up with various alternatives, which have in common at least this much, that none of them seems to be very satisfactory. There is certainly no generally agreed view, nor any near prospect of one. As an example, let us look at just one of these views, one which, though it has antecedents going back at least as far as Spinoza (1632–77), dates in its modern form from the 1950s, when it was introduced mainly by a group of Australian philosophers. It is usually called the identity theory of body and mind, though various versions of it are also called physicalism, central state materialism, or just materialism.

As the theory is concerned to answer the question of how mind is related to body, one would expect it, from its name, to say that mind is identical with body, that I am two sorts of thing, as I am a don and a house-owner. As it stands this is much too crude, if only because there are many parts of the body that pretty clearly have nothing to do with mind at all. What then is identical with what, according to the theory? There is no simple answer to this, and the theory takes various forms according to various answers that are given. The general idea is that the mind is not a separate entity over and above the body, and conscious experiences are not separate entities over and above bodily phenomena, but are identical with some of them, in particular with certain states or processes in the brain, or perhaps in the central nervous system (whence the name 'central state materialism').

At first sight this probably seems rather bizarre. When I see, say, an after-image I am not seeing something happening in my brain. But this would be a misunderstanding. The theory does not say that the after-image is something in the brain, but that the experience of seeing, or having, the after-image is a state or process existing or going on in the brain. Admittedly this is not what it seems like. The experience does not present itself to us *as* a brain-process. But lots of things are not what they seem. Lightning does not seem to be an electrical discharge, until the scientists tell us that that is what it is, and heat does not present itself to us as molecular motion. That lightning is an electrical phenomenon and that heat is molecular motion are empirical discoveries. Lightning and heat might have turned out to be quite different things from what they in fact are, and indeed for many centuries were thought to be quite different. In the same way, our theory claims, sensations, etc. might not have been brain processes, but this is what neurophysiology suggests that they are. Of course neurophysiology is relatively in its infancy, and we cannot be as sure that sensations are brain-processes as we are that heat is molecular motion. But what the identity theorists insist on is that there are no *philosophical* objections to their being so. Whether they are in fact so, and if they are, which sensations are identical with which brain-processes, are for physiology to say.

An important feature of the identity theory as normally held is that the identity is contingent. Similarly, it is not claimed that statements about sensations *mean* the same as statements about brain-processes, any more than 'I see lightning' means the same as 'I see an electrical discharge'; people talked about seeing lightning long before electrical discharges had even been heard of.

One of the avowed motives of the identity theorists might be called ontological economy: they want to keep to a minimum the number of distinct things that are postulated to exist. They appeal to 'Occam's razor', a maxim of method which says: Entities are not to be multiplied beyond necessity. We do not want to postulate minds or conscious phenomena as separate entities in addition to bodies and cerebral phenomena, if we can help it. In this motivation we can surely agree with the identity theorists. The simplest hypothesis may not, as such, be more likely to be true. But if two hypotheses are otherwise equally balanced, we would accept the simpler as a matter of explanatory convenience. It is generally accepted as a principle of method that we should explain things as economically as possible, other things being equal.

But how much is achieved in the present case? Even if we can get rid of sensations, etc. as separate entities, are we not left at least with certain extra *properties*, beyond those which apply to material objects like the brain? For suppose I see a red after-image. It is unlikely that any brain-process is red. True, it is the having of the after-image, not the after-image itself, which is supposed to be identical with the brain-process. But red is involved in the having of the after-image in a way it is not involved in the brain-process.

J. J. C. Smart, one of the original proponents of the identity theory, deals with this by saying that when we talk in what might be called sensation language – when we talk of having sensations, or seeing after-images, etc. – we talk in a way which is essentially less specific than the way we would talk in if we talked in terms of our brain-processes, supposing we knew enough physiology to do so. When we say 'I see a red after-image' we mean something like this: 'There is something going on which is like what is going on when I see a tomato in standard conditions.' The way in which it is like what is then going on is left undetermined, and Smart thinks that by leaving it so we can say what we want to say without mentioning any special property, like redness, which is involved in having the after-image but not similarly involved in the brain-process. Also we need not know what physiological things are happening in the brain. The 'something' that is going on is simply some brain-process or other. (See C. V. Borst (ed.), *The Mind/Brain Identity Theory*, pp. 59–61.).

We might wonder whether this analysis is worth the effort. Even if we allow the use of 'like' where the respect in which the two situations are being compared is left completely indeterminate, we have the apparent arbitrariness of having to bring in a tomato, or a pillar box or anything else we might substitute. But anyway can we really avoid mental properties, or 'psychic' ones, as Smart calls them? If sensations really are brain-processes, then they will have the properties, neurological or other, that brain-processes have, as Smart admits (p. 61). We may not talk of them as having those properties, but that does not matter. We don't normally say that the evening star is sometimes visible in the morning, but it is true that the evening star (i.e., the planet Venus, which is also the morning star) *is* sometimes visible in the morning. But if sensations are brain-processes, and therefore have the properties of brain-processes, is it not equally true that brain-processes, or some of them, are sensations, and so have the properties of sensations? Suppose I have a feeling of anger, and claim that it is justified. Must I also claim that the brain-process with which, on the theory, it is identical is also justified? But can we really talk of brain-processes being justified or unjustified? In view of what we have been saying it seems that we must, though we might add that it is only as a consequence of being identified with the feeling that the brain-process can be called justified; we do not first have to find out whether it is justified in order then to conclude that, since it has all the properties of the feeling, it is identical with the feeling (see T. Nagel in the Borst volume, especially pp. 221–2).

There is one device the identity theorist might call in aid here. Some adjectives can only be applied to an object when it is described in certain ways. A large mouse is not a large animal. A qualified architect may be a quack doctor and an illegitimate son. Such adjectives are called attributive, as opposed to predicative adjectives like 'red', which can apply to an object however it is described. Attributive adjectives are of different kinds. The large mouse could not have been a large animal, though an animal can be large. The qualified architect could have been also a qualified doctor, thought not a qualified son, since sons can be legitimate but hardly qualified. Now suppose a certain experience is vivid or justified and a certain brain-process is confined within a cubic inch. If they are identical, the experience should be confined within a cubic inch and the brain-process should be vivid. Perhaps the truth is that they are, but that the situation is only properly described by saying that the entity in question, which is both an experience and a brain-process, is vivid *qua* experience and contained within a cubic inch *qua* brain-process. The son after all is also qualified – though only *qua* architect.

But if we take this line we have not got rid of the presumably 'psychic' property of being justified. What we have done is rather to show that the identity theory does not have to get rid of it but is compatible with the reality of such properties. So far so good for the identity theory, if such properties do indeed exist, as they seem to. But we cannot at the same time claim it as a merit of the theory that it gets rid of such properties and so satisfies our Occamite inclinations. We have defended the theory, but only at the price of removing one of its motivations.

Before going on let me mention a point against Smart's version of the theory by J. Cornman (see the Borst volume, p. 126). As we saw, Smart translates a sentence like 'I see a red after-image' into something essentially more general, like 'There is something going on like what goes on when I see a tomato in standard conditions'. But why is this not equally good as a translation of 'I see a round after-image', given that tomatoes are round? Even if we replace 'tomato' by a group of objects which have in common only that they are red, we can still ask why the resulting sentence would be a translation of 'I see a red after-image' rather than of 'I see a coloured after-image'. Smart's appeal to generality and unspecificness does not seem to do the trick he wants.

One thing our discussion of Smart does is make us raise the question of what the identity theory is really trying to do. I introduced it by saying it was often known as materialism. But there are various versions of the theory, and not all of them are on the face of it materialistic. If sensations are identical with brain-processes, all the properties of sensations are properties of the relevant brain-processes, and all the properties of these latter are properties of the former. But in that case it is just as true to say that (some) brain-processes are sensations as to say that sensations are brain-processes. But why should that be called materialism in particular? Why should it not equally be called idealism, since it makes some brain-processes out to be spiritual to just the same extent that it makes sensations out to be material? Or perhaps one should prefer the neutral-sounding 'double aspect theory', since the theory says that sensations and brain-processes are two aspects of the same thing, much as the evening star and the morning star are Venus considered from different points of view? The point is that the material and the non-material are put on a level and treated symmetrically.

The version of the theory I defended a few paragraphs ago, starting from Smart's version but ending up by removing its Occamite motivation, is of the kind I have just sketched. Psychic properties were rescued from Smart's attack and put on a level with material properties, and the defence of the theory consisted in showing that this move freed it from a possible objection it faced in the form in which Smart originally stated it (the objection that brain-processes do not seem able to have properties like being justified or unjustified). But the theory is usually thought of as having more bite than this. It is a theory of sensation, and other things, claiming that they are brain-processes, not a theory of some brain-processes, claiming that they are sensations. Sensations and brain-processes are simply not treated symmetrically.

Let us compare 'Sensations are brain-processes' with two other sentences (partly following R. Rorty, and also C. Taylor, in the Borst volume): 'Demons are really germs' and 'Heat is molecular motion'. When we discover that diseases are caused by germs we abandon the theory that they are caused by demons, and we say demons don't exist, or anyway not in the sphere of diseases. What we are denying the existence of is things which, if they did exist, would have properties other than just that of causing diseases; perhaps they would have pointed ears and barbed tails and malignant intentions. When we find that heat is molecular motion we do not follow this up by saying that heat does not really exist (and we feel less inclined to express our discovery by saying that heat is 'really' molecular motion, unless we are rebutting someone else who held that it was, say, phlogiston). But we are still somehow not putting heat and molecular motion quite on a level. It is heat that is molecular motion, not molecular motion that is heat, though admittedly there are circumstances in which we might say this instead. The reason is presumably that we are much more familiar with it as heat, and are more likely to know of some phenomenon in front of us that it is heat than to know that it is molecular motion. But the point of the discovery seems to be beyond this. We can now keep tabs on that familiar phenomenon, heat. Since we have a theory about molecular motion, we can explain the properties of heat in terms of those of molecular motion and perhaps predict that heat will have other properties we might not have thought it had. In principle we could do the thing the other way round, and predict the properties of molecular motion from those of heat. But we are less likely to do this. We derive our knowledge of molecular motion from the theory in which it plays a part, but we have no similar theory in which to derive any properties of heat that are not obvious to us from experience – or rather the theory about molecular motion just *is* the theory with which we do this.

The asymmetry of heat and molecular motion, then, is an asymmetry of familiarity and explanatory power. How about sensations and brain-processes? Identity theorists do not seem to want to say that sensations do not exist. What they do seem to mean is that sensations do not have any nature of their own beyond what brain-processes have. The properties they seem to have in their own right they really have only because they are brain-processes, and their having them can ultimately be explained in terms of a theory constructed to deal with brain-processes.

At any rate, this seems to be part of what makes the identity theory tick. But unfortunately the matter is not all that clear. What do we mean by 'a theory constructed to deal with brain-processes'? Presumably one which only uses terms that we would intuitively apply to brain-processes rather than to sensations, etc. But if sensations are identical with brain-processes, why should a theory of the latter be limited in this way? What is the justification for excluding from it terms like 'red', 'smelly', 'lustrous', 'fading', 'justified', unless it is that we have at the back of our minds the feeling that these terms do not really apply to brain-processes at all? Is it that we find a theory that excludes these terms more amenable to scientific development, perhaps because these terms don't admit of measurement (we can measure Angstrom units but not colours: one thing cannot be twice as red as another)? This sounds promising, but it will not do as it stands. Colours, after all, may be properties of sensations and after-images (though not of the *having* of after-images), but they are also normally ascribed to physical objects, which presumably come on the brain-process side of the fence. But perhaps a more fundamental point is this: What sort of scientific evidence can we imagine that would convince us that sensations, or the having of sensations, are identical with brain-processes *as opposed to* being regularly correlated with them in the way that other theories than the identity theory will allow? Must we appeal to economy and simply *postulate* identity on the grounds that it fits the facts no worse than correlation and is scientifically simpler?

So far we have considered things like sensations and feelings. If the identity theory is to be a solution to the mind/body problem it must cover other mental phenomena as well, such as thoughts. We have already come across a difficulty concerning what is sometimes called the phenomenology of thinking, when I introduced the example of the thought that Peter might drop in for a drink. 'Phenomenology' means, literally, 'description of appearances' where 'appearances', like 'phenomena', need not carry any suggestion of unreality. The problem is to describe what actually happens, in terms of events of which we are

129

conscious, when such a thought occurs to us. But there are other difficulties too about thoughts, of which two are relevant here.

One concerns how thoughts are connected with time. There is good reason to say that our brains are active when we think. Brain-damage, senility, fatigue or under-nourishment can all affect our thinking, and 'He has a good brain' is almost synonymous with 'He has a powerful mind' or 'He is intelligent'. But brain-processes take time. One thing, or several things, happen, and then some more things happen, and so on. Brain-states similarly last over time. But thoughts seem to do neither of these things. When the thought about Peter occurs to one, how long does it take to occur? Which part of it occurs first and which next? Or how long does the thought last? A brain-process could be interrupted in the middle and a brain-state could be brought to an end. But how could a thought — a simple thought, not a train of thought — be either interrupted halfway through or brought to an end? It could be driven out of our minds, but that is different; it is not the end of the occurring of the thought, but the end of our remembering it or bearing it in mind; the occurring was completed before any driving out could occur, and irrespective of whether it did occur. The expression of a thought is given by a sentence, which has a structure, and whose utterance takes a time. But neither the structure nor the time seems to apply to the occurring of the thought itself. It does not occur by first a part corresponding to 'Peter' occurring and then a part corresponding to 'might drop in'; it seems to occur all at once. We cannot go further into this problem here, but it clearly raises a difficulty for anyone saying that the act of thinking is either a brain-process or a brain-state. The identity theorist might comfort himself with the reflection that it is a difficulty no one seems able to solve satisfactorily. But for the dualist it is merely a piece of unfinished business, and not an objection specifically to dualism as such.

The second difficulty about thoughts is that they have what is called intentionality (sometimes spelt 'intensionality' with an 's'; this difference in spelling marks an issue, but we must not stop to discuss it). This means that they are about something, and are directed at something, either the external world or something else, such as numbers. Roughly, thinking is called intentional because the mind is 'intent upon' something. Being intentional in the sense of 'deliberate' is just one way of being intentional in the wider philosophical sense. Take the thought 'Oh golly, I promised to have lunch with my aunt!' How could this thought be what it is if neither my aunt nor the institution of promising had existed? Yet brain-processes do not seem to depend for their existence on aunts and institutions. (Cf. N. Malcolm in the Borst volume, pp. 176–8, and also T. Nagel, *ibid.*, p. 225.)

The identity theorist will presumably reply that the thought could very well occur without the aunt. I could have imagined I had an aunt, and in principle could even have invented the institution of promising, *ad hoc.* What makes the thought one about my aunt is that she played some causal role in my having the thought: it is because I have met my aunt, or been otherwise influenced by her, that I have an idea of her at all. Suppose I had dreamed her up, as it were, but unknown to me I did indeed have an aunt precisely resembling the image I dreamed up, but whom I had never met or heard of. Presumably then the thought would not be called a thought *of* my aunt; but it could be the same thought and the same brain-process.

There is another feature of thinking that might seem to make against the identity theory: namely, its rationality. Often when a thought occurs to us this is because another thought has occurred to us with which the first has some rational connection. Whatever may be going on in the brain at these times, it seems that we could neither predict nor explain the occurrence of the second thought merely by examining the brain and without taking into account the first thought, considered *as* a thought. Though our mental and physical lives are obviously closely connected, it does not seem that the purely material causes that the physiologist deals in could ever be enough to account for the course of events in our mental life.

Remarkably enough, however, this has been used as part of an argument *for* the identity theory. D. Davidson, whom we have met before, has an interest in philosophy of mind second only to his interest in philosophy of language. In an article on 'Mental Events' (in L. Foster and J. W. Swanson (eds), *Experience and Theory*) he insists that there are no strict psychophysical laws, i.e., laws which connect mental and physical phenomena by saying that whenever a mental phenomenon of a certain kind occurs it is always accompanied by a physical phenomenon of a certain kind, and vice versa. For example, such a law might say that whenever anyone is thinking of his aunt a neural pattern can be observed in his brain, or that whenever such a neural pattern can be observed the person concerned is thinking of his aunt. Davidson combines this with two other principles: first, mental events do cause physical ones, and vice versa. The thought that I promised to have lunch with my aunt causes me to leave my house, and leaving my house causes me to think how cold it it outside. Second, whenever one event causes another, they are connected by a law, saying that events of the first kind are regularly accompanied, or followed, by events of the second kind. But now we seem to have a contradiction. For if *a* is a mental event which causes a physical event *b*, there must be a law linking events of kind *a* with events of kind *b*; but how can this be so if there are no psychophysical laws? It is here that Davidson brings in the identity theory to rescue him. For suppose *a* is identical with some physical event *a'*. Then if *a* is the cause of *b*, *a'* (being the same event as *a*) is also the cause of *b*, and there is nothing to stop *a'* and *b* being linked by a law. We then have this situation: *a* and *a'* are the same event looked at from different points of view. In its capacity as *a'* it satisfies the demand that it be linked by a law to the event it causes. A similar argument would apply in the case of a physical event causing a mental one.

This may well seem a strange way to defend the identity theory. One thing it depends on is Davidson's view of causation as linking events, however described, so that if *a* causes *b*, so does *a'*, and vice versa. Some philosophers hold that causation links facts rather than events. On that view one might say that the fact that I thought of my promise to have lunch with my aunt caused me to leave the house; but even if when I thought this my brain was in a certain state, the fact that it was in that state would not be the same fact as the fact that I thought as I did, and so would not be the cause of my leaving the house. It would be open to philosophers who take this view to say, if they dislike the identity theory, that the fact that Davidson is led to that theory is an argument against his view of causation.

Perhaps Davidson's argument is also a bit of a cheat. For if *a'* is linked by a law with *b*, and *a* is the same as *a'*, surely *a* too must be linked by a law with *b*? Actually this is not so, and the reason why it is not brings us to an important distinction we have so far glossed over. Though Davidson makes the distinction, it perhaps comes out more clearly in a development of his view by C. McGinn. McGinn insists that at least in principle a mental state could always be realised in quite different physical states, of the brain or anything else. In fact he thinks we can know this *a priori*, without having to examine particular cases. He compares the case of clocks (p. 211), which could have the property of registering noon by quite different mechanisms. One clock might do it by having its two hands pointing vertically upwards, another by chiming, and another by its dial turning a certain colour. If things like thoughts can be realised in indefinitely various ways like this, there cannot be psychophysical laws, McGinn thinks. But he also brings out that one version of the identity theory is blocked. This is the version which identifies type thoughts, etc. with type brain-processes.

Consider our old friend, the sentence, 'The cat is on the mat.' How many words has it? Six, if you count them up; but then 'the' occurs twice, so it only has five different words. What it has six of are called tokens, and what it has five of are called types. It is types that we look up in the dictionary, and tokens of those types that can be written in red ink, or illegible. This distinction among words can be applied by analogy elsewhere. If on Monday it occured to you that your aunt was a spy, and the same thought occurred to you again on Tuesday, then you had two token thoughts of the same type thought.

The version of the identity theory which is blocked is that which identifies type thoughts with type brain-processes, which says, e.g., that the thought that Hitler was a house-painter, no matter who has it and when, is identical with a certain pattern of neurone-firings, etc. Maybe the rational fish sometimes said to inhabit the methane seas of Jupiter have no neurones but do their thinking by a complicated arrangement of bits of copper wire. But this leaves it open that your act of thinking, last Tuesday afternoon, that Hitler was a house-painter should be identical with whatever brain-process it was that on that occasion enabled you to think it. The identity theory Davidson espouses has got to be a token identity theory.

At the end of the last chapter I promised to show how Kripke's theory of reference and names has repercussions on the philosophy of mind. We are now in a position to see what they are. We saw at the beginning how the identity theorists insist that the identities they postulate are contingent. Kripke's point was that identity statements whose terms are rigid designators are either necessarily true or necessarily not true. Now phrases like 'The thought that Hitler was a house-painter' or 'Pattern X of neurone firings', where we understand 'pattern X' as short for some scientific description, presumably are rigid designators. They could hardly refer to different thoughts or brain-processes in different possible worlds, in the way that a phrase like 'The thought John had at noon last Tuesday' could. So the statement that the thought about Hitler is identical with pattern X will be necessarily true, if true at all.

How does this relate to our intuitions that thoughts or sensations and brain-processes could exist without each other? On Kripke's own view the fact that a statement of identity is necessarily true does not imply that we must know it *a priori*; we might have to discover it empirically. But there could still be a problem about why we think the statement false, if it is in fact true. Let us take Kripke's main example, that pain is identical with a physiological process called C-fibre stimulation. If they are the same, how can it be conceivable, as it seems to be, that they are not? Kripke argues that one way out is blocked. This way is to ally the case with that of heat and molecular motion. If heat is molecular motion it is necessarily so; but we might have the sensation we call that of heat from something else instead (the presence of a special 'caloric' fluid, for instance). In that case our sensation would have been qualitatively the same, but it would not have been a sensation of heat. But this could not happen with pain. If pain *is* C-fibre stimulation, it could not be that we got the same sensation from another source, say, D-fibre stimulation, and that it was therefore not a sensation of pain. The reason is that pain cannot be distinguished from the sensation of pain in the way that heat can be distinguished from the sensation of heat. We cannot then use the heat case to explain our feeling that pain and C-fibre stimulation could exist without each other.

Kripke argues mainly against a type version of the identity theory, identifying pain in general with C-fibre stimulation in general, and he rejects it for essentially the same reason as we have seen for rejecting it if we say there are no psychophysical laws because mental states can be realised in matter in indefinitely many ways. How does a token version fare here? Your act of thinking last Tuesday that Hitler was a house-painter will have to be necessarily identical with the relevant brain-process, if identical at all. Does this clash with any of our intuitions? Suppose we become convinced that they were identical. Do we find it conceivable that *that* act of thinking – yours on Tuesday – could have occurred without the brain-process? Why do we need to say this, rather than simply that *an* act of thinking it could have so occurred? Similarly with a pain: do our intuitions make us say we could have had the same pain as one we did have, had the brain-process been absent? Or merely that we could have had a similar one, one indistinguishable *qua* pain, but different simply because it was not a brain-process? The token version seems to avoid this particular objection, about clashing with our intuitions.

In some respects, then, the token version of the identity theory seems better placed than the type version. But this does not mean it is free from objections. If different occurrences of a thought about Hitler, or of a certain kind of pain, are, or could be, identical with quite different material events, how is it they are so similar? What is it they have in common? In the clocks case what they had in common (registering noon) was a role dependent on human conventions, which has no analogue in the case of thoughts and pains. Perhaps the events which were or embodied the same thought had in common certain causal features (Hitler played the same causal role in respect of each of them, for instance), though this would not explain why they have the same appearance to us, i.e., how we should know, if we had both of them, that they were both about Hitler. Moreover, it seems conceivable that such thoughts and pains could occur without *any* embodiment, which is hardly true of registering noon. However, it must be admitted that this is difficult territory, and that it is not easy to think of alternative theories that are not open to equally grave objections.

It seems then that our verdict on the identity theory must be rather an open one. Perhaps the token version is a bit easier to defend than the type version, and we may feel obliged, if we follow Kripke, to allow that the identities are necessary identities where they exist at all. If the theory is to be worth anything as a solution to the mind/body problem, it must cover all the various kinds of mental phenomena, such as thoughts, perception, sensations, pains or after-images, though we must expect these diverse cases to raise diverse issues in some respects.

In this chapter we have discussed two solutions to the mind/body problem, dualism and the identity theory. There are others, which I can only mention, such as psychophysical parallelism (mental and physical events correspond to each other in certain ways but do not cause each other), epiphenomenalism (physical events cause mental events but not vice versa), behaviourism (mental events are to be analysed in terms of how we behave and react), and some others, which it is not easy to characterise briefly, associated with such people as Strawson and Aristotle.

Before leaving this chapter I want to mention an objection to Kripke which will lead us on to another philosophical topic. It occurs in a defence of a type version of the identity theory by S. Williams, who says, 'The fault lies ... in his uncritical view of pains as phenomenal objects immediately and incorrigibly recognisable by only one person, yet ... rigidly designated in a language of public reference.' I shall not discuss the validity of this objection (I am not sure myself how much to concede to it), but I will try to fill in the background to it in the next chapter.

8 Scepticism and language

Philosophers from the beginning of time have set themselves all sorts of tasks. We have seen earlier how hard it is to pick out anything that they all have in common. Still there are certain perennial themes that have gripped the attention of at any rate large numbers of philosophers at widely scattered times and places. One of these has been called in recent times the egocentric predicament.

'No man is an island,' said John Donne. But many philosophers have disagreed. Every man for them is not only an island but one set in a misty ocean out of sight of any other land. One of the remarks by which C. P. Snow infuriated Dr Leavis in the famous 'two cultures' debate of the 1950s was, 'We die alone'. The philosophers we are concerned with would have expressed our troubles rather by saying, 'We are born alone', thereby infuriating Wittgenstein, as we shall see, if not Dr Leavis.

For the trouble basically is: how can we ever get to know that anything else exists besides ourselves? That we exist ourselves might perhaps be hard to doubt. Descartes at any rate (1596–1650) claimed that he could establish that he himself existed, because when he tried to doubt it, the doubting itself was a form of thinking, and anything which engaged in thinking must surely exist in order to do so. This is the argument known as the Cogito, from the sentence 'Cogito ergo sum' ('I think therefore I am') in which he expressed it. Philosophers have been at his, and each other's, throats ever since about this argument, not so much because they doubted whether Descartes, to say nothing of themselves, ever did exist, but because they were not clear just how much the argument establishes: what exactly does it establish the existence of? How far does it *establish* anything at all? What are its premises and assumptions, and what is the justification for them in their turn? And does the argument really involve a process of inference, as the 'therefore' suggests? But let us leave this particular question, though to be fair to Descartes's memory I should add that the expanded form which I have offered of the argument, to show roughly what it was about, is one he rejected himself: he insisted one did not have to start by knowing the *general* premise that anything which thinks must exist. Let me allow that I exist. How do I know that anything else does? 'Well, it's pretty obvious,' the reader might say; 'just look around you.' Yes: there are lots of sights, sounds, smells, touches, and tastes, no doubt; what nowadays are called sense-data. But what do these tell me? I certainly do not deny that I have experiences. But I also have them when by general admission I am asleep and dreaming, so how do I know I am not dreaming at the moment? This is another argument Descartes used, though it is at least as old as Plato. Even when awake I am obviously sometimes deceived, so how do I know that this is not one of these times, and that what I am experiencing at the moment is in fact not a total illusion, or at any rate quite different from what it seems to be? Take sight, for instance, and suppose I am seeing an apple. According to our present view of the matter light-waves must bounce off the apple, travel through a possibly distorting medium to my eye, and then hit my retina, where some rods and cones are activated, and electric impulses travel along my optic nerve to a certain part of my brain, where a whole lot of neurones fire in a certain pattern, and as a result of all this I get the experience of 'seeing an apple'. But the apple seems an awfully long way away from the real me, on this story. To use a simile at one time common among philosophers, it is as though the real me, the me that had the experiences, was seated in a telephone exchange, bombarded with a stream of messages from reporters stationed outside, whom I had never met, and whose reliability I had to take on trust.

Philosophy nowadays is in a mood where this sort of argument is not very popular, and the reader who has any acquaintance with the subject at all will almost certainly have already met and rejected such arguments, though I have tried to make them sound at least plausible enough to show how philosophers of the calibre and recency of Bertrand Russell could have been captivated by them. Other readers might like to sharpen their philosophical wits by trying to say, in a reasonable amount of detail, just what is wrong with them. As I want to go on to discuss other things, I will confine myself to a single hint: what sort of a thing is this 'real me' supposed to be? An inner person, like a telephonist, with another even realler me inside it, which in turn is an even innerer telphonist with inside it yet another ..., and so on? Some of the things we said in the last chapter will soon become relevant again here.

This egocentric predicament which I have tried to describe represents one form of scepticism. There are many forms of scepticism, and they perhaps deserve a paragraph to get us orientated before going on. The sceptic may deny that something exists, or is real, or is the case, as the atheist denies that there is a God. Or he may deny that something can be known, as the agnostic denies that it can be known whether there is a God or not. The atheist can be called a dogmatic sceptic and the agnostic an agnostic sceptic. The term 'dogmatic' incidentally is a technical term here, as in another usage it is in theology; it is not intended as a term of character assassination. The atheist, the agnostic, and the theist can be equally dogmatic in the sense of laying down the law and brooking no argument. But there is a complication. One of the things that can be denied to be the case is that some alleged thing or fact can be known. So the dogmatic/agnostic distinction applies also within scepticism about whether something can be known. To continue with the religious example, a dogmatic agnostic, as it were, will say that it definitely cannot be known whether there is a God or not, while an agnostic agnostic will simply insist on suspending judgment on whether it can be known whether there is a God. The agnostic agnostic may himself become dogmatic, if he says that it cannot be known whether it can be known whether there is a God. But in fact some sceptics have simply refused to assert anything at all and have insisted on complete suspension of judgment, while others have asserted that nothing can be known, or even that nothing can be more probable than anything else. These positions, of course, provide plenty of scope for that favourite philosophical game of shooting one's opponent down with his own weapons. For how can the sceptic who asserts that nothing can be known himself know, or feel himself justified in asserting, anything at all? And as for the sceptic who refuses to commit himself to anything, it is hard to see how, if he is consistent, he can make his presence as a philosopher felt at all: does he, for instance, venture to commit himself to any reasons in favour of his extreme modesty? Finally, and this brings us back towards our muttons, the sceptic may apply his doubts universally or in various different spheres. We have met two sceptics so far: the solipsist, as he is called (literally: 'solely-oneself-ist'), who doubts whether anything exists or can be known by him except himself, and the dream sceptic, who does not deny that an external world exists, but is troubled about how we can know we are in contact with it at any given moment. A further type of sceptic accepts that there is an external world, and that he is in contact with it, but has doubts about whether it contains any other minds but his own: the 'other minds problem'; for minds seem to be less substantial and accessible parts of the world than bodies and chairs and tables.

We cannot possibly discuss all these kinds of scepticism, which between them have attracted a vast amount of philosophical attention, starting from some of the earliest philosophers known to us (Xenophanes and Heraclitus, writing about 500 BC). But in recent

138

decades discussions of scepticism have been influenced, like so many other philosophical spheres, by the fascination philosophers have felt for the study of language. Whether we are born alone or in company, as it were, it is certainly through language that we communicate with one another, and an attack on certain kinds of scepticism has recently been developed, primarily by Wittgenstein, which has become known as the private language argument.

Language is the main device we use for communicating with one another. So if we are born alone, we must somehow get hold of this device so that we can start doing the communicating. We start off surrounded by our own sensations, sights, sounds, feels, or whatever they may be, and so presumably these are what we must start talking about. Normally it is other people, such as our parents, who teach us language, but they themselves can only appear to us through the sensations we have of them, as when they make noises to us; language is usually a matter of noises, presumably because we are physically capable of making a large number of different noises with very little effort. So what can we do with these noises but attach them in some way to various of our sensations, or to groups or patterns of these sensations?

This is the kind of picture, or one of the kinds of picture, that Wittgenstein attacks. It says that language is essentially a private thing, constructed by each of use for ourselves, albeit on stimulation from outside, which ensures that we construct it in parallel ways to each other. Wittgenstein holds that a private language is impossible.

However, it is not at all easy to see yet just what it is that he thinks is impossible. Surely something like the above picture must be true, for we do after all acquire language, and we do get our knowledge of the world basically through the five senses. Let us start by asking what sort of things might count as a private language.

The most obvious thing the phrase suggests is the sort of thing that probably most of us indulged in in childhood, when we made up secret codes so that we could safely write in our diaries all sorts of nasty things about our friends and parents. Clearly there was no difficulty about doing this. But equally clearly we used our ordinary language as a basis and simply encoded it in some way, e.g., by writing its words back to front. If we were reasonably ingenious, our friends could probably never have learned the language unless we wanted them to; but they would have had little difficulty in learning it when we did want them to; we could easily teach it to them. But how about a language that we could not teach them? Could there be a language which at least one person knew, but which it was logically impossible that anyone else should learn? The 'at least' here raises a minor problem to start with. It is usually assumed that, if such a language could exist at all, only one person could know it. Strictly speaking there would not, for anything we have said so far, be any objection to several people knowing it, provided they could not *learn* it; they would have to know it by some sort of magic, as a man might, as far as logic goes, be born like Athena from the head of Zeus, speaking fluent English (or Greek presumably, in her case). But this, apart from not being very interesting on a practical level, would only be possible 'for anything we have said so far'. It might turn out that the reasons which made it logically impossible for anyone but its first speaker to learn the language (and he after all invented it rather than learned it) also made it impossible for more than one person to speak it. This would be so if, for instance, what it was used to speak *about* was something that only one person could have access to, so that anyone else could no more use the language than learn it.

Now is there not for each of us one kind of thing which is indeed accessible only to ourselves: namely, our sensations? If a language is specially geared for talking about them, so that they provide the meanings of its words, then is it surprising that only we can understand it, since only we can have or know about these sensations? (The wary reader will note two things about this last sentence: the vague phrase 'provide the meaning of' and the casual disjunction 'have or know about'.)

There then is the general picture. A private language is one which it is logically impossible for anyone but its speaker to learn. One reason that would make a language private in this sense would be that it was used to talk about things which it was logically impossible for anyone but its speaker to have access to (to use another vague phrase). Since our sensations seem to be things of this kind, and since we can apparently know about other things only by means of these, is it not inevitable that at least part of our language, and that part the part we start off with, should be private in this sense? I use the word 'pain' or 'red' and so do you; but must we not mean different things from each other, so that really we are not speaking a common language at all, but two different languages which are conveniently homophonic to each other? Or if it is not in this way essential that our language should rest on a part which is private, is it not at any rate possible that there should be such a language or part of a language?

Before discussing this let us note one or two further distinctions. I have just distinguished between 'a language' and 'part of a language'. One might mean by a private language one which was entirely private in that all of its words, and presumably its syntax, satisfied the condition of being unlearnable by anyone but its user. But more commonly it is tacitly assumed that we are talking only about part of a public language, say English, the part in question consisting of certain nouns and adjectives, and their adverbs, of the kind I have mentioned already, such as 'pain', 'tickle', 'red', 'sweet', 'pungent', 'glad', 'sad', 'hungry', and perhaps 'nauseous', and verbs like 'desire', 'believe', 'suffer'. Other words, like 'house', 'hot' (applied to what thermometers can measure), 'eat', 'smiling', and the other parts of speech, together with the rules of grammar and syntax, are assumed to be public. Another distinction is between saying that a private language could be, or even must be, our first language, or the first part we construct of the language we eventually end up with, and saying it is something we can construct, but only after we have already got a public language to give us a basis for it. We have already distinguished between the interesting case where the language is logically private and the trivial case where it is only contingently so. A related question, though not quite the same as any of the above, is whether a Robinson Crusoe, abandoned in infancy on a desert island, could invent a language for himself. An opponent of private languages might say that he could not, or might say that he could (he could after all be born with one, like Athena), but that such a language would be only contingently private: Man Friday would have no difficulty in learning it when he came along.

Wittgenstein was not a very straightforward writer. He worries at a topic like a dog at a bone, returning to it many times in different places and even different books, and often either repeating himself or at least apparently contradicting himself. The main connected passage where he attacks the notion of a private language is in his *Philosophical Investigations*, the main book of his later period, where his thoughts came as near to a final expression as they ever did; but there are many other relevant passages, and philosophers still dispute over just what his attack amounts to, or indeed just what he was attacking.

Anyway let us start with §243, where, after observing that people can soliloquise and might even in principle be imagined to use language for no other purpose, he asks:

> But could we also imagine a language in which a person could write down or give vocal expression to his inner experiences – his feelings, moods, and the rest – for his private use? – Well, can't we do so in our ordinary language? – But that is not what I mean. The individual words of this language are to refer to what can only be known to the person speaking; to his immediate private sensations. So another person cannot understand the language.

Wittgenstein presumably does not mean that words like 'the' and 'of'

141

are to refer to private sensations, so let us assume he is talking of a private part of a language. If he can show that even part of a language could not be private, it would seem reasonable to assume that a whole language could not. That he does mean this is confirmed by another famous passage in §258 (too long to quote), where he imagines that I might have a special kind of sensation, which I invent a name for – say, 'S' – and then whenever I have the sensation write 'S' in my diary to mark the occasion. This is sometimes called the diary argument (C. W. K. Mundle in his article reprinted in O. R. Jones (ed.), *The Private Language Argument*, p. 104).

Before going any further I had better reassure the reader that I am not going to plunge him into the minutiae of Wittgensteinian scholarship. Since Wittgenstein is by common agreement one of the greatest modern philosophers, the forms in which he states a problem will probably be those which bring out what is most interesting about it – this is why we pay so much attention to the history of philosophy – but our main interest nevertheless is to discuss the problems themselves, and in a work like this it would not be feasible to get straight precisely what Wittgenstein may have thought.

Let us return to the diary problem. I have some peculiar internal sensation, as we often do, and I write 'S' in my diary to mark its occurrence. Then when it recurs a few days later I write 'S' again. What could be simpler? Well, the first question is, how do I know it did recur? How do I know the second sensation wasn't of a different kind, which I ought to have marked by some other symbol, say 'T'? Obviously because I remember it is the same. But do I? How do I know I am not misremembering?

We have now passed through the cultivated paddy-fields and are reaching the edge of the swamp country. What exactly is the problem here? I often have misremembered things, and I know this because later I have found out the truth. No doubt I have also misremembered some things which I have never found out about, but I could have done so. The special sensation we are considering, however, is supposed to be accessible only to me, and this as a matter of logic, not just contingently, for it is my sensation and mine only. Once it has passed, then, how can I ever recall it? I can recall it in memory, but here I meet a dilemma: either any remembering I claim to do may always be a misremembering, or this is not so. If it is not, then indeed I cannot be in error, not because I am immune to it, but because there is nothing to be in error about, any more than when I first christened the sensation 'S'. But now I am simply not doing what I set out to do. I am not christening a sensation 'S' and then referring to it as 'S' when it returns, but simply calling a new sensation 'S'; any question of how this new sensation is related to the previous one simply does not arise. Let us call this horn of the dilemma horn one. Horn two will then be that I always may be misremembering, and simply have no way of finding out whether I am or not. But if there is no way, even in principle, can we really say there is anything there to be found out?

This is beginning to look rather like our old friend from Chapter 6, the verification principle: if it is impossible even in principle to verify that this sensation is the same as the previous one, then the assertion that it is is meaningless. Some versions of the private language argument have been accused of saying just this (see J. J. Thomson's article in the Jones volume, though she is attacking not Wittgenstein himself but his American disciple Norman Malcolm). Taken on its own merits the view that the assertion is meaningless does not seem very plausible. Surely it does make sense to ask if the new sensation is the same as the old, however irretrievable the old one may be. Suppose I try to remember my dream last night: what possible method can there be for verifying whether I am right? Yet surely it makes sense to suppose that whereas it now seems to me that I was chased by a lion, actually in the dream itself it was a tiger chasing me; i.e., I then saw it as a tiger. This does not mean that an obvious description is always available for a dream as it really was. Dreams can be very odd. But that is another story.

Whatever Wittgenstein's own position here may be, it certainly has some affinities with this second, verificationist, horn of the dilemma. He insists on the availability of a check on my claims if they are to be claims at all. In another famous sentence, still from §258, he says: 'One would like to say: whatever is going to seem right to me is right. And that only means that here we can't talk about "right".' It is as though we tried to balance our impressions, but found we were using only the impression of a balance in order to do so (cf. §259, if I interpret it aright).

The argument so far might be put into three steps: (1) If I am not merely to apply 'S' in a christening ceremony, but to *use* it as a name thereafter – if I am to opt for horn two and not horn one – my use of it must follow some rule. (2) If I am to follow a rule, there must be something which would count as my following it, and something would count as my failing to follow it. (3) Therefore it must be possible, at least in principle, to find out whether I am following it or not. And in the diary case this seems to mean I must appeal to unsupported memory.

It is step (3) that brings in verificationism. As I said, we are not primarily concerned with Wittgenstein's own views, even though the whole discussion is inspired by him, but I will venture one general remark: I think he would insist on the first two steps, and would insist on the third only if it really does follow from those two.

It is also step (3) that brings in memory, so let us look at it more closely. There seems to be two things one might say about it with a view to undermining the argument. First, it surely will not do to object to any proposed checking process that it will involve unsupported memory, because in the last resort almost any knowledge we have at all will involve this. If I check my memory of a public event by asking you to corroborate it, I am asking you to rely on your memory. I am also assuming that I remember who you are, and what you or I said a moment ago, and that the English language is as I suppose it to be. Virtually if not quite all checking and all use of language, public or private, involves memory, so where is the sense in demanding that memory be always publicly checkable? (See, e.g. Ayer in the Jones volume.)

Someone might object that what I have just said commits a logical fallacy, akin to that of arguing that if every nice girl loves a sailor, there must be a sailor that every nice girl loves. Maybe every checking process must end with an unsupported memory. But it does not follow that there must be, nor even that there can be, some memories which can support various checks but cannot themselves be checked; and it is this sort of memory that the defender of private languages seems to need. But this brings us to the second comment on step (3) (for which see H. K. Castañeda's article in the Jones volume, pp. 153–4). Why does it matter so much whether the impossibility of verifying that a memory claim is correct is theoretical or only practical? If any given checking process ends in some memory claim that is not in fact checked, why is it so important that it should be theoretically possible to check it? If the vital witness to a crime dies, this does not render the trial of the suspect senseless. So why should it matter if, as with remembering a dream, no such witness could ever have existed?

The way these two comments claim to undermine the private language argument, as presented in these three steps, is by saying, first, that appeal to unsupported memory is a thing we have to live with anyway, so can hardly be made an objection to any particular view; and second, that if the argument proves anything it proves too much, for it ought to render senseless any memory claim that cannot be checked, whether the reason is theoretical or only practical, if not indeed any memory claim that *is* not checked.

But perhaps step (3) does not really follow from the others, and should be dropped. Let us see what happens then. Step (2) seems much less controversial. If a rule exists at all, surely something must count as violating it, just as, if a statement is to be other than vacuous, something must count as being inconsistent with it. Perhaps one reason why step (3) has been thought to follow is that, if engaging in a rational activity, such as keeping a diary, involves following a rule, it surely involves (consciously) *following* it, not just complying with it, as one might comply with a law by accident without even realising the law exists. Two things might plausibly be thought to follow from this: that I must think that I am following the law, and that I must know what would count as following it. It does not follow that I must *know* that I am following it. However, how can I (rationally) even think I am following it unless I have some grounds for so thinking, and how can unsupported memory supply these? Here we come to the key point of this stage: it is true that *this* memory is uncheckable, but memory in general is not – even though to check on any one memory I may ultimately have to rely on other memories. I cannot check this particular memory, and so I am no doubt less well off than I am in many other cases (and so I cannot claim to *know* I am not deceived by it); but I have the same reasons I usually have for trusting a memory: namely, that I have ordinary inductive grounds for thinking my memory in general is reliable. It is true that the very act of appealing to these grounds involves me in assuming that *some* memories are reliable; but this, as I have argued, is part of the human condition, and to discuss it further, though interesting enough, would take us too far afield; the sceptic at this point could not attack private languages without attacking a great deal else as well.

What then do steps (1) and (2) really commit us to? In Chapter 6 we looked at some of the difficulties Wittgenstein saw in saying that the meaning of a name is its bearer. Putting labels on to pieces of luggage is an empty activity unless we make clear what the point is of doing so. I have a certain sensation, and write 'S' in my diary. Why? So that I can write 'S' again the next time I get the sensation? That seems a bit pointless! We christen our children so that we can then call them and talk about them by their names. I cannot affect a sensation, as I can a child, by addressing it, so perhaps I name it so that I can talk about it. To whom? Someone presumably who understands the name and knows what I am talking about. But the sensation is something private to me and no one else can know about it; at least this is what the advocate of a private language is supposed to hold, since otherwise the language would not be private. So I cannot use the name to talk to anyone else. Can I then use it to talk to myself? This, of course, is what the private language supporter thinks I can do. What does it matter, he will say, whether anyone else can understand me? Wittgenstein on the other hand will say that, if I cannot, logically cannot, talk to anyone else in this language, then I cannot talk to myself either. Why not? Because it is not really a language. Why is that? Because a language must be governed by rules, and if the language is confined to myself, then I lay down the rules; but then if I pretend to be acting under the discipline of following the rules as I use the language, that's a mere sham: I am making up the rules as I go along, and I cannot claim to be submitting myself to any 'discipline' in 'following' them.

We are now getting near to the middle of the swamp, and the going is not easy. We are coming round in a circle, and we can see, a few paces ahead there, the point about checking waiting for us to stumble over it again. Still, perhaps it will be worth having another look at it, from a slightly different angle. Either there is nothing there for 'S' to be the name of, so that 'S' has nothing to do but is like an idle knob on a machine, which does nothing when you turn it (horn one of our dilemma: cf. §§270–1 in Wittgenstein); or else there is something there, in which case why cannot anyone else see it? (Horn two, from a different angle: last time we said, if no one, not even myself, can see it, there cannot be anything there.)

Well, *can* we name our sensations? Isn't 'pain' just such a name? Yes, but in English, not in my private language. Since I was taught English by others, my use of 'pain' is what it is only because those others got me to use it in connection with pains, including and perhaps starting with my own, and they could only do this if they knew when I had those pains – which indeed they did: I made jolly sure of that in my early years!

So now perhaps we can feel something of a path under our feet, at any rate to the next tussock. 'Pain' can indeed be the name, in ordinary public English, of a kind of sensation, and we can use it to talk about our pains. But it only manages to be this because pains are not just things we suffer in silence; some pains we no doubt do, if they are small enough, but not all of them. Pain has certain natural expressions (crying, groaning, etc.), and it is only because of this that our parents knew when we were in pain, and so could teach us a way of communicating with them about our pain: by using the word 'pain'.

We have now reached the next tussock, but not the end of the marsh, so let us have another look round. Wittgenstein certainly gives the impression that he is constantly inveighing against the use of 'pain' (let alone 'S') as a name. He seems to think of it as having meaning in something of the way that 'ouch!' does; at least, this is suggested when he says that 'the verbal expression of pain replaces crying' (§244). He adds that it does not describe crying, but he talks as though it does not describe (or name) pain either. However, at least two commentators have doubted whether he does really mean to deny that sensations can have names (N. Malcolm in the Jones volume, p. 38; and A. Kenny, *ibid.*, p. 209), and in §244 itself he introduces the bit I have quoted as part of an answer to the question, 'how does a human being learn the meaning of the names of sensations?' Perhaps the lesson he wants to teach us is this: not that sensations cannot have names, but that what it is to have a name is not the same as what it might seem to be at first sight. As he puts it in §257, 'a great deal of stage-setting in the language is presupposed if the mere act of naming is to make sense'.

So far, so good. But pain has a natural expression, and it is perhaps part of our very concept of pain that this is so: people might be more heroic than they are, but can we really conceive that people had pains just as they now do but had no tendency to cry out or take avoiding action, etc.? 'S', however, was introduced as naming the sort of sensation that has no natural expression – and surely there are all sorts of internal sensations of this kind. How then can parents ever teach 'S' to their children as a word in ordinary English? If 'S' is to be a word at all, surely it must be invented and used by the only person who knows when the sensation exists, namely, the person experiencing it?

But before discussing 'S' any further, here are three preliminary points. First, how about an ordinary public word like 'red', which also seems to refer to a kind of experience, but one for which there is no natural expression? Unless we are bulls, maybe, there is no reaction like groaning or shrinking back which we tend to display when confronted by red objects but not by green ones. Yes, but 'red' is a word we apply to red *objects*, which are public enough, and not primarily to red sensations. It is plausible, if no more, to say that when we call a sensation red we mean it looks like a tomato, rather than vice versa. But we will return to red sensations in a minute.

The second preliminary point is this: only I can have or feel my pain. Normally I feel it in some part of my body, though not just any part: not in my hair or toenails. Occasionally I may feel a pain outside my body, though near to it (the 'phantom limb' pains felt by people after amputations). I can conceive that I might yelp with pain when you stick a pin in the chair I'm sitting on, and in principle perhaps I might if you stick it in someone else's body; but it would still be my pain I was feeling, not his, even though it was his body I was feeling it in; he might or might not feel a pain in the same place at the same time. It is a truth of logic, in a fairly wide sense of that phrase, that only I can have or feel my pains, just as only I can have my seeing of a tomato. You may see the tomato too, and if the conditions are right it may look exactly the same to you as to me; but you still cannot have my seeing of it. But it does not follow from this that only I can know of the existence of my pain. All

147

that follows is that only I can know of this by one particular route, by having it. You may know that I am in pain, either because I tell you and you know I am honest, or because I am writhing around with so many pins stuck in me that I quite clearly could not be pretending. This leads to a third point. Apart perhaps from some very odd circumstances only you can doubt whether I am in pain: I cannot myself. This fact is sometimes treated as though it supported the idea that only I can really know that I am in pain, but for Wittgenstein it has exactly the opposite force. For him, if I cannot be wrong about something, I cannot be right about it either, as we have seen, so that this reinforces his tendency to say that 'pain' is not a name, on the grounds that 'I am in pain' is rather an expression of pain than a description of myself, like 'I have a decaying tooth'. Since we must stop somewhere I shall suggest bluntly that, if Wittgenstein does think that I cannot know I am in pain, he is wrong − though the reader will realise by now that interpreting Wittgenstein is a tricky business. One point, whether or not it hits Wittgenstein, is this: it is not the same thing to say that if I know something it must be possible for me to doubt it, and to say that if I know something there must be some content to what I know, and therefore some content also to the denial of what I know. But even here there are difficulties: I surely know that twice two is four, but what is the content of either it or its denial?

Now to return at last to 'S'. Not only has S no natural expression (if S had, it would be like pain or nausea, with nothing special about it), but 'S' is not, like 'red', applied to objects. It is these two features that make it private in the sense required. If others can know that I have pains, or that my dream images are red, because I tell them so, why can they not similarly know that I have S? The answer to this is of course that they don't know what the word 'S' means, and I can't teach them, because I have no independent way of knowing, through S's natural expression, when they have S, so that I could say 'There's S for you!' So far as this argument goes, they could know something of what 'S' means, namely, that it means a sensation; but not what sensation; they might therefore know I am having S, but not quite what I am having. But why can I not myself know that I have S? What we saw earlier was that for 'S' to be a name it must not simply be 'attached' in some vague and unspecified way to an object. It must have a use, and it can only have this if it is part of a language. But since I already have a language, and know what it is to be a name − I have a concept of names − can we not now say I have enough equipment to know what I am doing when I introduce 'S' into my language *as a name*, not just as a noise mysteriously attached to an object, even though this time only I can use the name?

If we accept this, we are saying that a limited private language is possible, in that a private word can be introduced in the framework of an already existing public language. Can we go any further? What we have said is in effect that to introduce a word we must already have a language: we must know *what words are*. Even Wittgenstein would probably agree (see §243) that Crusoe could have a language on his own, if only because he could be born with it; but it would, for Wittgenstein, have to be a language other people could learn. It would have to be usable to talk about public objects, or sensations which had a natural expression in the sense we saw earlier. But we might ask this question, similar to one we asked earlier about verifiability: if Crusoe could develop a language without anyone else actually understanding it and using it with him, because there was no one else there to do so, why would he be any worse off if no one else *could* understand or use it? Presumably because then he could not understand or use it himself. And now we are no longer talking of adding an extra item to a framework of concepts already possessed by the speaker, but we are talking of how he could acquire that framework itself, and indeed of what such a framework, limited to the items in question, would consist in. He must presumably be able to say things like, 'There's S again!', a sentence, in which 'S' is only one word. But how could he have concepts like 'there', 'is', 'again' without any reference to publicly accessible things like times and places and objective existence? Let us re-emphasise one point: it is not just a matter of how he could acquire the framework, but of what the framework would consist in.

Our discussion had led to something of a compromise. There could not be a language which it was logically impossible for anyone but its speaker to learn, because such a thing would not be a language at all. This is not because we have arbitrarily defined the word 'language' to make this so. It is because anything which ordinary common sense would be willing to call a language must be understandable and usable by its speaker, if only in his diary, and anything of which this is true is also understandable and usable generally. But there is nothing to stop a speaker inventing words to talk about his own sensations, even if these have no natural expression. His own understanding and use of these words can be justified by memory, and particular appeals to memory can be independently justified. Others can learn these words from him. For instance, they might mean by 'S' 'the sensation Smith says he has before breakfast every morning', and they could know he had it to whatever extent they could know that he was generally reliable, not given to lying, possessed of a good memory in other circumstances, etc. But they could not know what the sensation was like, as they can know what a toothache feels like. They could not know whether it was the same as the sensation they felt themselves after supper each night. They would have the sort of knowledge a blind man has of red.

Let us end by discussing a few implications of all this, starting from this last point and redeeming the promise I made a few pages back to return to red sensations. A famous problem is this: I call blood red and grass green, and so do you; but how do I know that what you see when you look at blood is not what I see when I look at grass, and vice versa? There are standard colour-blindness tests for whether we make the same discriminations as one another, and for finding out that, for example, most non-human mammals cannot see colours. But how do we know our experiences are not systematically different in the way described? Wittgenstein raises the problem at §272 and elsewhere (see, e.g., the extract from him in the Jones volume). According to one commentator, the private language argument, i.e. the argument against private languages, is partly concerned to show this question is nonsensical and that 'the doubts it conjures up are spurious' (A. Kenny in the Jones volume, p. 205). Others are less certain (C. W. K. Mundle, *ibid.*, p. 114), while a detailed attack on just what the problem involves is made by N. R. Hanson. I must leave the reader to pursue the problem, with just three remarks. First, the compromise view we have arrived at suggests the question is more respectable than followers of Wittgenstein tend to allow. Second, it is important to compare different kinds of example – not just red and green, but hot and cold, round and square, pains and tickles, etc. – and to ask just how radically our experiences can differ, if they can differ in this sort of way at all. And third, there is a related problem which may not be entirely academic, but may affect our judgments of each other: I once attended a school where, for good or for ill, we were beaten on our backsides for various misdemeanours. Our reactions varied. Some of us squirmed and wriggled. Others seemed to bear the whole thing with a bland stoical indifference. Was it stoicism or was it indifference? Were they manly creatures, good at bearing pain, or did they scarcely feel any pain? It is not easy to answer such questions, but they can trouble us long before we have heard of Wittgenstein or the sceptics he attacked.

One final remark about Wittgenstein's approach to the private language argument: he attacks a view which says that in sensation we are aware of private objects. He does not seem to have considered a view such as G. E. Moore's, that in sensation we are aware of public universals, like red. The problem here would take the form: how do we know which universal the word 'red' refers to? This clearly has some affinity to the problem we have just been discussing.

The influence of the private language argument has been immense. Its importance for the philosophy of language hardly needs mentioning. In epistemology or the theory of knowledge it has been used, as we saw earlier in this chapter, to attack the coherence of certain kinds of scepticism. We approached it ourselves from the philosophy of mind, when we saw at the end of the last chapter how S. Williams defended a version of the identity theory against Kripke by arguing that Kripke, in effect, ignored the private language argument by treating pains as things which were incorrigibly known to only one person but could still be rigidly designated in a public language. But from another point of view the private language argument might itself be seen as an attack on the identity theory, because that theory is just as committed as Kripke is to treating pains as things that can be referred to. J. W. Cornman defends the identity theory against this attack in turn by saying that even if we allow that sentences like 'I am in pain' are not reports of *private* psychological entities, it does not follow that they are not reports at all. The argument can also be used to attack Cartesian dualism (see N. Garver in the Jones volume, pp. 100–1). One might well ask what Wittgenstein's own view of the mind/body problem is; but we had better not, except to point out that he is plainly not, as sometimes used to be thought, a behaviourist, i.e. he does not say that pains are somehow unreal or illusory and that all that really exists is pain-behaviour. Apart from his explicit, if not entirely lucid, denials of this (e.g., §§304, 307, 308), he could not, at least without incoherence (as commentators have pointed out), say both that 'I am in pain' says something about my (publicly observable) behaviour and that it is senseless to suppose I could doubt it: I can certainly doubt statements about publicly observable things like behaviour. (C. W. K. Mundle in the Jones volume attributes to him a modified theory which he calls 'linguistic behaviourism'; for discussion, cf. the ensuing paper (*ibid.*) by L. C. Holborow.)

So the private language argument is relevant to philosophy of language, epistemology, and philosophy of mind, at least. Could it also have any bearing on ethics? Take the question I mentioned above about assessing the amount of pain that people feel. Various ethical theories depend essentially on the possibility of measuring or comparing things like pleasure and pain. They would be considerably embarrassed if it turned out that such an enterprise was senseless – though whether the private language argument does imply this might itself be debated. Let us at any rate turn our attention in that general direction.

9 The basis of morals

We ended the last chapter by noting that if it turned out that human experiences were irremediably private and incommunicable, this would have disastrous effects for certain theories in ethics. For one famous ethical theory, utilitarianism, holds that it is our duty to produce as much happiness as possible. Strictly, a utilitarian is one who says our duty is to maximise value, and we need not think that happiness or pleasure is the only valuable thing; G. E. Moore is one who did not, and is often called an 'ideal utilitarian'. But most utilitarians in fact take happiness to be the only valuable thing. In philosophy, incidentally, 'utilitarian, does not have its everyday connotation of ignoring the more refined values. But if we are to maximise something we must be able to calculate, at least in general terms, how much of it a given policy will produce, and whether one policy will produce more than another. To do this with happiness we must somehow be able to compare the happinesss of different people, and this is what we plainly cannot do if experiences are private in the above sense. It is hard enough to do even if they are not. For it is hard enough to compare experiences of one's own, and even if the experiences of others are not completely inaccessible to us, they are seldom as easily accessible as our own.

Whatever the difficulties – and it might be said that if we cannot compare human experiences at all, then ethics is in a bad way anyway – utilitarianism at least has some plausibility. Would not many people agree, at least on first hearing, that basically our duties are concerned with producing happiness for someone, and especially with not producing unhappiness? In fact what could be the point, one might ask, of an action which had no connection whatever with the production of happiness for anyone? Utilitarianism may then step in and claim to systematise and simplify such intuitions. The most obvious objections arise when we ask about distribution. Would it not be wildly unjust to produce a maximum of happiness for people in general if this could only be done by inflicting extreme unhappiness on a few? It depends: many people see nothing wrong in expecting extreme and hideous sacrifices, in fact unlimited ones, for the benefit of the community in time of war; conscripted soldiers are expected to endure whatever the enemy chooses to throw at them. Someone might object that they are only expected to risk these sacrifices; even soldiers are not expected to face literally certain death, and those who do usually get VCs, etc.; they have acted beyond the call of duty. Still, the line between risks and certainties is a pretty thin one. After all, even if you walk straight into a machine-gun, there's always a chance that it will jam at the critical moment.

Another way risk enters in is that we often feel justified in adopting policies that will result in virtually certain death for some, provided that the 'some' are unknown and indefinite. We travel by car, though we know that several thousand people will die next year as a result. Would we accept cars so cheerfully if we knew that Mr Smith would be among the victims? But this distorts the case: if it is *known* that Smith will die, then he will have the additional agony of living in fear of it. But would we really feel much better if only we, or some government agency, knew, and Smith lived his last year in happy ignorance? Similarly it is often thought that bomber pilots feel happier about their activities than those who have to stick a bayonet into someone's stomach right in front of them. Is this mere psychology? Is it merely that what we actually see or know about affects us more vividly? Or have we a genuine ethical intuition that evils are more justly distributed if there is an element of indeterminacy in whom they fall on?

Perhaps we feel it is fairer that those who make decisions, however impartially or altruistically, should themselves share the risks that result, though this will not distinguish the bomber pilot from the bayonetter, nor explain why we feel, if we do, that genetic hazards to future generations from radioactive pollution are more acceptable if there is no way in which either we or the eventual victims can know whether their disease is caused by our pollution or inevitable background radiation.

We feel, no doubt, that if not evils, at any rate risks of evil, should be spread equally. Egalitarianism, the view that in some sense all men are, or should be, equal, is a deep-rooted feature of our ethical feelings. The trouble comes with the 'in some sense'. In intelligence, ability, experience, tastes, sensitivity, virtue, personality, in fact pretty well every respect one can think of, men are plainly anything but equal. An Archbishop of Canterbury (Dr Fisher, talking in an African context) once said that 'All men are equal within the love of God but not within the sight of God'. Whatever we may think about the precise way in which he expressed it, he was surely getting at something true. All men

153

may have equal rights, but rights to what? To money and material goods? But the needs of some are vastly greater than those of others, and tastes differ: some are happy enough to sun themselves at a cottage door, while for others a villa at Cannes is a virtual necessity. Additional complications, since we must deal with the world as it is and not an ideal world where we can start from scratch, come over expectations and gradients. If Smith has ten thousand a year and Jones has two thousand, and we redistribute so as to give them six thousand each, we are most unlikely to make them equally happy; and we all know how differently we feel on two otherwise similar half-cloudy days, on one of which the sun is beginning to break through while on the other it is vanishing into the gathering murk. Any realistic account of the human condition must recognise that it progresses through time.

This sort of consideration could be used by utilitarians to defend themselves against the charge that they ignore the demands of justice. Let us return to Smith and Jones, whose incomes we equalised a moment ago. The loss Smith suffers is 40 per cent of his resources, but the gain Jones enjoys is 200 per cent of his. Similarly if we leave them as they were but have an extra thousand a year to distribute, if we give it to Smith we shall increase his resources by 10 per cent, but if we give it to Jones we shall increase his by 50 per cent. If we assume that increments of happiness are proportional to percentage increments in one's resources, we can maximise the happiness of Smith and Jones taken together by equalising their resources. If justice involves equality of resources, this argument suggests that utilitarianism does not clash with justice but prescribes it.

But the argument will only go a little way. It says nothing about the injustice of, say, punishing an innocent man where it so happens that this will benefit society, perhaps by deterrence, or by quelling a mood of popular hysteria. And anyway we have seen that justice need not involve equality of resources, at least if what we really have in mind as just is equality of happiness. And if we have, the utilitarian's defence collapses; for it said that to equalise resources was a way of maximising happiness; it said nothing about how happiness itself was to be distributed; it said nothing to stop us taking a small amount of happiness from an unhappy man to give a larger amount of happiness to an already happy one. The most it could say is that we shall seldom have a chance to do such a thing, but that is not a point in favour of utilitarianism.

The last two paragraphs have been a digression, so let us return to the question of what equal rights are rights to. If not to resources, should we say to opportunities? This sounds rather better, but there are still difficulties. Should we waste resources on providing opportunities for those who don't want them, or for one reason or another can't use them? How much should we spend on educating the ineducable? How should we apportion our funds between scholarships and kidney machines? Should we equalise opportunities to satisfy desires? Or to form desires? Or to satisfy needs? Or what?

Another plausible candidate for at least part of what we mean by justice is equality under the law; it is certainly a slogan we often use when assessing conditions in our own or other countries. But equality under what law? Are we justly treated if we are all equally subjected to a law forbidding, say, black-skinned or hook-nosed people from holding certain jobs? Equality under the law may not be a vacuous notion. It at least restrains oppressors from treating people in arbitrary and unpredictable ways which have not been sanctioned by some general and previously known law-making procedure. But it does not take us very far. It is compatible with the police having unlimited powers of arrest 'on suspicion'.

Yet, as we saw before, it is hard to get away from the idea that somehow justice and morality involve equal treatment and equal rights for all men: we are all equal 'within the love of God'.

One reason for our rejecting all our candidates seems to be that they do not lead to equality of happiness, which as I suggested a few paragraphs back is perhaps what we are really getting at. So why not get at it head-on and say men have a right to equal happiness? Granted, there are some horrible difficulties about comparing people's happiness, but we had better not make too much of them because, as we saw at the start of the chapter, any sane ethical theory will surely involve such comparisons somewhere, and we constantly make them, however rough and readily. Anyway ethics, we might think, should not wait upon practicability. If it is true that men have a right to equal happiness, then it is true; and if we cannot make the calculations needed to implement such rights, that is just one more unfortunate feature of the human predicament. Maybe God will straighten it all out one day.

But *is* it true? One difficulty is that so much of our happiness depends on our own efforts, on what we do with what we've got. Some people can manage their lives better than others, who are otherwise equally placed. The choices people make obviously depend on things like intelligence and character. How far these choices can be called 'their own fault' would lead us back into the freewill problem, but if we say people should have equal happiness in all respects not subject to their own choice, we shall be led back in effect to equality of resources or opportunities. Also my choices often affect others; but have I no right, within limits, to spend my money or choose my friends to suit my own pleasure, not other people's? I certainly shall not be very happy if I haven't. But anyway, *should* we always equalise happiness? Faced with a Nazi camp guard and one of his victims, should we simply try to make them equally happy? And even if so, should we equalise this happiness over the whole of their lives, or only over the part yet to come? Note that this question is not the same as the one we have just considered, about how people's happiness often depends on their own choices. Rewards and punishments come to people in a way through their own choices, but not as a natural result of these. If we punish the Nazi (for retributive reasons; deterrence and reform introduce complications that I am ignoring) he will not lose happiness because he muffed his opportunities, but we shall affect his happiness because of our own evaluation of his choices. If he *knows* his choices may lead to punishment, this of course is a factor he must take into account along with everything else. But this does not alter the fact that our policy will no longer be one of ignoring his choices because they lie outside our control. Also, we must distinguish between punishing and inflicting pain to equalise happiness. We might do the latter to someone who had merely been very fortunate, as, more plausibly, we might compensate, but not reward, the unfortunate; and we might still punish the Nazi, even if less severely, if by some lucky accident his victim had not actually suffered anything.

One intuition about justice, then, tells us that sometimes happiness should be proportioned to moral desert. But how about non-moral desert? We feel, as one of the most important strands of justice, that someone should get something when he has a claim on it, irrespective of his total state of happiness. Perhaps he has worked for it, or been promised it, or owns it. Here we come to one of the most fundamental criticisms of utilitarianism: namely, that it is purely teleological, which means it seeks to justify actions solely in terms of some future good to be achieved. (*Telos* is Greek for 'end' or 'purpose'.) But justification is often backward-looking. One standard utilitarian reply to this is to argue that backward-looking considerations are important only in so far as they affect future happiness or expectations – which they usually do. But this misses the point. It is partly because they already have the moral significance they have that they do affect our happiness or expectations. If you steal my property I shall be unhappy, but this will be partly because I feel I had a right to it.

It is easy to get confused here, for two reasons. First, in one sense every action is forward-looking, or at least not backward-looking. We may sing in our bath simply for its own sake, and not to ensure some future good, such as the possession of a practised voice, or the departure of the man in the flat below. But we cannot affect the past. Any act not done purely for its own sake is aimed at producing some situation, even if this is simply the situation that the act has been performed (as when I climb Everest in order to have climbed Everest; I don't normally sing in my bath in order to have sung in my bath). But though the situation must lie in the future when I begin the act, the justification for it may well lie in the past.

Second, the justification for keeping a promise lies in the past (even if it can be overridden: as Plato once said, you would not return a knife to someone, however much he owned it, if he had become a homicidal maniac since you borrowed it); but the point of making a promise, or of having promising among our social institutions at all, may well be that it is useful. This second point is relevant for utilitarianism, which comes in two varieties, act-utilitarianism (AU) and rule-utilitarianism (RU). AU says our duty on any occasion is to do that act which will have the best total consequences. RU says we should base our morality on rules, but only on those rules which would have the best consequences if generally followed. But this leads to various difficulties. Should we obey a rule which would have the best consequences if generally followed, but which we know will not be generally followed? But which of the following two views is RU really maintaining? (i) That we should engage in a practice like promising, and make it part of our social equipment, if and only if making and keeping promises will have better results overall than dispensing with promises altogether. (ii) That the justification for keeping any particular promise is backward-looking, but that the justification for accepting as valid the rule to keep promises in general is forward-looking. (i) is innocent enough, but goes dangerously far from utilitarianism. For it allows that our obligation to keep particular promises is backward-looking, and simply tells us that we should avoid making them in the first place if the result of making them is likely to be unfortunate. It says nothing about other backward-looking obligations, which may not promote overall happiness but are less easily avoidable. (ii) tries to abolish such inconvenient obligations by fiat, but is surely incoherent. Suppose that showing gratitude to parents wastes resources that would produce more happiness if used otherwise. If my own particular obligation to show such gratitude has a backward-looking justification (that my parents produced me), how can this fact have a forward-looking justification? If it is true, it is true; and it can no more be 'justified' by its results than the statement that twice two is four can. This is quite independent of the point made above that promise-keeping, etc. only do have good results because people think they have an independent justification. RU can also be brought in to simplify the complex calculations entailed by AU. This leads to difficulties of its own, but I think we have said enough to see that RU has all the hallmarks of an unhappy compromise.

II

So far we have come across three intuitions that don't seem to sit very happily together. First, an action or policy that had no connection whatever with promoting happiness would seem quite pointless. Second, justice and morality somehow involve equal treatment and equal rights for all men: we are all equal 'within the love of God'. Third, the justification of at least some actions seems to be fundamentally backward-looking. We might call these, for short, the teleological, egalitarian, and deontological intuitions respectively. (These are rough and ready titles. 'Teleological' means forward-looking, without any necessary reference to happiness. *Deon* is Greek for duty, whether forward- or backward-looking, but in practice 'deontological' is normally applied to backward-looking theories. I shall return briefly to the teleological intuition in Part Two.) Can we find a compromise? One notion we might look at, which has had a long history and has been recently reinvigorated, is that of contract. Perhaps all men can somehow be viewed as equal partners in a contract, and it is in this sense that they are equals 'within the love of God'.

The idea that our duty to obey the law rests on a 'social contract' goes back at least as far as Plato's dialogue, the *Crito*. It flourished in the writings of Hobbes (1588–1679), Locke (1632–1704) and Rousseau (1712–78), and has recently been revived as the grounds not just of civil obedience but of morality in general by Russell Grice (*The Grounds of Moral Judgment*, 1967) and John Rawls (*A Theory of Justice*, 1972, based on earlier articles).

A social contract can be seen as holding between a people and its ruler. The people promise to obey the ruler, who in turn promises to behave in certain ways. But more commonly, and in all the above writers except Plato, the contract is seen as made by people with each other. They agree to set up and be bound by certain institutions and procedures for making laws. Of course no one now thinks such a contract was ever historically made. People so primitive as to be in what Hobbes called a 'state of nature', everyone fending for himself like animals, would hardly be able to understand what was meant by a contract, let alone travelling to some primitive Geneva to sit down and make one. This might seem rather obvious, but it is not without significance. If our ancestors really had signed a contract we might give an ordinary backward-looking justification for their having certain duties as a result, and we might argue that we ourselves had somehow inherited those duties. Sometimes people argue, as Socrates did, if we trust Plato, that we ourselves have implicitly signed a contract simply by continuing to live in our society and accept its benefits without emigrating. Perhaps that sounds rather strained, especially in an age of immigration restrictions and work permits; such a contract would hardly be one entered into by equal parties. But anyway writers like Grice and Rawls do not appeal to any historical contract, explicit or implicit.

What they do argue is that our duties can be seen by reference to a hypothetical contract. Grice's general position is that we have a duty to do something if it would be in all our interests that everyone, including ourselves, should make a contract to do that sort of thing in certain relevant circumstances. This is not the same as it being in all our interests that everyone should actually do the thing in question; it might well be not in my interest that everyone, including myself, should (say) pay their taxes, while remaining in my interest that everyone, including myself, should contract to do so, because only if I contract myself can I get others to contract.

In some ways Grice's position is an odd one, because in spite of basing morality on the backward-looking notion of a contract (cf. pp. 78–9: 'the reason for keeping our promises is, quite simply, that we promised'), he insists that his view is basically teleological rather than deontological (pp. 7, 177), despite 'some quasi-deontological elements' (p. 46). This is because of the central place he gives to interests. What he calls 'obligation principles' differ from mere edicts in that they cannot be in the interests of an arbitrary group, such as a ruling class. They are therefore in the interests either of no one or of each of the members severally of a given society. Grice than adds (p. 91), 'I take it that the first alternative is too absurd for discussion', and so takes the second. This is all very well. No doubt it would be odd if obligation and interests – interests in general, not necessarily one's own – were always disconnected. But they may be sometimes. A philosopher as great as Kant could hold that society had a duty to execute murderers, for purely retributive reasons having nothing to do with deterrence or satisfying the victim's relatives. If we want to disagree with Kant we ought to have reasons for doing so.

To return to Grice. His argument is tortuous, but goes roughly like this (pp. 93–8): Let X be a kind of action which it is in everyone's interest to contract with everyone else to do. Then it is in everyone's interest to be under an obligation to do X, provided everyone else is, for a contract is a mutual promise, and promising just *is* putting oneself under such an obligation (p. 51). (Actually one might jib here. If it is in my interest to marry the prettiest girl in the world, and the prettiest girl happens to be a murderess, does it follow that it is in my interest to marry a murderess? Is it enough for Grice to reply that promising is not just accidentally connected with obligation, as prettiness with murderousness?) It is in everyone's interest then that everyone be required to do X. Now suppose Not-X is obligatory. Then it is in everyone's interest that everyone be required to do Not-X (he takes this to follow from adopting the second alternative on p. 91). But this cannot be so, if it is in everyone's interest that everyone be required to do X. So Not-X is not obligatory, i.e. (presumably) X is not morally forbidden. So X is either obligatory or neutral. But part of what is meant by calling X neutral is that its performance does not, unless for some accidental and irrelevant reason, affect other people. So if X is neutral it cannot be in everyone's interest to contract to do X. But *ex hypothesi* it is; so X cannot be neutral. So X is obligatory.

Such, I think, is Grice's argument; and it is surely fallacious in its last step. For X is only shown to be obligatory if it is neither forbidden nor neutral, where 'neutral' means neither obligatory nor forbidden. But it is no part of what is meant by calling X neutral is this sense that its performance does not affect others. The argument seems to depend on an ambiguity in 'neutral'.

Whether or not I am right in accusing Grice of this fallacy, there is a great deal more of interest in his book. See, for example, the argument at pp. 131–5 that if it is in everyone's interest to contract to do something, everyone has a reason for doing it, and a better reason than any selfish reason they may have against doing it. Space forbids further discussion of Grice, but the reader might ask whether 'rational' on p. 134 means *prima facie* rational or resultantly rational.

Rawls's book is both larger than Grice's and more famous. It has spawned a secondary literature of its own, with titles like *Reading Rawls* and *Understanding Rawls*. Like Grice, Rawls seeks to base morality on a hypothetical contract, though he is more concerned with the justice of institutions than with the rightness of actions. Rawls's approach is less overtly teleological than Grice's. In fact he explicitly rejects teleology (p. 330), and insists that the notion of what is right is prior to that of what is good (pp. 31, 560). But the position is complex, as we shall see.

For Rawls the rules of justice are those which would be unanimously agreed upon by people present, as it were, at the founding of a society into which they would later be born as members. But there are restrictions on the people doing the choosing, and on the circumstances in which they do it (what he calls the 'original position'), and these restrictions are vital to the nature of Rawls's enterprise. The choosers are not just people in general, or the whole human race, but rather idealised people, supremely intelligent but not very knowledgeable, and motivated by self-interest alone. This restriction on their motives does not mean they are egoists, but simply that they do not take account of the interests of the other parties to the contract, the other choosers. But they can, and and indeed must, take account of the interests of some third parties. We are to think of them as heads of families, desiring the welfare of their nearest descendants (p. 128). They are 'not to view themselves as single isolated individuals' (p. 206), and must ensure that their choice of principles will 'seem reasonable to others, in particular their descendants, whose rights will be deeply affected by it' (p. 155). The choosers are intelligent, in the sense that we are not concerned with what actual people would actually choose, as a matter of psychology, but rather with finding 'the only choice consistent with the full description of the original position. The argument aims eventually to be strictly deductive' (p. 121).

Finally, the choosers choose from behind a 'veil of ignorance'. As the process goes on and they come to choose the more specific institutions they are to live under, this ignorance is gradually removed, but at the start they know practically nothing about the kind of society they are choosing for (its population, resources, etc.), or about their place in it, or even about themselves and their own individual natures and desires. These restrictions are obviously to ensure impartiality, and that the principles chosen will, at the most general level, be suitable for any kind and condition of society. Knowledge is allowed to filter in as it becomes necessary for deciding how the original principles are to be justly applied in various cases; e.g., it might be hard to decide whether a given economic policy was just unless one knew what resources were available; the justice of a certain scheme of petrol rationing might depend on whether public transport was available (see §31).

The veil of ignorance, however, hides from the chooser not only his status and circumstances in the social set-up, but also his own nature. He is not even to know his own conception of the good, or things like what religious beliefs he holds. All he knows is that he will desire certain 'primary goods', defined as those which a rational man wants, whatever else he wants. These include 'rights and liberties, opportunities and powers, income and wealth', and also self-respect (p. 92).

There is one other type of knowledge the chooser is allowed, and that is certain contingent facts about human nature, which can be summed up as 'the general facts of economics and psychology'. These include not only general facts to the effect that human beings are what they are, but such ideas as 'that in a competitive economy (with or without private ownership) with an open class system, excessive inequalities will not be the rule. Given the distribution of natural assets and the laws of motivation, great disparities will not long persist' (p. 158).

The chooser, being rational, will adopt a 'maximin' policy; i.e., one which maximises the amount of liberty, welfare, or whatever, that would occur in the worst case allowed by a given choice of principles – it seeks to maximise the minimum of liberty, etc., and in this respect is a safety first policy.

What shall we make of all this? Whatever we may think of the rather cheerful outlook described two paragraphs ago, it seems reasonable enough that the choosers should be allowed to know that they will be human beings and living among human beings. 'Some philosophers have thought,' says Rawls (p. 159), 'that ethical first principles should be independent of all contingent assumptions, that they should take for granted no truths except those of logic and others that follow from these by an analysis of concepts. Moral conceptions should hold for all possible worlds.' Such philosophers would be following the general spirit (though not the detail) of Kant, who of all philosophers tried hardest to derive morality from reason. But until such time as we meet some green-eyed monsters from outer space, let us be content if we can elaborate and give grounds for a morality suitable for human beings. After all, if we are going to speculate about other beings, how do we know that *morality* will apply to them at all? How do we know that their lives will not involve totally unknown concepts as different from morality as morality is usually thought to be from common prudence? Of course these are not the only alternatives. Humans might be somewhat differently motivated from what they are without ceasing to be recognisably human. But let us return to Rawls.

The restrictions imposed on the 'original position' by the 'veil of ignorance' mean that the choosers will be fairly idealised creatures, not very like ordinary flesh-and-blood men and women. (They will not be of any particular sex, for instance.) They have been deprived of all individual personality, all indiviudal ideals and beliefs. What is the point of demanding unanimity of such choosers (p. 122)? What features of them are left that could possibly produce any variety in the way they choose? And indeed if they do come in various types, then surely we must go further and ensure that all possible types are represented, or all types that actually occur in the human race, or some types of actual people will find themselves not catered for. Once we abandon the idea that the contract is between *all* human beings, we seem forced to fall back on a single ideal chooser, the Rational Man perhaps. Rawls in fact admits this: 'we can view the choice in the original position from the standpoint of one person selected at random' (p. 139; there are some complications about different generations (p. 140), but they are relatively minor). The choosers are made plural presumably just to signify that they are, in choosing, committing themselves to live with a similar choice made by other people who will differ in their conceptions of the good, even though no one knows how (p. 327). The one respect in which a sense of justice must be built into them, despite any danger of begging the question thereby, is that they 'can rely on each other to understand and to act in accordance with whatever principles are finally agreed to' (p. 145).

The choosers are fairly artificial creatures then. But what determines the restrictions that are built into them? It is here that we return to the question of teleology. The choosers are making a contract to promote their own (and their families') interests. This is presumably meant to reflect the fact that we accept as principles of justice principles that will be effective in certain ways in promoting the interests of people in general. But the restrictions are evidently built in *ad hoc* to ensure that the contract reflects accurately what we want it to reflect, our intuitions about justice. Consider, for instsnce, the 'special assumption' on p. 143 that 'a rational individual does not suffer from envy', which is put to work at, e.g., p. 103. The contract can hardly be, as it might be for Grice, a way of *finding out* what is just. We might gain real help in finding what is just by asking with Grice what contract would be in the interest of all actual people. But this would leave quite unexplained why Rawls's restrictions are as they are. What then is the role of the hypothetical contract? The best answer seems to be that it is intended to systematise our intuitions about justice. 'What we are doing,' he says (p. 587), 'is to combine into one conception the totality of conditions that we are ready upon due reflection to recognise as reasonable in our conduct with regard to one another.' Reliance on intuition is to be reduced but not eliminated (p. 44). (Cf. §20.) One thing Rawls evidently feels is that systems like utilitarianism can have intolerable results in hard cases, and that a contract approach can avoid this (p. 175). One of the early articles from which Rawls's view developed was called 'Justice as fairness', and this is a slogan he has kept. The fairness refers to the position of the choosers behind the veil of ignorance (pp. 12–13). He also seems to think it may justify our views as well as systematise them (p. 122). But it is not obvious how it can do this except in the way that systematising a view prepares the ground for justifying it by making clearer what the view really amounts to. The contract itself is not only hypothetical, but also abstract in the sense that the choosers are too artificial to be really human. Rawls reckons to deduce by logic how they would choose, but, as we have seen, he has to appeal to our ordinary intuitions to supply the right premises for the argument; i.e., the right restrictions on the original position in terms of what the choosers can know and what motives they are allowed.

I implied in the last paragraph that Rawls's outlook is only within strict limits a teleological one. Let me mention one more notion relevant to this, that of 'pure procedural justice', of which Rawls makes some use (§14). This obtains when a situation is justified not in terms of its own nature but in terms of how it was reached (p. 86). If you have more property than I have, you might justify this by pointing out that you acquired it by just and legitimate procedures, such as filling in a football pool when I also filled one in but was less lucky. This plainly backward-looking procedure, I might add, also plays a large part in another recent influential ethico-political theory, that of Robert Nozick's *Anarchy, State and Utopia*.

The maximin policy is controversial. But I am afraid I must leave the reader to consider it on his own, starting perhaps from §26. It plainly corresponds to an intuition about helping the lamest duck. The question is: would it in fact be the rational policy for those in the 'original position'?

So much for the general nature of Rawls's position. The bulk of the book is concerned to work out what principles of justice the choosers would actually choose. The result is two basic principles (the second having two parts) linked in a certain order of priority. They are finally stated on pp. 302–3, where the general conception underlying them is summarised like this: 'All social primary goods − liberty and opportunity, income and wealth, and the bases of self-respect − are to be distributed equally unless an unequal distribution of any or all of these goods is to the advantage of the least favoured.'

Let us conclude by noticing a few features of Rawls's final position. First, there is a strong emphasis on liberty. One might well expect choosers behind the veil of ignorance to hedge their bets by leaving themselves as much freedom of choice as possible for when the veil is lifted and they find the places they have been born into; the veil of ignorance is well calculated to support intuitions in favour of liberty. One of the books in the secondary literature Rawls has generated is called *The Liberal Theory of Justice*, by B. Barry.

Second, equality is emphasised, but gives way to inequality if the least favoured get more thereby of whatever is being distributed than they (and everyone) would get in an equal distribution. It is clear enough here why the choosers must not have envy among their motives, but Rawls admits that envy exists and can even be justified (§80); he thinks that implementing his principles would not in fact lead to too much justifiable envy (§81). Does Rawls succeed in accounting for the equality of men 'within the love of God'? Even if citizens have equal liberty, their ends and well-being need not be of the same worth (p. 329). The hypothetical choosers, however, are all 'equally moral persons'; i.e., equal *qua* being moral persons (*ibid*: of course they are, since they are to all intents and purposes indistinguishable, but does this show anything about actual people?); §77 is devoted to this issue, and Rawls seems to conclude that the main qualification for being treated justly is that one has (or can acquire, to cover children) the capacity to act justly. Rawls treats this as amounting to the capacity to act as one of the hypothetical choosers, but this seems problematic: how could anyone, while remaining himself, become such an abstract and bloodless creature? Does Rawls really mean the capacity to think out the basis of justice, the capacity to write, or anyway to read, Rawls's book? Presumably not, though defects of intelligence, etc. are allowed not to count, provided they are the fortuitous results of birth or accident. Rawls implicitly thanks goodness that there is no 'race or recognised group of human beings' that systematically lacks this 'capacity for moral personality' (p. 506), though it does not seem very clear why it matters whether those who lack it do so systematically or fortuitously. He allows that we do not have duties of justice to animals, though we do have duties of compassion and humanity to them (p. 512). He admits that the contract theory may not explain these, but seems to think that this is to be expected, since it is a theory of justice and not of morality as a whole.

This chapter has been about the basis of morals and political philosophy, or at least about the basis of an important part of them: namely, justice. As we have seen in going along, especially in discussing utilitarianism towards the beginning, ethics is also concerned with the notion of value. There are various different kinds of value. Apart from the general notion of value, which strictly speaking is the subject of a study called axiology, we can speak of moral value, aesthetic value, economic value, and of other kinds as well. One of these kinds, aesthetic value, is the subject of another branch of philosophy, aesthetics. So let us end our tour with a brief look at that area.

10   Works of art

What is aesthetics all about? Works of art, might be a first-go-off answer. It will not do as a final answer, because everyone would agree that there are lots of other things which provide us with aesthetic experiences, or provoke aesthetic responses from us. Gazelles, roses, snowflakes, tennis-strokes, friendships, and arguments can all be called beautiful, to go no further than that traditionally rather overworked adjective; but none of them is really a work of art. Perhaps we should say the subject-matter of aesthetics is everything we can describe by words like 'beautiful', 'graceful', 'neat', 'fine', 'sublime', together with their opposites like 'tawdry', 'squalid', 'ugly', 'awkward', 'shallow', 'mediocre'. But this would include just about everything in the universe, and it would be very hard to know just where to close our list of adjectives. 'Mediocre' expresses an aesthetic judgment when applied to a painting, but does it when applied to an essay, or a batting average? 'Tepid' does when applied to a novel, and not when applied to a bath, but is this a mere ambiguity in the term? Have we really two terms, spelt the same way, one an aesthetic term and one not? Surely not. To call a novel tepid is to put a general word to an aesthetic use, and we can do this with a vast number of words. In fact to list them would be in principle impossible, if a critic may properly use words in evaluative ways in which they have never been used before. To take a fairly trivial example of the stretching of uses, could one not praise a film by saying, 'Its portrayal of the gambling saloon is deliciously squalid'? Someone might say it is the saloon, not the film or the portrayal, that is being called squalid. But what is it that is being called deliciously squalid?

To mark out aesthetics by a special set of words, or by the objects such words might be applied to, seems hopeless. There are many alternatives left. We might try to single out a special set of feelings, or of experiences, or of attitudes. Or we might abandon any attempt to give a hard and fast definition, and content ourselves with picking our certain primary instances, such as looking at pictures and listening to music, and saying, 'Aesthetics is concerned with that sort of thing.' All these courses would have their difficulties. But let us leave them there and return to works of art; for everyone would agree that these at least form a large part of what aesthetics is all about.

So what is a work of art? It is easy enough to give examples: *Hamlet*, the *Eroica*, the Mona Lisa, the Venus de Milo. It is less easy to say what they have in common, or where to stop. Is the Parthenon a work of art? Or is it rather a religious building which happens to have great aesthetic merit? Could it even owe some of this merit to its present ruined state (originally it was garishly painted)? And to descend from the sublime to the merely lofty, how about the Eiffel Tower? Or the Koh-i-Noor?

Perhaps this particular difficulty is not insuperable. A work of art is something deliberately created to embody aesthetic value or arouse aesthetic responses, and our problem arises mainly because many things are created for more than one purpose, and the aesthetic purpose may be dominant to various degrees. A wedding march may be composed primarily as a piece of music but secondarily to fulfil a certain role in a religious ceremony, while the Hermitage, say, was built primarily to house the Czars but secondarily to give them pleasure while they were in it. In these cases we need say no more than that being a work of art is a matter of degree – which is different from saying that being successful as a work of art is a matter of degree. At one extreme we can talk of poems or symphonies as pure works of art, while at the other we shall have functional objects which, while we are at it, we try to make as beautiful as possible. So far as our immediate question, 'What is a work of art?' goes, we need say no more, though a whole field of questions for aesthetics in general arises when we ask how the functional criteria an impure work of art must satisfy, i.e., the criteria for success in its other capacities, are related to the aesthetic criteria it must satisfy to be a successful work of art. For instance, a good car is one which is safe, fast, easy to manoeuvre, economical on petrol, and so on. It is an added merit if it looks nice. But what counts as its looking nice? In particular, should it look as if it would be fast, safe, etc.? Considered purely as an abstract pattern, a square or star would seem to be on all fours aesthetically speaking with a circle or oval. A square or star-shaped car would probably be a very clumsy instrument for swift and economical travel, but would this fact stop it from being a nice-looking car? I suspect most people would say yes, at any rate if they were considering whether it was a nice-looking *car*. The case need not be simple, of course. The aesthetic criteria need not coincide exactly with the functional ones. But they certainly seem to be related. In general perhaps a thing is a nice-looking so-and-so if it looks as if it would do well the sort of things so-and-sos are supposed to do.

167

This has the interesting result that our aesthetic judgment on an object may vary according to what sort of an object we think it is; and if we have no idea what it is we may find it hard to pass any aesthetic judgment on it at all. However, we are talking here of objects produced with a purpose in mind which is to serve some non-aesthetic function, or anyway some function which does not depend directly on the object's own aesthetic properties – I add this to cover things like pianos. But let us return to works of art, where these are things whose sole or primary purpose is to be aesthetically pleasing.

I said that one problem about the examples I gave above was to know what they had in common, apart from being created to be aesthetically pleasing. The Mona Lisa is a piece of canvas with paint on it, hanging in the Louvre. It was created in the sixteenth century and will presumably perish at some time. Indefinitely many slides and postcards of it exist, and probably a fair number of copies painted on canvas of the same size. But none of these is the Mona Lisa, which is a unique material object. The same is true of the Venus di Milo. But what about *Hamlet* and the *Eroica*? Beethoven wrote the *Eroica* on a piece of paper in about 1803. But nobody thinks that piece of paper is the *Eroica*, and it is preserved, if at all, simply as a curiosity in some museum, or perhaps as an authoritative source for the precise nature of the *Eroica*; but even this does not make it into the *Eroica* itself; a photograph of it would do just as well.

So what is the *Eroica*? To have its effect it must be performed. Probably no two conductors will perform it in the same way, but provided they stay within certain vaguely defined limits they will all be giving performances of the same thing, the *Eroica*. The performances are many and the *Eroica* is one, so they are not it; they are *of* it. They are not copies of it, in the way the slides are of the Mona Lisa, for the Mona Lisa is totally independent of the slides, while in a way the *Eroica* seems to have to be performed in order to become completely actualised. It is true that trained musicians are sometimes said to get as much satisfaction from silently contemplating the score as from hearing it performed; but presumably they must give it some sort of internal performance of their own. If they don't in any sense inwardly 'hear' it, how can the *Eroica* be called auditory at all – and whatever else music is, it is surely that? Music goes beyond what can be expressed on paper, which is hardly, if at all, true of a poem.

We must be careful here. Of course the *Eroica* must be heard, with inner or outer ear, if it is to be appreciated at all. But so must the Mona Lisa be seen. So why does the *Eroica* stand in need of performance to become fully actual, more than the Mona Lisa stands in need of being seen? For the Mona Lisa is the Mona Lisa, as actual as actual could be, whether anyone sees it or not. But the analogue here would be this: a performance of the *Eroica* is a perfectly good performance, whether anyone hears it or not. With the *Eroica* we have three things, the symphony, the performance, and the hearing, but with the Mona Lisa only two, the painting and the seeing; there is nothing corresponding to the performance. Perhaps someone might say there *is* something: it must be exhibited, and in particular illuminated, if it is to be seen. But exhibiting and illuminating are hardly on the same level as performing. Art gallery directors and lighting experts, with all due respect to them, necessary though they are, have not quite the role of a Toscanini.

Anything to be seen must be illuminated. The Mona Lisa is a visual object, and is just as complete and actual as any other. The *Eroica* seems to be an auditory object. But apart from the performances, which are not the *Eroica*, the only object we have is Beethoven's manuscript, which is not an auditory object. The only auditory objects we have, the performances, are not what we are looking for. So is the *Eroica* perhaps not an object after all, in the sense of a material object located in space and time? Perhaps it is something abstract, a sort of blueprint for its performances.

Something along these lines must surely be true. But there are difficulties. The view in question seems to make the *Eroica* into a universal, where universals are what often represented in English by words ending in '-ness', '-hood', '-ity', etc. Hardness, fatherhood, and generosity are universals; they are so called because they embrace or cover or apply to the whole of a certain class of objects, such as hard things. (But words of this form do not always denote universals; when you join the Brotherhood you join a society, not a universal. Nor presumably is the Deity a universal.) Now is the *Eroica* a universal? If so, the instances of it, the class of things it applies to, will presumably be actual or possible performances of it. They would be related to it as hard things to hardness, or dogs to doghood or caninity.

To start with there are some objections which sound rather verbal. We don't talk of *Eroica*-ness or *Eroica*-performance-hood. And we say the *Eroica* lasts fifty minutes, meaning that performances of it do, or should; but we do not say that doghood lives for about fifteen years, meaning that dogs do. Is this a mere stylistic accident, or should we take some other view of the *Eroica*? Is it perhaps a special sort of performance, the paradigm or average or typical performance? It cannot be a paradigm performance, for this would have to be some actual performance at a certain time and place, which serves as a model for other performances. There could be such a performance, say one

169

conducted by Beethoven himself; but there does not have to be, and we don't say things like, 'The *Eroica* took place nearly two centuries ago.'

'Average' and 'typical' mean different things. The average man has about two and a half children, but the typical man, at least of my acquaintance, has an integral number of children. The average man can have a property even though no actual men have it. The typical man can have a property only if most men have it. It might seem that even the typical man can have a combination of properties no actual man has. Suppose these are ten independent properties, A, B, C, ..., each possessed by 90 per cent of the population, but the 10 per cent that lack A is distinct from the 10 per cent that lack B, and both are distinct from the 10 per cent that lack C, and so on. Then the typical man will have all ten properties, though no actual man will. However, this will be so only if 'The typical man has A' and 'The typical man has B' together entail 'The typical man has A and B', which they may not, any more than 'I can marry Joan' and 'I can marry June' entail 'I can marry Joan and June'. Also there are complications when we come to second-order properties like 'having exactly nine of the properties, A, B, C, ...'. I think the typical man, unlike the average man, can only have combinations of properties an actual man *could* have. *A* typical man is either the same as *the* typical man, or is the typical member of some not too way-out sub-class of men. The typical Cornishman is a, but not necessarily the, typical Englishman. But the typical snub-nosed left-handed acrobat is hardly even *a* typical Englishman. An average man could similarly be the average member of a sub-class of men; but in fact I suspect that the phrase 'an average man' is usually used synonymously with 'a typical man', probably because we don't have much occasion to say things like, 'The average Cornishman is an average Englishman', interpreted in the strict way I have been suggesting. Of course 'average' and 'typical' can be used loosely for each other.

Is the *Eroica* then the average, or the typical, or a typical, performance? It could hardly be the first two of these. For some, if not most, performances presumably lie in the future, so how can we possibly say what the average or the typical performance is? Is it just *a* typical performance, say the typical one of those so far, or of those at present? This would suggest that the *Eroica* is constantly changing, and in a way this is not as absurd as it sounds, for with developments in instruments, etc. what we think of as the *Eroica* probably does sound rather different from what Beethoven thought of it as. But there is a worse objection: typical performance of what? How do we know which performances are candidates for being a typical performance of the *Eroica* unless we already know what the *Eroica* is?

We seem pushed back again towards the universal. But another difficulty is that the *Eroica* had a beginning in time. It was composed in about 1803. But a universal is surely a timeless thing. How could hardness have a beginning, even if at some time in the past there were not yet any hard things? Hardness is something like a possibility, and the possibility of hard things was surely always there. Perhaps the *Eroica* is a possibility, which was always 'there' but was only actualised when Beethoven came along. Perhaps it is basically a structure of sounds. This would explain why it is true, if it is, that someone else might have composed that very same symphony before Beethoven did – though there are problems about this, which I will mention later. If we do take this view, we shall have to explain how Beethoven's act of composing the *Eroica* counts as an 'actualising' of it.

Also we shall still have to allow that some things we say about the *Eroica* must be taken not at their face value. 'The *Eroica* lasts fifty minutes' will have to be interpreted as something like, 'The *Eroica* is a pattern such that any proper performance of it lasts fifty minutes'; while 'The *Eroica* is Beethoven's third symphony' will not be so translatable. We might compare a sentence like St Paul's 'Charity endureth all things', which means that anyone who is to be charitable must endure all things. (This example has given rise to the term 'Pauline predication', and has proved to be important in connection with some issues in the metaphysics of Plato.)

This chapter is about works of art, and we have been concerned with two kinds in particular, paintings and symphonies, which we have so far treated as quite different kinds of thing; paintings are material objects existing at a certain place for a certain time, while symphonies are abstract structures, whose relations to space and time are more complex. But should we rest content with dividing works of art into such fundamentally different kinds? After all, these two kinds at least, paintings and symphonies, appeal equally to the senses, and the fact that one appeals to the eye and the other to the ear should not make all that much difference. How big really is the difference between them? Symphonies have to be heard and paintings have to be seen. But while symphonies can be heard only if they are performed (in the mind if nowhere else), a painting is, as it were, its own performance. Suppose that musical notation did not exist, and the only way of publishing a symphony was to perform it – this would be easier with a sonata, but it makes no difference in principle. Then the original performance by the composer would naturally become invested with a certain authority. Other performances would have to look to it, rather than to general instructions like 'allegro', to know not only what the notes were but what interpretation was intended. It would be hard for the composer, even if he performed it several times, to indicate a *range* of permissible interpretations, as he can with terms like 'allegro', rather than certain isolated permissible interpretations. Suppose a painter painted different variants of his picture, as many have done: does this allow us to paint further, perhaps intermediate, variants and call them all manifestations ('performances') of the same picture? Maybe if painters issued instructions like 'Bright red in the top right corner' we could do this. But as things are, paintings are produced by producing manifestations of them, and even with colour photography and all the gadgets of modern reproductive techniques we do not feel competent to put on a level with the original any other manifestations of it, whether produced by human imitation or by mechanical means. When painters themselves produce different versions we either call them different pictures or else different versions of the same picture; but we do not allow further versions to be anything but copies.

Naturally enough, far more could be said about works of art, both about what they are and about how we evaluate them. I will mention just three further questions. The first one raises the issue of how far even paintings and symphonies make their appeal solely to our senses. Would we regard a painting in the same way if we found that by some freak of chance it had arisen from natural causes, say as colouring on a flower or a vein of marble, or because the wind had knocked some pots of paint over? We might not *call* it a work of art then, of course, but would we *judge* it any differently? How important is the context in which the work was produced? Are we helped if we know anything about the civilisation in which it was produced, and its artistic conventions, or about the artist's intentions? A case of some interest here concerns originality. When we discover that an apparent Vermeer is a forgery by Van Meegheren its price usually goes down, but should our evaluation of it? Are we evaluating it *simply* as something presented to the senses?

A second question grows out of this. Miss R. L. Meager imagines that Browning's 'Pippa Passes' was recomposed all unknowingly by a modern African poet who had never heard of Browning but had a girl-friend called Pippa. Have we one poem or two? And suppose that since Browning's time some of the words in the poem have changed their meaning, as 'silly' and 'obnoxious' have over a longer interval, or perhaps just their emotional tone, like 'propaganda' and 'militant'? It is here that problems arise about someone's anticipating Beethoven's *Eroica*.

The third question again arises from Meager's article (p. 54). She is discussing the relations between the work of art we call Michelangelo's

David, the piece of marble he carved, which is now in Florence, and the many copies since made from it. Speaking of the marble in Florence she says it might be called a 'model-universal': 'at one and the same time an individual thing, and the defining model of a class of things, more or less imperfect copies of it, which take their identity as works of art (though not as blocks of marble) from it.' One issue this raises is whether two things can be the same under one description but not under another. Can two things be the same work of art but not the same block of marble? This is a question that has been debated recently in metaphysics, involving the nature of identity. But here we reach a frontier of aesthetics, where it borders on metaphysics.

I have taken the question 'What is a work of art?' as a convenient example of a question in aesthetics, and also as one which shows something of how aesthetics is linked to other parts of philosophy. Obviously there are indefinitely many other questions one could take. Questions about representation and expression, in particular, are in fashion. What is an artistic representation? Is it a copy, and if it is, why make such a copy? And if a work of art is expressive, must there be something which it expresses? What is meant by calling a piece of music 'sad', and how completely can we describe the emotion a work of art expresses? And, finally, some questions which take us back again to other parts of philosophy: How relevant to a work of art are notions like truth, sincerity, and morality?

Part Two

11   A map of philosophy

We have now completed our tour of the philosophical park. It has probably left the reader with a number of feelings. One perhaps is that the goal we have been aiming for, or even the general direction we have been following, is unclear. This is not surprising, because there has been no such goal. We have simply been exploring the territory on a circular trip, prowling around the various sights as we came across them, and taking the most convenient route from one to the next. We have not arrived in triumph at a central shrine, but have slipped out at the nearest exit after seeing ten sights, which was all we had time for.

Now we can sit back and see where we have been, and try to construct some sort of map of philosophy generally. There is no very obvious place to start; but another feeling the reader may have had is that there has been quite a lot of emphasis on logic and questions about meaning, so let us start there. This emphasis on logic has not been accidental, for three reasons. The first is simply that logic is a difficult subject, at least in the sense that many undergraduates say they find it the hardest part of the course. In another sense all the philosophy that philosophers spend their time on is difficult, and necessarily so; for otherwise they would not need to spend their time on it. The easy questions, if there are any, are dealt with easily and got out of the way at the start, or as they arise. But logic tends to be technical, and so a lot of time has to be spent in mastering the technicalities, as we have seen in the two longest chapters in this book, on truth and meaning. Also, and here we come to the second reason, the ideas of logic are among those which most widely underlie philosophy as a whole. When we had finished discussing truth in Chapter 2 we moved on to a question about value judgments which mainly belongs in ethics, but since we were asking what role truth and falsity had in connection with them, it would have been hard to reverse the order of those two chapters. And then when we wanted to discuss laws of nature in Chapter 5 it seemed necessary to say something first about conditional statements and the ways in which one statement can imply another, a topic which again belongs to logic. The third reason is that an approach to philosophy through logic, or making use of logical techniques and ideas, an approach which is closely linked to an emphasis on language and its problems, has been dominant in English-speaking philosophy for many years. No doubt if I were writing a century ago or in a century's time I would have to write very differently. But of this more anon.

I have mentioned truth and meaning, notions intimately connected with language, as topics which fall under logic. Another, and perhaps the most central, is reasoning, which we have already seen something of in the reference to implication just above. Philosophy as an academic discipline is concerned to argue for conclusions. One can do this, of course, without studying argument itself. But philosophy, as we saw earlier, is a very self-conscious subject, ever concerned with where it is going and what tools it is working with, and apart from the intrinsic interest of studying the processes of valid reasoning our chances of arguing well are likely enough to be improved if we ask what kinds of argument are available to us. You don't have to know much about how a car works in order to drive it; but it can help, if you want to economise on petrol.

So a philosopher, in his capacity as a logician, will study our reasoning processes; not, as a psychologist might, to find how we actually do reason, but to find how we ought to reason if we want to be rational, what reasoning processes are legitimately available to us. But though a philosopher pursues truth, and therefore facts, he is not interested in just any old facts. Like the mathematician he wants to know what *must* be the case, but unlike the mathematician he also wants to know what this word 'must' means. The study of necessity and possibility forms a branch of logic normally known as modal logic (though to be exact, modal logic studies some other notions as well).

Logic forms one of the central pillars of philosophy, at any rate of modern English-speaking philosophy, and one could certainly add ancient Greek and medieval philosophy. There are perhaps two other pillars that might be called equally important. One of these concerns knowledge. A philosopher – and from now on I will not keep repeating that I mean primarily a modern English-speaking philosopher and secondarily the tradition from which he springs – is nothing if not a cagey individual. If anyone claims to know anything the philosopher instantly wants to know how he knows it. There are many ways in which we apparently come to know things – and by 'things' I mean both objects, places, people, etc., and facts. We can perceive them, remember them, be told about them, infer them, sometimes perhaps intuit them. Some things, like the position of our limbs, or what we are thinking about, we seem to 'just know' without having any way of knowing. Throughout the ages philosophers have been fascinated by questions about the ways we come to know things, and about what we can know by those ways. Scepticism in one form or another has been a constant bogey. Some philosophers have embraced it cheerfully; but most have striven desperately to push it aside and then wash their hands thoroughly to show how cleansed they are from any defiling contact with it. Questions of this kind fall under epistemology, or the theory of knowledge (*episteme* is the Greek for 'knowledge'). We have seen something of them when we discussed private languages in Chapter 8, for one thing which motivated the search for a private language was the belief that whatever we know about the world we must ultimately know because of the data of our senses, so that these data are the things we really and primarily know, and so must be what our words primarily refer to. There was also an epistemological flavour to our discussions of positivism and the anti-realist views of Dummett in Chapter 6, for those views demanded that if we are to make sense of the world, and talk about it, we must be able to say in principle how we would find out, or recognise, whether what we say is true: if we cannot do this, say these views, our language fails, as it were, to make contact with the world, and so fails to have meaning.

These two pillars of philosophy, logic and epistemology, both in a way have to do with the relations between us and the world, and to that extent support the conception of philosophy which we saw in the Introduction has affinities with existentialism and Kant. This is particularly clear with epistemology, since knowledge obviously forms a link between us and the world. But logic, as we have seen, concerns thought and rationality; basically the world provides us with the objects of our thought, and rationality is exercised both in thinking about and in acting in the world. Logic also concerns the nature and working of language, though nowadays this has occupied so much attention and led to so many ramifications that its study is often thought of as a subject on its own, the philosophy of language; and language again relates us to the world, since it represents an indispensable tool for understanding the world, and dealing with it in those ways that require the activity of more than one person; and for that matter for solo activities too, since thinking, at least of certain kinds, seems to require language, as we saw in Chapter 7.

The third pillar I referred to concerns things like being or existence and what there is, and this, it seems to me, fits rather less easily into the conception of philosophy I have just mentioned. There is surely a certain fascination in the idea of making an inventory of the universe on the

179

grandest scale. Of course we shall not be bothered with the details, with the tree in my garden and the pen of your aunt, nor even with listing the large-scale things like stars and galaxies – that we leave to the physicist or cosmologist, though we might express a certain enquiring interest when he starts discussing whether the universe is finite or infinite, or whether it contains some axis of symmetry, or whether time could run backwards. But we are mainly interested at the moment in what *kinds* of thing exist. Material objects, like trees and pens and galaxies, are the obvious things to start with, though we might enter discussion with our physicist friend about electrons. But are there any non-material objects, like spirits? This we discussed in Chapter 7, and we might have extended the discussion to ask whether persons form a special kind of thing. But material objects carry other things with them. They have surfaces and shadows, and often when struck emit sounds. They have qualities and stand in relations. They undergo changes and thereby form part of events. The list of even the kinds of thing that are, or have been thought to be, is almost endless. The task of compiling it belongs to ontology (the stem *ont-* is Greek for 'being'). But the task is complicated by the question of whether being itself is an unambiguous notion. Some philosophers (e.g., A. Meinong, 1853–1920) have thought a special word like 'subsist', should be used for some of the more shadowy things like universals or numbers or the difference between red and green.

Ontology is a part of metaphysics, which differs from it by being wider and covering other questions as well, questions like those we have already mentioned about space, time, and infinity; or about causation and whether there is any necessity or purpose in the world; or about unity and identity: what makes a thing the thing it is, and under what conditions would it no longer be the thing it is? Could you, while still being you, have been born in China in the twentieth century BC? Or from another than the one that succeeded of the half million or so sperm cells that competed to bring you into being? Unlike ontology these other branches of metaphysics don't usually have special names. None of our ten chapters has been devoted single-mindedly to metaphysics, but we have touched upon it several times. In Chapter 1 we asked whether it was fated that things should be as they are. In Chapter 2 we asked whether Jones, who lived such a sheltered life that he never met danger, could have been 'really' brave, and whether there are facts, and if so, what are they, while in Chapter 3 we asked much the same questions about values. The question about Jones's bravery was part of the general issue of realism and anti-realism, and of whether there can be truths beyond our ken, which we took up again in Chapter 6, and which can be regarded as both metaphysical (if we emphasise the question whether there *are* such truths) and epistemological (if we emphasise the 'beyond our ken' bit). In Chapter 7, as I said a moment ago, we discussed whether there are spirits or souls separable from bodies, and then finally we ended Chapter 10 at a point where we were verging on metaphysics with a discussion of identity.

I have described logic, epistemology and metaphysics as the three central pillars of philosophy, for various reasons. One is simply that that is how most philosophers treat them, I think. Papers in them tend to be among the compulsory papers in university examinations in philosophy. The papers on the history of philosophy, which in practice concentrate mainly on the early Greeks, to the death of Aristotle, and on the seventeenth and eighteenth centuries, are mainly composed of questions that, in a broad sense, belong to these same three spheres, or more particularly perhaps to the last two, since logic was rather in the doldrums in the seventeenth and eighteenth centuries, because it was considered that the main work in it had already been completed by Aristotle; most philosophers now, I imagine, would regard this as a grave limitation on the philosophical outlook of those centuries.

A second reason is that these subjects provide an underpinning for the other regions of philosophy, and supply them with concepts and arguments in what is rather a one-way traffic. We saw an example of this a few paragraphs ago in the way in which our discussion in Chapter 3 of the role of truth and falsity in ethics grew out of the treatments of truth and falsity themselves in Chapter 2; in Chapter 3 we were applying them and taking further the results of Chapter 2. Similarly the discussion in Chapter 3 of certain kinds of implication in ethics led us on to a general logical study of implication in Chapter 4. In both these cases our discussion in ethics required us to ride horses (truth and implication) which were born in the stables of logic.

A third reason, or perhaps really the basis for the second, is that the concepts and questions of these central areas are general. In them we study truth in general, implication in general, knowledge in general, being in general, while the other philosophical subjects tend to have more restricted subject-matters. This might not seem all that obvious. Does not a subject like ethics study goodness in general and duty in general? Yes, it does, but these notions themselves are not as general as truth, knowledge or being. These latter notions pervade ethics in a way that goodness or duty do not pervade logic, epistemology or metaphysics. Ethics spends quite a lot of time asking questions like whether moral utterances can be *true*, how, if so, we can *know* their truth, whether values *exist*. Duty and goodness do not in this way occupy the attention of the logician, etc. when he is on his home

territory and not simply applying his conclusions to ethics as an example
or as one sphere among others. At least this is true in general, though the
distinction is admittedly not quite as clear-cut as I have drawn it. There is
a topic, for instance, called the ethics of belief, which asks how far belief
is subject to the will: can we *decide* to believe something or suspend
judgment, as against deciding to act or refrain from acting on our
beliefs? It then asks whether, if we can, we ought to believe certain
things, and can be held responsible for our beliefs. This is not an
application of epistemology to an ethical sphere, as when we ask how
we know, if we do, moral truths as against other truths. It is rather a
matter of ethics invading a central epistemological area, the assessment
of beliefs and judgments. To claim that beliefs can be assessed in an
ethical dimension as well as in the logical one of validity is to claim
something important about the concept of belief itself, and the concept of
belief, especially when considered in connection with the kinds of
justification it is open to, is a central topic for epistemology.
Nevertheless, this is a rather minor matter. Even if at this point we
cannot do our epistemology without taking some ethical notions into
account, ethics is nothing like as pervasive in epistemology as
epistemology is in ethics, where we would be hamstrung over enormous
areas if we could not bring in notions from epistemology like belief or
judgment.

These three subjects then are central to philosophy in the ways I have
tried to explain. But this does not mean that the other parts are without
importance or are any less philosophical. Much of the most important
work being done in philosophy now belongs in these more specialised
areas, as it is perhaps most fair to call them. I will say a few words about
the most important of them.

Many readers will probably have been slightly shocked to be told that
ethics is not one of the central pillars of philosophy. If good and evil are
not at the very heart of philosophy, what is? I have already explained
the sense in which, I think, ethics comes outside the very central area,
but let me now make partial amends and say that, even on the criteria I
have used, it is not far outside. It has fundamental notions of its own:
good, evil, duty, etc., to take only the most general ones, which cannot,
or certainly cannot obviously, be derived from other parts of philosophy.
The position is rather that it has to borrow notions (truth, knowledge,
etc.) from the central parts in order to do its own work, while its own
special notions it tends to keep rather to itself, without significantly
lending them in return to the central areas. Plainly nothing follows from
this to derogate from the intrinsic importance of these special notions
when considered in their own right. Ethics in fact comes usually next in

line to the central subjects in respect of being compulsory in university examinations.

We could contrast ethics with a subject like philosophy of history. Here we have a branch of philosophy that has its own special subject-matter – or it would hardly be worth calling a separate branch at all – but few special notions like good or duty. It is related to philosophy of science, which is itself a sort of amalgam of logic and epistemology, applying to science in particular the general conclusions about rational argument reached by logic, and asking how we can justify our claims to knowledge in that particular area; it also examines notions like causation, and asks in what sense there is anything that could be called necessity in the world of nature. Philosophy of history asks how far the methods and conclusions of philosophy of science can be applied to a subject which seems on the face of it to be much more concerned to treat events in all their particularity and uniqueness, rather than to subsume events under general laws. In fact one of the main current disputes in philosophy of history could be expressed just like this: is it really just a part of philosophy of science? Suppose we say no: what peculiarities shall we have to attribute to it? It will no doubt refer to freewill, and it will couch its explanations, or some of them, in terms of intentions, purposes, and motives. But these are not terms peculiar to itself. They are terms shared with other branches of philosophy, and they are not themselves the subject of examination: philosophy of history is not concerned to say, for instance, what counts as having freewill, or how a motive differs from a purpose. Philosophy of history, then, is rather a fringe subject in the sense of not being central. Its subject-matter is relatively limited in scope, and its concepts are derivative and shared with other subjects; or if it has concepts of its own, like, say, progress, these bulk far less in it than ethical ones do in ethics. But this does not mean it is at all a fringe subject in the sense of not being properly philosophical. Its questions, methods, and conclusions are just as philosophical as those of any other branch of the subject, central or peripheral. Our ten chapters did not, I think, contain anything that could be called philosophy of history; but we did touch on philosophy of science in Chapter 5, and in one or two incidental remarks elsewhere, such as pp. 93–4.

Notions like intention, motive and purpose, which we mentioned just above, find their proper home, along with the freewill problem, in philosophy of mind or, as it is sometimes called, philosophical psychology. The general study of what exists is ontology, as we have seen; but the fact that the world contains minds, or things (persons, living bodies) which have mental properties, is a rather striking fact about the world, and it is not surprising that is has managed to acquire a branch of philosophy of its own. We saw something of the freewill problem in Chapter 1, though our approach for most of that chapter was oriented rather from a logical or metaphysical direction, since we were mainly concerned with whether things in general, including human action along with all the rest, were subject to fate, and how truth is connected to time. To ask whether there is a special force or necessity at work in the world, and whether the future is somehow already there, waiting to walk on to the stage, is to ask metaphysical questions, while to ask what is entailed by a statement saying that something is true is to ask a logical question. Philosophy of mind comes centrally into the picture when we go on to ask how human actions differ from events in the non-human world Philosophy of mind also formed the main topic of Chapter 7, when we raised the central question of what we ourselves are.

Like ethics, philosophy of mind is a relatively central subject. It covers quite a wide field, and has many important concepts of its own: namely, in general, those associated with mentality. It has even spawned a sub-species of itself called the philosophy of action, dealing with concepts like intention, motive, purpose and will. It might be said to cover questions of analysis where epistemology covers questions of justification. Epistemology asks when our beliefs are justified, while philosophy of mind asks what counts as believing something. But, like most demarcation lines of this nature in philosophy, this one is rather vague in practice and not all that important. The analysis of what it is to know something or perceive something, where questions of justification are at least in the offing, is usually called epistemology; but epistemology also asks how we actually come by various of our ideas and beliefs, whether or not we are justified in doing so. (This last is sometimes called 'naturalised epistemology'.) The concepts belonging to philosophy of mind, especially those concerning action and freewill, are obviously of vital concern to ethics, and here philosophy of mind plays the role of a central subject in feeding other subjects. In fact it is really only its subordinate position to metaphysics, in that its subject-matter is less general, that stops me calling it a fourth central pillar, though it does not have quite that role in modern university curricula. There is one other overlap between it and metaphysics that deserves mention, and that concerns personal identity. What makes you you and me me? I have already mentioned the question about your being born in ancient China when talking about metaphysics a few paragraphs ago. At this point philosophy of mind simply acts as one sub-species of metaphysics, examining the general concept of identity as it applies in one particular sphere, where the difficulties are especially great.

There are two other subjects that might be compared to ethics, though in different ways: political philosophy and aesthetics. Political philosophy, like ethics, concerns norms of human action, though on the collective rather than individual scale. Its special concepts include things like liberty, equality, democracy, authority and sovereignty. It can be studied independently of ethics, but it seems more natural (and is more common in university courses, I think) to treat it as following on from ethics. Perhaps the rationale for this is that collective action is after all still action taken by individuals, even when they are acting in an official rather than private capacity. One notion which very much straddles the border between political philosophy and ethics is the virtue of justice, and our discussion of Rawls in Chapter 9 – and in fact the whole of Chapter 9 for that matter – has just about equal claims to be assigned to ethics or to political philosophy.

While we are talking about political philosophy I might mention another branch of philosophy concerned with man in society and acting collectively. This is social philosophy, which links political philosophy with philosophy of mind and philosophy of science, and also has some relation to philosophy of history. It studies people in groups, but whereas social psychology asks how they operate, social philosophy asks how they ought to operate, and how far the study of them can be compared to that of individuals on the one hand and that of the world of nature on the other.

Aesthetics does not so much have a common subject-matter with ethics, but is rather analogous to it. They both concern different types of value, and if aesthetics is generally treated as less central than ethics, this is at least partly because of a feeling that its subject-matter is less intrinsically important. We *can* live without art, but we should not get far without morals of some sort. But just how far the treatment of aesthetic questions can parallel the treatment of ethical ones is itself a question of some interest. For instance, is there any comparison between the role of general rules as precepts for producing works of art ('Avoid consecutive fifths', 'The horizon should never bisect the picture') and as precepts for how to act rightly ('Always tell the truth', 'Never harm the innocent')? We saw something of aesthetics, and of its relation to metaphysics, in our final chapter.

There are a handful of other branches of philosophy that I might as well mention for completeness. Logic is concerned with reasoning, and reasoning, at least when explicit and laid out for inspection, invokes language. A large part of logic is concerned with the materials for reasoning, and so with language, but this study has grown so enormously in recent decades that it is now often treated as a separate subject, known as philosophy of language (not to be confused with linguistic philosophy, which is a movement or approach, not a subject). A great deal of what we said about meaning in Chapter 6 could come under philosophy of language, and its overlap with logic is great, so great in fact that university examiners are often embarrassed to find that they have set virtually the same questions on the logic paper and the philosophy of language paper in some examination.

On the other side of logic, where it becomes rather mathematical in nature, the more technical developments tend to shade off into the philosophy of mathematics, which studies the concepts of mathematics, such as the nature of numbers, the status of different geometries, the relations between truth and proof, etc. The main reason for this development is that logic itself constructs and uses abstract systems which in many ways resemble those of mathematics; so it is not surprising that when logic turns to study these systems it finds itself studying mathematical systems at the same time, and asking, for instance, how closely the two kinds of system are in fact related to each other.

Almost any subject or sphere of human activity can generate certain philosophical problems, which, if there are enough of them, will become known as the 'philosophy of' the subject in question. One sometimes hears, for instance, of the 'philosophy of biology', which singles out those questions in the philosophy of science which arise particularly in connection with biology. It asks, for instance, how one should define life, or what counts as evolution, or whether there is such a thing as teleological explanation (explanation in terms of goals or purposes). Two spheres which have particularly well established philosophies of their own are law and education. Finally, there is a subject which is quite wide in extent, but has suffered various vicissitudes in recent decades, for reasons which I hope will become clear later, the philosophy of religion.

So there is our map of philosophy, with its three central pillars of logic, epistemology and metaphysics, branching out through the still relatively central subjects like ethics and philosophy of mind to the rich foliage of the fringe subjects I have just been portraying, subjects, to repeat, just as philosophical and just as respectable in the philosophers' eyes as the central pillars themselves; the outer twigs are just as much part of the tree as the main trunk. But, alas, metaphors usually come unstuck eventually, even when they try to get the best of both architecture and botany like this one. Our tree should perhaps be a banyan tree, which I believe is joined to the ground by a number of different trunks. The point is that we must not think of each twig as being joined to only one branch, and each branch to only one trunk.

Before going on, let me add one or two remarks about the map and our own journey. First, how important is the map? It has, I hope, a modest intrinsic interest, but how important is it that we know where we are when we are doing a piece of philosophy, and can say that this question belongs to logic and that one to metaphysics, etc.? Apart from the tribulations of those who have to arrange for university examinations, whose papers have to have titles to them, the answer is: not very much. It is obviously interesting to have some idea of the general structure of philosophy. But to insist on classifying any given problem in just one pigeon hole would be little better than pedantic, and might even be worse. For not only have the branches of philosophy no clear dividing lines, and often substantial overlaps, as we have seen with, say, logic and philosophy of language; but what starts as one problem might be looked at in different ways, which might tempt us to classify it differently. Suppose we ask how it is that we manage to think about things in their absence, a problem on the face of it in the philosophy of mind. We might ask what sort of things have to be going on inside us, whether any images or incipient movements of the vocal chords must be occurring, and if so, how they must be related to the thing we are supposed to be thinking of; this suggests a metaphysical approach, in so far as we are asking what sort of things must exist in this situation. Or we might ask what it is that justifies someone's claim to be thinking about, say, Julius Caesar; this suggests an epistemological approach, in that it concerns the justification of some mental state relating a person to the world. Or we might ask what the truth-conditions are for a statement that, say, it has just occurred to Smith that his wife's lover should be boiled in oil: what light is thrown on these truth-conditions, and on the meaning of phrases like 'his wife's lover' in sentences expressing such thoughts, by the possibility that his wife has no lover? This suggests a logical approach, concentrating on truth and meaning. The reader might like to compare the different approaches to this sort of problem of W. J. Ginnane, and of S. Blackburn and J. Heal.

Second, our own journey has been, of course, only one out of indefinitely many possible ones. I have tried to make it reasonably representative, and one point it illustrates is just this artificiality of insisting on too rigorous a classification of problems. I said, for instance, above that the discussion of fatalism in Chapter 1 touched on metaphysics. It could at least partly be classified under philosophy of mind, and the discussion of logical determinism that followed it could similarly be classified under philosophy of mind or under logic. Again we saw above that the discussion of Rawls in Chapter 9 fell equally under ethics or political philosophy.

Third, a feature of philosophy is that one must always expect the unexpected. In particular one must expect apparently quite remote parts of the subject to have effects on each other. For instance, one might be thinking about a problem in logic and suddenly realise that one's conclusions will radically affect one's views on something in ethics. We noted an example of this *en route*, when an argument from Frege against analysing negation in terms of the activity or 'speech act' of denying (Chapter 2, p. 32) turned up again in Chapter 3 (pp. 50–1) as an argument against a non-cognitivist analysis of moral judgments. We also saw the same argument appearing again as a criticism of Strawson's 'performative' analysis of 'true' (Chapter 2, p. 36). And there are other places too where it could be used. For instance, S. E. Toulmin offered a 'performative' or 'speech act' analysis of 'probably'. He thought that to say 'It will probably rain tomorrow' (in normal conditions, i.e. not acting in a play, etc.) was to assert that it would rain tomorrow, but to assert it only tentatively, half withdrawing it, as it were. Frege's argument could be used against this too, provided that 'probably' can occur in contexts like the antecedent of a hypothetical. Frege thought of this argument when he was concerned to analyse negation, i.e. in a logical context. But he might quite easily have thought of it first in, say, an ethical context, and only then realised its implications for logic. One's work in ethics can affect one's work in logic, just as one's work in logic can affect one's work in ethics. To say this is not inconsistent with what I said above about logic being more central than ethics, and nourishing ethics in a way that seldom happens in reverse. If Frege had thought of his argument while analysing 'good' rather than 'not', it would have been a matter of a logical point, or a point in philosophy of language, occurring to him an an ethical context: the point that a performative analysis cannot, straightforwardly anyway, give the meaning of a term that occurs outside the relevant performances. We do not feel tempted to say that what actually happened was that an ethical point occurred to him in a logical context, though the point that did occur to him was relevant to ethics.

What this third feature shows is that philosophy is a unified subject, despite what may sometimes seem the amorphous mass of problems that it covers. It also incidentally explains why universities are often reluctant to let students study philosophy in bits and pieces and without studying at least one or two of the central subjects. It is true that someone reading, say, modern languages might do a subsidiary paper in aesthetics or philosophy of language – and nothing I am saying is intended to discourage them from trying to; it is simply that there will inevitably be limitations on how far one can get in those subjects without doing at least a bit of the central core as well. Joint degrees are feasible enough – indeed at Oxford, the traditional centre of British philosophy, it cannot be studied in any other way – but there are usually restrictions on choice to ensure that a fair amount of the central core is studied.

12 Recent developments

So far in this Part, I have discussed philosophy in a static way, trying to show something of its structure, and making a few general remarks about it and our journey through it. But now we might have a look at it from a more dynamic point of view, to see something about how it is developing and where it is going, or has been going recently. This will involve us in a bit of history. Obviously this is not the place to start on a general history of philosophy, even a potted one. But what we might do is have a look at one or two recent developments, which have resulted in philosophy being where it is at the moment. In fact the claim of what follows is still as much philosophical as historical, for what I want to do for at least part of the time is show how certain philosophical developments arise naturally out of what preceded them, rather than get bogged down in the precise details of how they arose historically.

From the point of view of this particular enterprise there is one rather fortunate historical fact we can start from. This is the dominant position occupied by logical positivism in roughly the second quarter of this century. We have already looked in Chapter 6 at the verificationist theory of meaning associated with this, but now let us look at logical positivism in a broader context.

Throughout the history of philosophy there has been a tendency for philosophy to try to abolish itself. In logical positivism this tendency has come as near, if not nearer, to fruition as at any time before. There are two strands in the web of philosophical thought which help to explain this, both of which we have seen already. One is scepticism and the other is Occam's razor, and they are linked together. Epistemology is largely concerned to justify our claims to know what we do know, and so it tends constantly to pare these claims down, because the stronger the claims the harder they are to justify. Ages when epistemology has been a dominant concern of philosophy, as it has in modern philosophy and in the tradition leading up to it, have been ages when scepticism has never been very far round the corner. Occam's razor is a tool of the sceptic. It says: Don't assume the existence of any more things than you have to. 'Things' here can be taken in a very wide sense, and certainly need not be limited to material objects. It can include not only abstract things like numbers, universals, propositions, but also modes of valid reasoning, or ways one can claim to know things, or types of thing that can be known.

The effect of applying the razor is to dismiss as illegitimate a large number of claims to knowledge, and to cut down the number of things that one claims to exist. The resulting world tends to be rather sparse and Spartan, though not necessarily in a way that common sense might approve of. For common sense accepts ordinary material objects and rejects airy-fairy things like ghosts and unicorns, or the present king of France, whom we discussed in Chapter 2. It might also be persuaded fairly easily to dismiss things like universals or propositions, once its attention has been drawn to them, especially if those who claim that there are such things do so in the rather portentous way of the Platonist who suggests not only that they exist, but that really they exist rather more thoroughly, as it were, than anything else, material objects having only a sort of courtesy existence by comparison. But the wielder of Occam's razor is quite likely to cut out material objects, because how after all do we know them? Only through our senses; we can hardly know about them without using our senses. But our senses only tell us about our own sense-data, for reasons we discussed in Chapter 8. So sense-data are the only things whose existence we really know about. Material objects we either infer to exist, so as to have something to cause these sense-data, or else we construct them out of the sense-data rather as we construct the average man out of ordinary men (the view usually meant by 'phenomenalism': see Chapter 6, p. 94).

This sort of outlook is usually associated with empiricism (literally, 'experience-ism'), the philosophy that all our knowledge comes ultimately through the five senses, plus various kinaesthetic senses, etc. and perhaps introspection (cf. p. 87). There are a vast number of forms empiricism can take, but it is generally considered to have reached an extreme point in David Hume (1711–77), who said:

> If we take in our hand any volume; of divinity or school metaphysics, for instance, let us ask *Does it contain any abstract reasoning concerning quantity or number?* No. *Does it contain any experimental reasoning concerning matter of fact and existence?* No. Commit it then to the flames: for it can contain nothing but sophistry and illusion.

The two kinds of writing which Hume would save from the flames are concerned with what he elsewhere calls relations of ideas and matters of fact respectively. They correspond pretty closely to the two classes of statements admitted as meaningful by the logical positivists, which we discussed in Chapter 6; the first class are usually called empirical, and the second class analytic. The main burthen of logical positivism in fact is to insist that these two kinds of statement are indeed the only meaningful ones, because only they can be verified.

Logical positivism, then, is at least to some extent a variant of Hume's empiricism. Actually the degree of resemblance becomes rather less when one considers Hume's philosophical programme as a whole; but that is a historical matter which lies well beyond our scope. The term 'positivism' was invented by Auguste Comte (1798–1857) at a time roughly halfway between Hume and the logical positivists, but to go into his philosophy would again take us astray. One thing that is worth noting, though, is the term 'logical' which gets added on when we come to twentieth-century positivism, associated mainly with the so-called Vienna Circle of the 1920s (until Hitler did a great service to English-speaking philosophy by forcing many of the Circle members to become refugees in Britain or America, where they started writing in English). Hume asked what sort of thing we have the mental equipment to think about the world, while the logical positivists asked what sort of thing we have a meaningful language to say about it. All our knowledge, or at least all that we can pass on to anyone else (and here remember Chapter 8), must be formulated in language. So if there are certain limits to what language can do, there will be corresponding limits to what we can think. The logical positivists claimed that there are indeed certain limits to what language can do, at least by way of stating facts.

Language is a human creation: not, of course, a deliberate one – no one was silly enough to think men sat down in the jungle and invented language as they might invent a new way of catching animals – but still a creation that grew up to serve human purposes. One of these purposes, and the one the logical positivists usually treated as the basic one, is conveying information; others would include asking, commanding, expressing emotions, etc. Language conveys information, or rather we use it to convey information, because words and sentences have meaning. But, thought the logical positivists, the meaning of a sentence (of the relevant, basic kind: roughly, a sentence in the indicative) either is or is essentially based on the information it can be used to convey. So if we are to understand the sentence and know what it means we must know what this information is. And knowing this means knowing what the world must be like if the sentence, as used on a given occasion, is to be true; we add the clause 'as used on a given occasion' because the sentence may contain so-called 'token-reflexives' like 'here', 'this', or tense of verbs, which will make what it says depend on when it is used. So knowing what the sentence means is knowing what will verify it (make it true), or knowing how to verify it (find out if it is true).

This verificationist theory we discussed in Chapter 6. What is important here is the emphasis on language and meaning. Language is the instrument by which we possess knowledge, but it is a human tool and can only be used to do what it is capable of doing. When it is being so used it has meaning, and when it does not have meaning it is being misused and gets us nowhere. Meaning is a linguistic notion, and the laws of logic can be thought of as governing how we should use language, at least in such respects as avoiding contradiction, etc. This gives one reason for applying 'logical' to a philosophy which concentrates on asking what are the conditions under which what we say is meaningful, and so gives one reason for the term 'logical positivism'. But there is another reason for it, in so far as these positivists thought it was a matter of logic that their philosophy was correct. They seemed to think that nothing would count as a meaningful statement that was not empirically verifiable (making allowances for analytic statements, which I will return to in a minute); and to say that nothing else would count as meaningful is tantamount to saying it is logically impossible that anything else should be so; and so they are claiming as a matter of logic that only verifiable statements are meaningful. This gives another reason for the term 'logical positivism'.

Like Hume and the earlier positivists such as Comte and also Ernst Mach (1838–1916), the logical positivists are one variety of what are called reductionists; this means that in one way or another they reduce the richness of the world by claiming that some things either do not exist at all or are disguised forms of other things, as one might argue that ghosts are merely imaginary, or else are really small boys dressed up in sheets. What the logical positivists use Occam's razor to get rid of are allegedly meaningful statements that are not empirically verifiable. Statements that seem to be meaningful though unverifiable are either not meaningful or are not actually saying what they look as if they are saying but something else instead, and something which is empirically verifiable.

But philosophical statements are not empirically verifiable, so either there are no such statements or they are saying something else which *is* empirically verifiable; but in that case they are not really philosophical statements at all, so either way there are no philosophical statements. Philosophy has abolished itself.

Before we go on to see what happens next, I want to draw attention to one feature of logical positivism as I have described it, an affinity to the philosophy of Wittgenstein. Wittgenstein is not usually thought of as a full-blooded logical positivist, though in his early days he moved in that general area, and was on the fringe of the Vienna Circle. One of the remarkable things about him is that he is usually supposed to have originated not one but two movements in philosophy, one called 'logical atomism' in the first of his two main works, the *Tractatus*, and the other called 'linguistic philosophy' in his other main work, the *Philosophical Investigations* (written in the 1930s and 1940s, and disseminated orally, though published only posthumously). Just how distinct the philosophies underlying these two works really are is much disputed, but they certainly give quite different impressions when one reads them. Bertrand Russell was highly impressed by the first, and was himself the other main exponent of logical atomism, but he rejected the second with something approaching sheer disgust. To explain logical atomism would take us too far afield, though we can say that it was a reductionist philosophy. But it is Wittgenstein's second philosophy that I really have in mind, and that was not primarily reductionist, and in fact in some ways was just the opposite. We shall see more of this later, but for the moment I want to return to our discussion of private languages in Chapter 8.

Wittgenstein's hostility to the idea that there can be a private language, in the sense we saw earlier, rests largely on the demand he made that there should always be criteria of correctness in the offing when we claim to be doing something that involves following a rule; and he thought that using language did involve this. Otherwise, he thought, what we did would be quite undisciplined, and would amount to mere senseless rambling. To use one of his metaphors (*Philosophical Investigations*, §270), our words would be idling like a knob tacked on to a piece of machinery, which looked like a working switch but performed no function. What the logical positivists had in common with this was the search for some guarantee that when we talked our words were not just idling, and they found this guarantee in the notion of verifiability: as long, and only as long, as we ensured that what we said was verifiable we could be assured that we were talking meaningfully and not just rambling. (We are thinking only of assertive or statement-making talk here.) In fact although I have said that Wittgenstein's second philosophy is not primarily reductionist, which I will explain in a minute, there is one respect in which it is reductionist, and this comes out mainly in his treatment of mathematics, which comes in his *Remarks on the Foundations of Mathematics*, published posthumously like all his books except the *Tractatus*. His approach to mathematics is strongly anti-realist in the sense we saw when discussing Dummett's philosophy in Chapters 2 and 6. In fact Dummett was working largely under his inspiration in this respect. The general idea is that mathematical concepts, especially those involving infinity, and mathematical truths are only acceptable as genuine concepts and truths if the concepts are 'constructible' and the truths at least in principle verifiable. A concept is constructible if we can give a rule for constructing it. For instance, we can construct any finite number by using the rule, to put it loosely, 'Go on adding one to what you've got already until you get there'. It may not be so easy to give a rule for constructing infinite numbers, or transfinite numbers as they are usually called, such as the number of (finite) numbers, which is usually called, borrowing a Hebrew letter, 'aleph nought' or 'aleph-sub(script)-zero'.

On p. 104 I called Davidson's 'thin' theory of meaning reductionist because it effectively reduced a theory of meaning to a theory of truth; and we saw how Dummett's rival theory thought that this was not enough, and that not truth-conditions but assertibility-conditions, and so verifiability, had to be brought in. Yet now I am calling Dummett's theory itself reductionist, because it reduces the number of truths that we can accept, leaving out, not as false but as senseless, those alleged to exist beyond human comprehension. This gives us an excellent example of how a label like 'reductionist' can be applied, from different points of view, not only to one system but also to another which is opposed to that one on the very point for which that first one was itself called reductionist. In fact we must always be careful about classifications in philosophy, and be wary of attempts to classify philosophers simply as reductionists or anti-reductionists, or empiricists or rationalists, etc., without qualification. Of course we do use classifications of this kind – I am using them myself – but we should remember that they may be valid only from a certain point of view, or in a certain respect or context. We shall see more of this when we come later to discuss one or two philosophical '-isms'.

But now we must return to the logical positivists, who when we left them a page or two ago had just abolished philosophy. At the present day, some half-century later, I think it can be said that philosophy is flourishing. It is certainly being engaged in on a wide scale, and it is in an expansive and experimental mood. How did this happen? Somehow philosophy has risen from the carpet and fought its way back, and the history of philosophy since the Second World War is in no small measure the history of its doing so.

We looked very quickly in Chapter 6 at a handful of reasons why the verificationist theory of meaning was not found completely satisfactory.

But there is one point we might note now, not for its intrinsic historical importance so much as for what might be called its symbolic importance in the present context, where we are talking about how philosophy fought its way back from its apparent knockout. There is a certain paradox about philosophy abolishing itself, akin to the sort of paradox a physicist would find in the idea of a movement to end all movements (though admittedly the parallel is not quite exact). Aristotle, one of the greatest philosophers, once wrote a work called *Protrepticus*, which means roughly 'exhortatory sermon'. In it he asked, among other things, 'Ought we to philosophise?' He replied that we ought; for if we ought not, it would need a bit of philosophising to tell us that we ought not, so at least we ought to do that much philosophising. If the logical positivists abolish philosophy, are they not doing a bit of philosophy in abolishing it? They say that every meaningful statement must be either one that is ultimately verifiable through the senses or else an analytic statement, a tautology of logic or mathematics. But what about this very statement of their own position, the statement that every meaningful statement is either empirically verifiable or analytic? Is it itself empirically verifiable, or analytic, or what? If it is empirically verifiable, we shall need a great deal of evidence to persuade us to accept it, for it is after all a rather wide generalisation. It certainly cannot be used, as the logical positivists tried to use it, to *show* that statements such as those of metaphysics or ethics or religion, etc., are meaningless, or else not really statements at all but something else masquerading as statements; for unless we *already* have reasons to dismiss such alleged statements they will simply be counter examples to the generalisation which is supposed to give us our ground for dismissing them.

It is true that we might treat the verificationist principle as a well-founded inductive generalisation which we accepted as true because such a large number of meaningful statements turned out to be verifiable or analytic, much as we might accept that all cats have tails. We might then use the principle to dismiss metaphysical, etc. statements as meaningless because not verifiable or analytic. But this would be a rather shaky procedure. When we accept a principle on inductive grounds we do not do so simply because we have found a large number of cases which satisfy it. We do not accept that all cats have tails simply because so many cats obviously have. We want to know whether the cats in question cover a sufficiently large range of *types* of cat. If we know there is a type of cat, say Manx cats, which we have not yet examined, we shall suspend judgment on the generalisation until we have managed to examine some, however many millions of luxuriant Persian or Siamese tails we have seen. Similarly, the fact that masses of ordinary meaningful statements are verifiable or analytic should not persuade us that all meaningful statements are, if we know that there is one class of statements, metaphysical ones, which we have not yet taken account of.

Yes, the reader may say, that may be so; but am I not being a bit pedantic and rigorous? When we do have a well established generalisation, such as that all cats have tails, and then discover some apparent counter-examples like Manx cats, do we not often simply decide that Manx cats are not really cats after all? Yes, we do, but at a price. The price is that our generalisation is no longer an empirical one, open to evidence and counter-evidence, and capable of being used to say something significant and make predictions: it has become analytic. Nothing is to *count* as a tail-less cat.

Now at this point two comments are in order. The first is that this process by which an empirical generalisation becomes analytic by being clothed in an adamantine coat of mail against all counter-examples is a process which has its place in a certain setting. This is, roughly, that all reasonable hideouts of possible counter-examples have been examined and declared empty, but then some rather strange fringe cases turn up, which anyway are not very central instances of the generalisation. Manx cats are a bit of an odd breed, and maybe they differ from ordinary cats in other ways too when you really come to look at them, so not too much is lost if we just alter the definition of 'cat' a little so as to exclude them. But the kinds of statement which seem to be counter-examples to the verification principle − metaphysical, ethical, religious, aesthetic, political statements, and many more − are not a small handful of fringe statements that we discover only as an afterthought. Collectively they form quite a large part of our discourse, and they have been around all the time. We cannot treat them simply as an odd and minor phenomenon like Manx cats.

The second comment brings us to the second alternative open to the verificationists, that they should indeed treat their principle as analytic. This might seem a reasonable thing for them to do. It is after all a philosophical principle, not a scientific one, even if it was intended as a piece of philosophy to end philosophy; and philosophy might seem nearer to logic and mathematics then to science. But the trouble for the verificationists now lies in their own attitude towards analytic statements. For these statements, they hold, do not say anything. That is, they do not convey any information, or certainly not directly. They are 'true' in a sense, but true come what may. They do not exclude anything, and so do not tell us that the world is of one sort rather than another. If then the logical positivists take the line that their verification principle is analytic, they will have to say that it too is empty of content and does not say anything, which seems rather a cavalier way to treat one's own first principle.

This is not the end of the road for the logical positivists. They can say that the propositions of logic and mathematics are not usually thought to be of no interest, however we analyse them, and if their own principle is to be put on the same level with those propositions, it will be in quite good company. But it does show that the situation is not as neat and tidy as should be hoped for at the funeral of philosophy. Philosophy is beginning to fight its way back. The best bet for the verificationists, and one that some of them took, is probably to go on the offensive, to say that their principle is indeed not a statement at all, but a recommendation, that all statements not empirically verifiable or analytic should be regarded as either meaningless or not really statements at all, and then to challenge their opponents to find some better way of distinguishing the meaningful from the meaningless. Their principle does after all have a certain plausibility and appeal, as we have seen in discussing the outlook of present-day anti-realists.

II

There we must leave the logical positivists and go on to see what happened next. I have already mentioned Wittgenstein's second philosophy as inaugurating the movement known as linguistic philosophy, which dominated British (though not American) philosophy from the end of the Second World War until roughly the early 1960s. Wittgenstein's approach to philosophy was therapeutic. The aim of the philosopher, in a famous phrase, should be 'to let the fly out of the fly-bottle'. To be in philosophical perplexity was to be subject to a sort of disease, which Wittgenstein thought came upon us because we were ignorant and confused about the way in which language works. Schlick thought that if we said things that were meaningless, this was our own fault, because we had failed to *decide* what we really did mean (p. 86 above); the remedy was to make up our minds. Wittgenstein thought that if we got into philosophical perplexity, this was because we misunderstood the language we were using; the remedy was to understand it. The analogy is not exact, but it exists. Schlick and Wittgenstein both in their different ways show a rather dismissive attitude towards philosophy. This is odd in Wittgenstein's case, since he was known for the intense earnestness with which he engaged in philosophical activities. In Schlick's case this was because he thought philosophy had effectively reached its conclusion, and what remained was a matter of applying the main result to residual problems. In Wittgenstein's case it was because he thought the task of good philosophy was simply to free us from fly-bottles which only bad philosophy had got us into in the first place.

Since Wittgenstein thought that the troubles philosophy got itself into were the fault of philosophy itself, it was a natural corollary that he regarded ordinary thought and ordinary language as innocent, whereas Russell, for instance, thought that we could only understand ordinary language properly if we first translated it into an artificial ideal language free from its deficiencies. It is here that we meet the big contrast between logical positivism and the linguistic philosophy, or 'ordinary language philosophy', as it was often called, that followed it. Logical positivism was an ascetic system. Empirically verifiable statements were given full party membership. Analytic statements were admitted as indispensable aliens, without which the machinery of science would grind to a halt. Everything else was either rigorously excluded or else consigned to menial jobs like expressing emotions or attitudes and adding a bit of colour to things. Linguistic philosophy threw open the gates. The job of the philosopher was not to exercise censorship but to understand. Every sphere of human interest, science, ethics, religion, art, or what you will, had what was called, following Wittgenstein, its own 'language game', its own way of speaking and thinking and its special topics or problems to speak and think about. The job of philosophy was to examine these language games and give a sort of scientific account of their structure and how they operate. It was no more for philosophy to condemn or judge such spheres of interest than for science to condemn the tapeworm or cancer cell. Ways of speaking must not be dismissed as meaningless because they fail to satisfy some externally imposed criterion like the verification principle. Since they exist they must be meaningful somehow, and philosophy's job was to find out how. This was what I meant by saying above that Wittgenstein's philosophy is not reductionist.

So far, so good. The barriers were lifted and philosophy had freedom to expand in whatever way it would. Or had it? Many people, including Russell, thought not. To see why, we must ask whether philosophy had really emancipated itself as much as it might have thought from its logical positivist fetters.

Philosophy had now become above all a second-order subject. Its job was to study the concepts and methods of other subjects. It had no business to interfere in those other subjects, and indeed if it did, it would be in danger of distorting the very subject-matter it was trying to study. But these other subjects are 'ordinary' subjects engaged in by 'ordinary'

199

people. There is no mention of the traditional philosophical subjects like metaphysics, ethics, or aesthetics. These, if they *are* philosophical, must be second-order, and so must have a subject-matter provided by something else. Metaphysics for the moment remains still in the doldrums and 'metaphysical' remains a 'bad' word. Even if the verification principle has been abandoned, at least in theory, nothing has been suggested to take its place; and the new rules provide no subject-matter for metaphysics, since 'ordinary' people, which of course includes philosophers, outside their studies, do not engage in the sort of questions that seem to provide the subject-matter for it. (We will see later that this conclusion has to be modified.) But let us take ethics. Here there is a subject-matter, the moral judgments of ordinary people. Traditionally these have been taken to form part of the sphere of philosophy. People looked to philosophers, whether or not with much result, to tell them what was right and wrong. But the linguistic philosopher would never dream of doing such a thing. His job was to study moral judgments, not to make them, a job left to moralists and preachers. A sharp distinction was therefore made between ethics and meta-ethics, or morals and ethics: various labels were used, but the point is to distinguish between substantive moral or value judgments and a philosophical analysis of those judgments and the concepts they contain.

Here we can see both a reason for the dissatisfaction that was often felt with linguistic philosophy and also the lingering influence of logical positivism. The linguistic philosophers realised that moral judgments were not meaningless, but when they sat down to analyse them they could get no further basically than to take over and develop the 'speech act' approach of the logical positivists, who saw such judgments as primarily the expression of attitudes; the linguistic philosophers added a variation to this in the 'prescriptivist' analysis associated with R. M. Hare. We have already looked at some of the questions in this area in Chapter 3. The main difference perhaps between the linguistic philosophers and their predecessors is just that the linguistic philosophers were more willing to take this sort of task seriously. They were no longer trying to abolish philosophy, even if they had what a later outlook regarded as an unduly narrow idea of its scope. A work like C. L. Stevenson's *Ethics and Language* (1944) can be seen as bridging the gap from logical positivism to linguistic philosophy in this area.

The dissatisfaction felt with linguistic philosophers by people like Russell, and many others, was felt largely because they were thought to have abandoned their responsibilities. Their outlook was too permissive, with their insistence that 'anything goes' and that the philosopher's job is just to watch it going. They had abandoned the search for truth, in all but what seemed trivial respects. An example of this is the 'paradigm case argument', a typical tool of the linguistic philosopher, made most famous perhaps by its application to the freewill problem by A. Flew. Is there such a thing as freewill? Yes, of course, because there are paradigm cases of the use of an expression like 'He did it of his own freewill'. Flew's example is that of a newly married couple. They were not hypnotised. They were not drugged. It was not a shotgun wedding. They did it of their own freewill. To say they didn't, really, and that no-one ever really acts of his own freewill is to say there is no correct application of the phrase 'of his own freewill'. But plainly there is. It is meant to pick out ordinary cases in contrast to things like hypnosis or duress, and if there were no such contrast to be made it would be meaningless, which it plainly is not. Many people at the time felt rather short-changed by this sort of argument. In a way it seems to make its point, but that point is hardly the real point at issue. Surely the freewill problem goes deeper than these verbal considerations. That question, and whether the paradigm case argument is ever legitimate, we must leave aside. But the hostility to linguistic philosophy was real and widespread. I can remember myself when a philosopher could be almost literally button-holed in the street and told he was deserting his responsibilities.

In a way there is a certain irony in this hostility. The logical positivists often outraged respectable opinion by their scepticism. Metaphysics, ethics and religion were all thrown out of the window. Then along came the linguistic philosophers and let them all in again (or all but metaphysics, so far – a special case which outside opinion had little interest in), and what do they get for their pains but a clouting for their permissiveness? I cannot refrain from drawing a historical comparison with Plato's attitude to the Sophists, the itinerant professional intellectuals of his time. That he hated their moral outlook he was clear. But he often does not seem quite clear whether he was hating them for the sceptical egoism with which they subverted conventional morality and outraged respectable opinion, or for the fawning flattery with which they kowtowed to every whim of the Athenian public in their attempts to win favour and influence (and incidentally earn a living). In the modern setting the logical positivists were the outragers and the linguistic philosophers the kowtowers.

Actually this charge of triviality, of abdicating responsibility and lack of moral earnestness, has been levelled at other philosophers than those we have been discussing. Moralists of other schools, who were neither sceptical nor permissive, have been accused of triviality because of the sort of examples they use. As this is quite a common charge it might be worth saying something about philosophical examples by way of interlude before we go on. Examples are intended to clarify, but they can be of very different sorts according to the purpose in hand. In particular, if we want to illustrate some general principle, to show how it works or to bring out something about its general form, we need an example stripped to the bare bones of all distracting complications.

Suppose we ask, as philosophers have asked, how the practice of promising ever got going: where did the obligation attached to promising arise from? We might take an example like this: I have an apple, which you want. You have a banana, which I want. It is in our interests to exchange. But can we trust each other? If I give you my apple you might just thank me very much and pocket it. So I say, 'I will give you my apple if you give me your banana.' How will this affect you? Will you assume I am likely to give it because I shall be under an obligation? But I shall not. Promising, *ex hypothesi*, does not exist yet, and all I can be doing is describing my intentions or predicting my behaviour. If I fail to live up to these predictions you might accuse me of being mistaken in making them, and you might even feel aggrieved because I misled you, but I have not broken a promise. How then can I come to make a promise? One condition seems to be that I shall only have actually made a promise if you take it that you have been promised. For instance, if you are deaf and don't hear my promise it seems fair to say I didn't succeed in making one, though I tried to. Clearly we are on the verge of a paradox here, and I must leave the reader to continue the argument on his own, perhaps with the help of H. A. Prichard. My point is simply that for cases like this the best kind of examples seem to be nice simple ones about apples and bananas. At this stage their very artificiality is an advantage, enabling us to focus on the logic of the thing and the motives of ideally rational people, without getting bogged down in the complications of actual human psychology, or the moral complications that arise when we consider all the intricacies of real-life situations, with their conflicting obligations arising from other sources, etc. In other cases, of course, quite the opposite will hold, and the examples should display all the subtlety and intricacy of a realistic situation. The position is really the same as in physics or mechanics, where one often illustrates a general principle by some idealised example where, say, friction and air resistance are ignored. In both spheres there is a place for each type of example.

The other main kind of example that philosophers are criticised for using is the bizarre. A philosopher will often object to a certain view by saying, 'Ah, but suppose the following occurred ...', and then sketching some completely absurd sequence of events. But here again such examples have their place. They often, for instance, occur when what is important is not whether some proposition is true but whether, though false, it is logically false or only contingently false. For the interests of common sense this might be quite irrelevant, but it might make all the difference if one is asking how a certain concept works, or is related to other concepts. L. J. Cohen, a contemporary Oxford philosopher, recently discussed the concept of seeing, a topic where bizarre examples involving illusions or hallucinations are often constructed. Commenting on this, Cohen says, 'It sometimes takes a rather bizarre counter-example to reveal a very deep-seated semantic feature, just because the latter supplies information which we so familiarly exploit as to be unaware that we are exploiting it.' For other examples the reader might return to the one about barking cats at the end of Chapter 6, and also look at one of the most famous articles in modern epistemology, just two and a half pages long, E. Gettier's 'Is justified true belief knowledge?'

After that interlude, let us return to our main theme. I introduced linguistic philosophy as a permissive philosophy, and so it was, in the sense that it had an open-hearted attitude to human ways of speaking and thinking outside philosophy. But in another sense it inherited the ascetism of logical positivism, and this was largely responsible for the criticisms we have been considering. This concerns its attitude to philosophy itself, for, as we have seen, it had very restrictive ideas about what philosophy could do. It tended to hold itself primly aloof from the activities it was studying. It saw a sharp distinction between things like meta-ethics and ethics, and also between philosophy and science, a distinction I have been concerned to emphasise myself, though I think not quite so rigorously. But just as logical positivism found some embarrassment in the question of how to classify its own principle, namely the verification principle, so linguistic philosophy betrays a certain ambivalence when we examine its own procedure. Officially it is strictly a non-scientific, non-empirical, study; yet it spent a lot of time in what was called conceptual analysis: analysing various concepts, such as duty, or freewill, or perception. This was all very well so far, and no more than what one would expect a philosopher to spend at least part of his time doing. But the concepts in fact analysed tended to be much more refined and subtle ones than the three general notions I have just mentioned. Philosophers tended to be interested in, say, the precise differences between acting mistakenly, inadvertently, and unintentionally, or between having a duty to do something, being obliged to do it, and being under an obligation to do it. These enquiries, which particularly occupied J. L. Austin and his followers, come very near to an empirical investigation of human speech habits, at least in their general tendency if not strictly in their intention; and Austin did not emphasise the gulf between philosophy and non-philosophy that many of his contemporaries saw. He and his followers were accused of losing themselves in pedantic distinctions of no real importance, an accusation usually quite unfair, I think, though Austin did occasionally sail a bit close to that wind. At the end of an article on 'Pretending' he justified himself with the remark, 'I dreamt a line that would make a motto for a sober philosophy: *Neither a be-all nor an end-all be*'.

This all added fuel to the charge that philosophers were neglecting real philosophy. But to see how the next stage in things emerged it is important to go back to the rigorous dualism between philosophy and non-philosophy that I have mentioned, for an important feature of what has been happening in the last twenty years or so has been the eroding or complicating of this dichotomy and of other dichotomies with it.

Again ethics will provide a good sphere to look at what happened, though it certainly happened in other spheres. In ethics the rigid dichotomy borrowed much of its force from an earlier strand in the British empiricist tradition, the emphasis on the so-called 'naturalistic fallacy' and the associated fact/value distinction, which sprang into prominence with G. E. Moore's *Principia Ethica* in 1903, though it goes back, as one would expect, to the empiricism of Hume and others in the eighteenth century. I have tried to bring out in Chapter 3 something of how the fact/value distinction tends to crumble away, at least in part, when one really examines it, so I need not repeat that here. But I might mention one other fact of the same issue.

One of the features of the sharp separation between meta-ethics and ethics, and of the insistence that the philosopher should keep his nose out of the business of preaching, was the view that any ethics could go with any meta-ethics. This was essential if the philosopher was to have his proper professional freedom in meta-ethics without committing himself to any particular substantive views within ethics itself. But this independence of meta-ethics and ethics proved not so easy to maintain. One region where it faces problems is when we consider what is called 'universalisability', a notion which was of central importance for one of the leading linguistic philosophers, R. M. Hare. To sketch the point very roughly, there seems to be a sense in which if a moral rule applies to one person it applies to anyone else equally placed, and if a moral administrator treats a person in a certain way he ought to treat similar people in the same way. But is this a point of ethics or of meta-ethics? If I hold that, say, philosophy dons ought to be exempted from taxes, and claim that this is a moral judgment, but cannot give any adequate justification for it, am I holding a wicked and selfish moral principle, or am I simply not holding a *moral* principle at all? And if I hold, as a matter of meta-ethics, that a principle is only a moral one if it involves impartiality, can I combine this with what sounds like the substantive moral principle that I am entitled to put my own interests first on all occasions: an absurd moral principle, no doubt, but one that ought not to be excluded simply because it clashes with a meta-ethical principle, if meta-ethics and ethics are indeed independent? In other words, can we use our views of what sort of thing a moral judgment is to exclude moral approval of selfishness?

The age of logical positivism and linguistic philosophy was in many ways a dualistic age, despite the hostility of many of its leaders to the sort of dualism that perhaps occurs first to many people, that of mind and body; for minds, or souls, tend to be rather inaccessible things with unverifiable properties. Its earliest part especially was an age of bright colours and sharp edges, and much of this survived into the linguistic philosophy period, though Wittgenstein's second philosophy would have to be excluded at this point. Philosophers of science distinguished sharply between fact and interpretation, while in epistemology perception was divided into the receiving through the senses of an unadorned 'given' (sense-data) and interpretations put upon this by the mind. The distinction between meta-ethics and ethics, and the more general one between science and philosophy, was associated with sharp dichotomies within the concepts philosophy used. We have seen how facts were separated from values, or perhaps simply from non-facts, since 'values' had to cover a multitude of things like attitudes and prescriptions. It was typical of the outlook that that side of the fence should be allowed to be a bit of a rag-bag: the important thing was that facts should be put together and isolated and safeguarded from contamination. This distinction relied upon a similarly sharp distinction between the analytic and the synthetic, for what separated the factual and the evaluative was that there could never be an analytic connection between them; i.e., no statement of the form 'If p then q', where p was a factual statement and q an evaluative statement, could be analytic. The analytic/synthetic distinction was associated with other distinctions, such as the *a priori*/empirical, necessary/contingent, and logically true/factually true ones, and aligned with them so that the first terms in each pair as I have listed them went together: all and only analytic statements were *a priori*, necessary, and logically true.

We have already seen at the end of Chapter 6 something of the attack made on this by Kripke. Attacks of one sort and another on this general position had actually begun much earlier. In fact it is typical of the complications of things that, though I have emphasised the ascetic and cut-and-dried nature of the logical positivist outlook, a strong early attack on this very feature was made by one of the Vienna Circle, Friedrich Waismann (1896–1959), who spent his later years in Oxford as a leading member of the linguistic philosophers. It was then that he wrote a famous series of articles called 'Analytic', where he was mainly concerned to attack the sharpness of the analytic/synthetic distinction, drawing attention to various examples which were hard to classify, like 'I see with my eyes', 'Time is measurable', and 'Space has three dimensions'.

A stronger attack, which challenged the whole distinction and not just the sharpness of the borderline, was made by the American philosopher, Quine, who belongs in the general tradition of a logical approach to philosophy stemming from Frege and Russell, but has stood, like most Americans, rather outside the logical positivist and linguistic philosophy movements. In fact, during the 1950s he constituted perhaps the main rival to the latter. He advocates a holistic approach which is right at the opposite extreme to the European cut-and-dried-ness. He rejects not only the analytic/synthetic distinction but the others as well, for he thinks that our discoveries about the world might make it expedient to replace not only our laws of science, as we should presumably all agree, but also our laws of logic (cf. the end of Chapter 5, above). In fact we have a choice, he thinks, about how to deal with the facts confronting us: any statement we like, including even the laws of logic, can be rejected, provided we make sufficient adjustments elsewhere in our system.

To give a simple example, it is open to me to reject 'Paris is the capital of France', provided I make such consequential adjustments as rejecting 'What atlases and newspapers say about the capitals of countries when they have no reason to deceive us is usually true', or perhaps 'Atlases and newspapers have no reason to deceive us about the capital of France'. Of course rejecting either of these might involve us in further consequential adjustments. Quine agrees that some adjustments are far more likely to be made than others, but he thinks that no statements are absolutely immune from rejection. This outlook leads him to a further thesis which he has made famous, the so-called 'indeterminacy of translation'. Whenever we are confronted by a sentence in a certain language and we want to translate it into another language – or into another sentence in the same language for that matter – there is no unique way of doing this, he claims (apart from certain simple cases, which he allows). We have to adopt a hypothesis about what the sentence means, and there will always (except in the simple cases) be alternative hypotheses which we could adopt compatibly with our evidence. What is more, these alternatives will not only provide different meanings for the sentence but also different truth-values for it.

In his most famous example he imagines we hear a native of some newly discovered tribe cry out 'Gavagai!' in circumstances where we feel tempted to offer 'Rabbit!' as a translation. But how do we know the native did not think of it as 'Part of a rabbit!' or 'Surface of a rabbit!' or 'Time-slice of a rabbit!', where a time-slice of something is the thing considered only during one period of time; a Monday-rabbit-slice may be a different time-slice of the same rabbit from a certain Tuesday-rabbit-slice, rather as the boy I once was is a different time-slice of the same person (me) from the adult I now am? If you see a rabbit on a Monday, are you seeing a rabbit or a Monday-rabbit-slice? Quine thinks we could say either. To see a rabbit and to see part of a rabbit are the same thing: one can never see the whole of a rabbit at once, for if one could it would have to be transparent, and then we would not see it at all. As sentences 'Gavagai!' and 'Rabbit!' can be called synonymous because they give us the same information, but they may do so in different ways, if the *terms* 'gavagai' and 'rabbit' have different meanings. But with more complex sentences the case is different. If our native says 'That gavagai weighs five pounds', we shall give his sentence a different truth-value according as we interpret 'gavagai' as 'rabbit' or 'part of a rabbit' (taking 'part' in the sense of 'proper part', i.e. not the whole). Suppose the whole rabbit weighs five pounds. Then 'That part of a rabbit weighs five pounds' will on the face of it be false. But we can always make it come out true after all by reinterpreting the predicate, 'weighs five pounds', to mean 'is a part of something which as a whole weighs five pounds'. This suggests how Quine's view that every statement is revisable if we make relevant revisions elsewhere goes together with his view that translation, or most of it, is inherently indeterminate. In the above example we can revise our view about what the native meant by the subject of his sentence, and still communicate successfully with him, if we correspondingly revise what he meant by the predicate; by 'communicate successfully' I mean that we both smile happily when the rabbit tips the scales at five pounds. Again, Quine does not deny that some interpretations are much more natural than others. (We might remember in passing that the selection of the most natural set of interpretations for the complete collection of utterances in a given language is what Davidson calls 'radical interpretation'.)

Waismann and Quine then provide counter-examples to the simplicity of the picture I have drawn of the spirit of mid-century philosophy. There are plenty of others. The sharpness of the distinction between meta-ethics and ethics can be seen already in a philosopher as alien to both positivism and linguistic philosophy as the idealist F. H. Bradley (1846–1924). An example of where logical positivism and linguistic philosophy blur a traditional dichotomy instead of emphasising it lies in their standard (though not universal) treatment of the freewill problem, where for the usual antithesis of libertarianism versus determinism they substitute the 'soft deterministic' or 'compatibilist' line that determinism is true but does not exclude freewill. However, what they are doing here is not blurring a dichotomy one might have expected them to accept, but blurring a dichotomy that one can accept both terms of only if one does blur it: one cannot accept the reality of determinism and the existence of freewill unless one thinks they are not in fact sharply opposed.

I have probably now said enough to show the embarrassment that faces any historian who tries to sum up a philosophical movement. Almost anything he attributes to it will be contradicted within the movement and anticipated before it. Also, while the criticisms from Waismann and Quine seem to come too early for what I have been saying, they are far from universally accepted even now. Many philosophers accept the reality and even the sharpness of the analytic/synthetic distinction. But let us note three points. First, any such dichotomy is less likely to be simply taken for granted. Second, even when accepted it may be complicated, in the sense that a proposition may be called analytic or *a priori*, etc., in one sense but not in another. Third, the simple alignment of the dichotomies, which Kripke attacked, is less likely to be taken for granted. But all this need not stop us from pointing to broad generalisations, provided we realise they are no more than that. So let us continue with our thumbnail sketch.

III

Linguistic philosophy in the sense I have been describing is a movement which has passed away, though this is not to say that we no longer use its method of careful attention to what ordinary language is actually like, of humility before the linguistic facts in place of dogmatic regimentation. A small example of its use in our previous discussions would be, say, the use we made on p. 29 of the fact that we talk of believing truly but not of disbelieving truly. The difference is that now such a weapon occupies a much smaller place in the philosopher's armoury.

I have spoken of the permissiveness of linguistic philosophy, of its humility before the linguistic facts. But this permissiveness was a limited one, applying to the linguistic activities of non-philosophers. What has happened within the last twenty years or so is a loosening of the bonds within philosophy itself, a growth of permissiveness towards the activities of philosophers themselves. We are no longer in the situation of *1984* (or Plato's *Republic* for that matter) where the proles could do pretty well what they liked while the activities of party members (or 'guardians') were jealously circumscribed. This has been accompanied, not accidentally, by an increased interest in the activities rather than merely in their linguistic expression: in moral behaviour, religious beliefs, aesthetic experience, political institutions, and so on. This change of interest naturally leads philosophers to pay more attention to questions of justification in the spheres concerned, and so to get involved, and also to be less willing to call themselves *linguistic* philosophers – though, as I said in the last paragraph, this does not make them abandon the analysis of ways of speaking as one tool among others. Furthermore, the study of language – the *subject* called philosophy of language, as distinct from the *movement* called linguistic philosophy – flourishes today as perhaps never before. But it is still just one subject among others, and it does not limit itself to a more or less piecemeal analysis of different language games, but engages in metaphysical issues, as we saw when discussing realism and anti-realism in Chapter 6.

I have just mentioned a transition from a piecemeal analysis to a more general outlook. But now, without I hope being too annoying, I want to point out that in some ways the last twenty years have witnessed a much wider step in just the opposite direction. William James's distinction between tough-minded and tender-minded is sometimes applied to philosophical outlooks. It is an obscure distinction in some ways, and it would take us beyond our muttons to analyse it here, so I shall just assume we have a rough grasp of it. The same applies to the political distinction between left and right. To put the point in very crude terms, subject to at least as much qualification as the other generalisations I have been making, philosophy has moved from an ascetic universalist left tough stance to a rich particularist right tender one.

The new open-mindedness towards the scope of philosophy itself which we have been looking at is one feature of this change. As we have seen, it is associated with a blurring or complicating of boundaries, including to some extent the boundary between philosophy itself and other studies, though I have tried in my Introduction to defend the borderline; this is quite compatible, I think, with letting philosophy dirty its hands with such things as substantive moral issues: I am simply claiming that it keeps to its own methods while doing so.

A second feature, and this is what I mean by talking of a shift from the universal to the particular, is a tendency to abandon simple square-cut

209

positions in favour of more complex, subtle, and less easily classifiable ones. This could be seen as another aspect of the blurring or complicating of boundaries. Admittedly it is not an obvious feature of the development we are considering, because one of the things linguistic philosophy firmly insisted on was its abandonment of grand overall systems in favour of a piecemeal approach. So it might be said that this feature is rather one which distinguishes both current philosophy and linguistic philosophy from both logical positivism and its predecessors (of which I have said little: I mean mainly the idealism that was prominent in Britain for the last half of the nineteenth century and the first quarter of the twentieth). Logical positivism was in its own way an overall system, if not perhaps a 'grand' one in the way we think of more speculative metaphysical systems as being; the point is that it offered a single basis from which answers to all succeeding questions could be derived as they arose. It might even be said further that current philosophy does not share this particularism with linguistic philosophy but has less of it, because metaphysics, and with it at least some of the underlying motifs of the older traditional systems, has come back into favour.

All this is true. But there is still a sense, I think, in which the beginning of the last paragraph is true too. An example comes in those philosophers who reject the alignment of the dichotomies, like Kripke, or like those who would accept with Kant that propositions can be both synthetic and *a priori*. The mere existence of such philosophers among the leaders of the profession means that even those who accept the old simplicities can no longer treat them as unquestionable presuppositions.

But perhaps a more striking example comes in ethics, where there is a strong, though not universal, tendency to reject systems like utilitarianism, and even to reject the existence of general moral principles, appealing instead to a sort of intuitionism which insists on treating each case on its merits. Utilitarianism has, at least at first sight, the appeal of simplicity and of providing a supreme court for deciding moral questions. We saw some of the difficulties attending utilitarianism in Chapter 9, but there has been a further attack on it recently which brings out something of the spirit of the age, so I will briefly mention it. Utilitarians, and indeed many other moral philosophers, have tended to take for granted that ultimately the only good must be a state of consciousness. How, after all, could the world contain any value if it did not contain any conscious beings? G. E. Moore, an eccentric utilitarian, as we saw, denied this, and argued that of two uninhabited and permanently inaccessible worlds, one of which was full of beautiful flowers, etc. while the other was simply a heap of filth, the former would have more value. But most of his successors have treated this as a mere aberration on his part, and have insisted that neither would have any value at all in those circumstances. And even Moore thought the *most* valuable things were certain aesthetic experiences and personal relationships; in fact, he later withdrew his view about beautiful deserts to the extent of saying that anything valuable must involve an experience, though he does not say it must be one.

Some current philosophers, such as D. R. P. Wiggins, have attacked the whole basis of this view, arguing, to put it roughly, that the satisfaction of desire could not be the ultimate value in itself, for its value is parasitic on that of the objects of desire, and these objects certainly include other things besides mere conscious states. There seems to be a certain incoherence in saying that the satisfaction of desire has value but the object of desire has none, at least in the case of one's own desires; and the satisfaction of our desires could hardly itself be the only object of our desire; at least if it were, we should be doomed to eternal frustration. Also one might ask whether the satisfaction of desires in general was itself a conscious state. It might constitute a set of conscious states, or more accurately the existence of such a set, but it would hardly be a conscious state itself. Therefore utilitarianism seems to be wrong, on its own showing, in saying that the only things that can ultimately have value are states of consciousness. Even if the only valuable things are either such states or the existence of sets of such states, this still revises and complicates their position. Perhaps one of the most interesting problems facing ethics today is to reconcile considerations of this sort with what I called the 'teleological intuition' in Chapter 9.

So far I have hardly mentioned metaphysics, except to say that it is primarily a philosopher's activity and so did not benefit from the tolerance extended by linguistic philosophy to those language games they took to be going concerns before the philosopher came on the scene. While philosophy was forcing its way back, in the manner I tried to illustrate earlier in this Part, metaphysics naturally came back too, though in a rather gradual manner. An early sign of its reappearance was Strawson's *Individuals*, published in 1959, though incorporating material from a few years earlier. In it Strawson distinguishes what he calls descriptive and revisionary metaphysics. 'Descriptive metaphysics is content to describe the actual structure of our thought about the world, revisionary metaphysics is concerned to produce a better structure.' He then classifies his own book, the details of which do not concern us here, as descriptive and not revisionary. Descriptive metaphysics, as Strawson brings out with the word 'content', is the more modest enterprise, and the least likely to cause offence to a linguistic philosopher. In fact, he finds some difficulty in distinguishing it from the conceptual analysis that was linguistic philosophy's stock-in-trade, and says they differ in 'scope or generality', meaning that descriptive metaphysics goes deeper and takes less for granted.

Strawson's claims for descriptive metaphysics are perhaps a bit modest. Unlike the more pedestrian linguistic analysis it does not analyse just our language, or particular concepts, but the structure of our thought in general. And it also claims, I think, to say not just how things are with us but how they must be. Kant, whom Strawson classifies as a descriptive rather than revisionary metaphysician, gave most of his energy to describing how any mind recognisably like the human mind *had* to think. For instance, it had to see the world as a set of substantial objects with qualities and relations to each other, and acting causally on each other – no matter what the world in itself might actually be like, which we could never know. Maybe there were other minds which thought differently, but we could know nothing of them nor have any contact with them.

How does all this differ from revisionary metaphysics? Clearly it can make us revise our ideas, or it would hardly be worth doing at all. Strawson seems to mean that it can revise our ideas about the structure of our thought, but cannot revise that structure, i.e., cannot provide us with a new way of thinking about the world in general. Bishop Berkeley (1685–1753), whom Strawson gives as an example of a revisionary metaphysician, held that what we think of as material objects are really ideas in the mind of God, for nothing could exist independently of being perceived, either by us or by God. The point is presumably this: Berkeley is saying that we normally think in terms of material objects, but we ought not to, for there aren't any; what we call material objects are really something else. Actually I think Berkeley would have called himself descriptive rather than revisionary – but that is another story.

What Strawson offers us is certainly more tame and homely than the traditional metaphysics. There is no wild violation of common sense, as in Berkeley's view that a table is an idea in the mind of God, or Leibniz's that it is a set of spirits. Nor does Strawson try to construct a grand metaphysical system about the nature of reality, as these earlier thinkers did. He does, of course, make certain claims, and his book forms a systematic whole. But he does not claim that his subject-matter is somehow illusory, or that the world is radically different from what it seems; though he does make some substantive metaphysical claims, notably on the mind/body problem, where he argues that persons form a distinct *sui generis* type of entity.

In a way metaphysics had never really disappeared. I said some time back (p. 196) that the logical positivists had to do philosophy to abolish philosophy. The same might be said about abolishing metaphysics, which after all comes to much the same thing. G. E. Moore was neither a logical positivist nor a linguistic philosopher, but his respect for common sense and ordinary language led to his being widely regarded as a precursor of linguistic philosophy. He was in fact doing a kind of metaphysics when he defended common sense against the wilder flights of speculative metaphysics. But though his philosophy was an exercise in metaphysics, this fact rather got lost sight of in the general shipwreck of metaphysics in the storm of logical positivism. Strawson's book shows metaphysics making a tentative return to public life in its own name, peeping from behind the curtain to see if the boos have died down. Since then it has emerged more confidently, and stands mid-stage along with the other main branches of philosophy. Perhaps in some ways it is still a little chastened. It is still reluctant to outrage common sense, or to go wandering off building great systems on a few strange bricks at the base. But it is no longer content to be bound by the austere fetters of verificationism. Some of the time-honoured tools thrown on the scrapheap by both logical positivism and linguistic philosophy have been rescued and put to vigorous use. Let me mention two in particular, causal necessity and essence.

The first all-out attack on causal necessity in modern Western philosophy was made by Hume, and causation has been rather groggy ever since. Hume argued that in cases where we say that *a* causes *b*, all we can ever observe is that *a* is always followed by *b*. Look as you will, you will never find any further bond connecting them. We may feel that *b must* follow *a*, but this 'must' is something we can never observe in the world itself, and so is something that we have put there. Hume did not abandon causation. In fact, he offered a causal account of how we come by our notion of causal necessity. Causation has been used too throughout this century, as in C. L. Stevenson's causal account of meaning and in causal accounts of perception. But causation has been an attenuated version of its former self, amounting in the end to no more than regular sequence, and this has made many fight shy of causation altogether and think such a notion not worth appealing to. But causal necessity has made a come-back, whether or not decently clad in a fitting analysis of itself. One result of this has been to widen the gap between determinism and belief in freewill; for the stronger the notion of causal necessity, the harder it is to reconcile universal causation with any meaningful freewill, as 'compatibilists' or 'soft determinists' want to do.

Essence is another notion connected with necessity, for a thing's essence might be described as the properties it *must* have to be itself. The main attack this time had come from a fringe logical positivist, Karl Popper. Popper stresses falsifiability rather than verifiability, though he is kinder to metaphysics than the logical positivists in general were: metaphysical statements are unfalsifiable, but need not therefore be meaningless; they are merely not scientific. However, Popper is not really very fond of metaphysics, and the fact that statements about essences cannot be falsified is enough to damn them in his eyes. But essences, like causes, have made their way back, through articles with titles like C. Kirwan's 'How strong are the objections to essence?' We have seen something of the importance of this born-again notion of essence in the work of Kripke described in Chapter 6.

One figure deserving a brief paragraph in any account of current philosophy is Noam Chomsky (1928–), who incidentally criticises Kripke's essentialism. Though strictly a linguist rather than a philosopher, he has had an immense influence on philosophy, partly no doubt because what he says is so much in tune with the way philosophy was going anyway. The feature of Chomsky's contribution that most concerns us here is his resuscitation of innate ideas. It has become traditional to date what is called 'modern' philosophy from the seventeenth and eighteenth centuries, and to see there a running battle between the 'Continental rationalists', mainly Descartes, Spinoza and Leibniz, and the 'British empiricists', mainly Locke, Berkeley and Hume. The rationalists emphasised the role of 'reason', which covered intuition as well as processes of inference; reason tells us about the world *a priori*. The empiricists on the other hand insisted that only the senses could give us the materials of knowledge, however much reason might manipulate and build on those materials once given. This picture, especially in its simple opposition of the British and Continental philosophers, is grossly oversimplified, but it has largely governed philosophy's view of its own development, and has enough truth in it for our present purpose. As I have tried to show earlier, logical positivism and the general philosophical ethos of the 1930s represents a flowering of the empiricist tradition, more akin to Hume than to any of the others I have just mentioned. Chomsky's appeal to innate ideas represents a return to the other tradition, the rationalists; and Chomsky himself flies the flag of Descartes at his masthead (though without agreeing with him all down the line). We have seen how twentieth-century philosophy, from logical positivism on, has taken a linguistic turn; so it is not surprising that Chomsky's influence has also had that flavour.

Chomsky's innate ideas amount to this: when a child is confronted with the morass of sounds from which he must somehow extricate and learn a language, he has a built-in tendency to prefer some

214

interpretations to others, to try certain hypotheses, as it were, about the grammar and structure of what he hears, while rejecting, or simply not thinking of, others. These tendencies are the same wherever the child is born, so it is not surprising that all known languages have certain structural features in common. This last point is itself an empirical or scientific hypothesis. Maybe Martian languages are different; but if they are, then an earthly child, one with the genetic make-up shared by all the human race, could never learn such a language – or at least could never learn it 'at his mother's knee', by picking it up as children do: he might later manage to acquire some mastery of it by devoting the sort of efforts to it that one devotes to advanced physics. Chomsky is not saying that Martian would be logically unlearnable, like a private language. The same would apply, presumably, to Martians visiting the earth. As one might expect, Chomsky's views are controversial. But they fit in well to a philosophy freeing itself from what it sees as the empiricist stranglehold of the last few decades. Incidentally, this is not incompatible with calling his hypothesis empirical, if we wish to do so. It is quite consistent to say, on the basis of observation, that not all our knowledge comes from observation. A hypothesis can be empirical but anti-empiricist. How much of Chomsky's theory as a whole is empirical is for philosophy to decide.

So where is philosophy and where is it going? I shall not try any crystal-gazing; but as for where it is, it is in a mood of tolerance and expansion. Barriers and rigidities are being broken down. The multifarious spheres of human activity and experience in morals, art, religion, politics, etc. are being examined, but no longer in the fashion of linguistic philosophy, eyeing the doings and misdoings of the human tribe with the aloofness of an anthropologist whose home is safely far away. The contemporary philosopher is likely to have views on whether abortion is wrong, whether God exists, whether equality is a good thing, and to be willing to use his expertise in defence of these views. And how about relations with Continental philosophy, a lot of readers will ask, with phenomenology and existentialism? Are the barriers coming down here too? Perhaps a little, but much more slowly. But I have just said that philosophers are more willing to stick their necks out and make critical judgments, so let me make one myself: must all the dismantling be done by us? Could not the Continentals make a few changes too, in the direction of greater accessibility and an appeal to rational criteria? But the justice of the implied complaint I must leave to the reader.

13 Some philosophical labels

It is always much harder to describe the state of philosophy at the time of writing than to describe it as it was twenty years ago, when one can stand back and see the trees as forming a decently shaped wood. But one thing the newcomer may find particularly puzzling is the way some of the labels are flung around, words like 'realist', 'Platonist', 'idealist', 'nominalist' or 'pragmatist'. So perhaps we might have a brief look at some of them. Perhaps the most important thing to remember about words like this is that they are seldom used simply to name identifiable movements with a home in space and time; and when they are so used they should be treated as extremely rough and ready marks, something like proper names which survive when they have lost their *raison d'être*, as the first Smith went on being called Smith long after he had put down his hammers, or long after it was realised that metalwork had only been a weekend hobby of his. They are rather the names of features or aspects of thought, and may occur in the most unexpected places. We have already glanced in passing at the 'Continental rationalists' and 'British empiricists'. Yet Descartes, the *a priori* rationalist, tried to cast aside all the *a priori* maxims and intuitions he had inherited from the medieval scholastics and to reduce his mind as near as he could to a blank tablet, albeit the tablet was never entirely blank; while Locke, the empiricist, thought we had *a priori* knowledge of morals as well as of mathematics.

We have said quite a bit in earlier pages about a dispute between realists and anti-realists. Etymologically, realism (from Latin *res* meaning 'thing') is any view which posits the existence of things or entities where this might be disputed, or holds that certain things are real or exist in their own right, or play some given role, as opposed to being derivative or analysable into other things. A realist theory of perception holds that we perceive things themselves, not just images representing them, or sense-data, etc. In ordinary life a realist is one who sees things as they are, rather than, e.g., as we would like them to be, or some popular theory holds them to be; as the realist ignores wishful thinking, etc., he also sometimes acquires the reputation of ignoring the finer aspects of

216

things and riding roughshod over the higher values. The realist in the above dispute is one who holds, according to the definition I borrowed from Dummett on p. 47 above, that 'for any statement there must be something in virtue of which either it or its negation is true'. Dummett himself on the contrary thinks that where such a thing, or state of affairs, would be inaccessible to us if it did exist, then it is senseless to claim that there is such a thing or state of affairs. The anti-realist's point, as I tried to show earlier, is that we are in no position to attribute existence, even hypothetically, to what is totally inaccessible to us. I said that Dummett was in the tradition of the verificationists, and that they in turn were in the tradition of the empiricists. This anti-realism fits well with the reductionism of the empiricists, who argued that *only* verifiable statements were meaningful, or *only* the senses could give us knowledge, or *only* what we were immediately acquainted with could ultimately be said to exist, etc. The current realists, on the other hand, are likely to emphasise also the existence of things like values. We have also seen the view that some things other than states of consciousness must have value. This is not obviously a realist view in itself, but it has a certain analogy to the realist view that things other than states of consciousness have existence. It is the reductionist strand in anti-realism and empiricism, a certain preference for the austere and square-cut over the richly textured and expansive, that tempts one to call these outlooks left and tough rather than right and tender. But this must not be exaggerated. We see this same preference for austerity in the realist Davidson's attempt to view meaning entirely in terms of truth conditions.

The opponents of the current realism are called by the innocuous name 'anti-realists'. Traditionally realism has been opposed to idealism and to nominalism (and conceptualism). Idealism is a complex notion of which I will say here only that its main theme is that the real is limited to what is mental. Realist opponents to idealism say that other things are real too. One form of idealism dominated British philosophy for some sixty years, centring on the turn of the century. It was a holistic outlook, associated with a coherence theory of truth. Propositions had truth to the extent that they cohered (in some sense) with other propositions, and only the whole set of propositions, a total description of the universe, was completely true. Since we could never know such a total description, we could never say anything that was more than partly true. It was perhaps the constriction on thought that this produced that gave such a feeling of relief and refreshment to the reaction in the direction of some kind of atomism ('logical atomism') led by Moore and Russell, especially in Moore's article 'The refutation of idealism' in 1903. Idealism took some time to lie down and die, but what is worth noting is how the logical positivist philosophy that eventually followed, whose mood seemed in some ways to be right at the opposite extreme, atomist, pluralist, clear-cut and reductionist, in fact found itself uncomfortably close to a coherence theory of truth, which some of its followers (O. Neurath, C. G. Hempel) accepted. Roughly this was because we could only know the world by constructing sentences about it. So we could only compare them with each other. This feature of logical positivism, and also the feature that we cannot make contact with reality itself but can know only our sense impressions, etc., are sometimes called idealist.

Another term which turns up in perhaps unexpected places is 'pragmatist'. As a sort of official label it applies to C. S. Peirce (1839–1914), and his followers William James (1842–1910), John Dewey (1859–1952) and a few others. But it can also apply to any view which appeals to usefulness or simplicity or convention, as opposed to truth, when deciding what statements to accept. Quine's view that we can accept any statement we find it useful to accept, provided we make adequate adjustments in the rest of our system, is often called pragmatist. Because of its holistic aspect, whereby we have to look at all our statements together when deciding which to accept, Quine's view is sometimes also called idealist. 'Conventionalist' is another label often used in this area, for fairly obvious reasons.

Nominalism (from Latin *nomen* meaning 'name' or 'word') was originally a medieval view about universals, saying there were only words, like 'man' or 'beauty', but no realities which they named; the only realities were men and beautiful things. This was contrasted with realism, saying universals were substantive entities, and conceptualism, saying they were concepts or ideas in the mind. This sort of realism, saying that certain abstract things are substantive entities, is sometimes called Platonism. It makes sense to ask how far Plato himself was a Platonist. In general a nominalist with regard to a given subject-matter is one who says that only words are needed to deal with it and not entities either inside or outside the mind which those words might stand for.

It is important to realise that all these terms can be applied differently, and often apparently inconsistently, in different contexts. When we learn at our tutor's knee that William of Ockham was a nominalist, Hegel an idealist, and Locke an empiricist, these are at best general labels for the dominant theme in their philosophies. But opposite labels can often be applied to the same person. For instance, Locke is a conceptualist with regard to universals, since he thinks that general words like 'dog' stand for ideas in the mind; but he is a realist in ethics, since he thinks that moral judgments can be true or false independently of human desires or beliefs about them.

218

Conclusion: Philosophy and 'the truth'

Finally, and far too briefly, let us again touch on the question we touched on in the Introduction: does philosophy seek truth, and if so, does it ever find it? I said there that philosophy goes round in circles. Plato and Aristotle argued about universals. So did the Middle Ages, *ad nauseam*. We are still arguing today, and a philosopher as respectable as Frege can be referred to as a 'Platonist'. The seventeenth and eighteenth centuries broke from what they saw as the shackles of scholastic philosophy (that of the medieval 'schools') and swept the place clean and started again from scratch (as they thought). This led to what, on the surface anyway, seems to be an extreme reductivist empiricism in Hume. Kant told us to stop doing metaphysics and first examine the human mind and ask what we *can* know, and what are the inevitable limitations of our thinking. Metaphysics bounced back grinning with a brand of idealism stemming from Hegel, only to be abolished again by the logical positivists with more clean-sweeping and reductionist empiricism. The neo-Kantian Strawson again asks us to examine the structure of our thought, and now metaphysics is back with us again and philosophers chat happily and unself-consciously about causal necessity and essences and moral intuitions. (This sketch is, of course, vastly oversimplified.) It is all very well for philosophers to say with Strawson (*Individuals*, p. 10) that it is 'unlikely that there are any new truths to be discovered in descriptive metaphysics. But [its task] has constantly to be done over again. If there are no new truths to be discovered, there are old truths to be rediscovered', and expressed in contemporary idiom. But this does make the philosopher rather like Alice, running desperately to keep in the same spot.

The topic we are now broaching could probably fill a book of its own. I shall finish with just two comments. First, perhaps the best image is not a circle but a spiral. Philosophy does repeat itself, but not exactly. New arguments are found for old positions, but the positions themselves rise from the grave in a new dress, and not in the decrepit state they were brought to by the misfortunes that put them there. We cannot envisage philosophy coming to completion. But can we envisage mathematics or science or the history of, say, the French Revolution coming to it either?

That brings me to my second point. Is philosophy really so different from science in that respect? Scientific knowledge increases: Hiroshima tells us that. But science too has its circles and endless progressions. Is the universe cyclic in nature? Yes, said Empedocles in 450 BC. And yes, say at least some modern physicists, who believe in an 'oscillating universe'. Is there a void? Yes, said the Greek atomists. No, said Aristotle and Descartes. Yes, said Newton. No, said the nineteenth-century ether-mongers. Yes, says modern physics, *but* – full of fields: the void in a new dress. What is the universe made of? Atoms? Electrons and protons, etc.? Quarks? Are we really within sight of a final answer? No doubt the revival of Kant/Laplace on planetary origins and that of Wegener on continental drift are minor hiccoughs; but along with the contrast succession of fads in medicine or nutrition or baby-care, each with a good basis in contemporary science when it starts, they suggest that even science would be well advised not to bury its past offspring too deeply. We need not go all the way (and I certainly would not) with T. S. Kuhn to realise that there are limits to the degree of blackness that the scientific pot should attribute to the philosophical kettle. Perhaps philosophy just has less effect on the human stage (though even here we must exclude political philosophy). Philosophy, thank goodness, has no Hiroshimas.

Bibliography

Introduction

A. C. Danto, *What Philosophy Is: A Guide to the Elements*, New York, Harper & Row, 1968. (Philosophy as dealing with the gap between consciousness and the world.)

J. L. Austin, *Philosophical Papers*, Oxford, Clarendon, 1961.

M. Woods, 'Scepticism and natural knowledge', *Proceedings of the Aristotelian Society*, 1979–80. (Says philosophy should try to explain our knowledge rather than to justify it, and attacks scepticism. Sees generality as the essence of philosophy, p. 232.)

I. Kant, *Critique of Practical Reason*, 1788, Part I, Book II, Chapter II. (God, freedom, immortality.)

B. Russell, *Human Knowledge*, London, Allen & Unwin, 1948, Part III, Chapter IV. (On what we see.)

A. N. Whitehead, *Process and Reality*, Cambridge University Press, 1929, p. 53: 'The safest general characterisation of the European philosophical tradition is that it consists of a series of footnotes to Plato.'

Part One

Chapter 1

Aristotle, *De Interpretatione*, Chapter 9. (Famous discussion of logical determinism in terms of 'sea-battle' example. Best read in J. L. Ackrill's translation, with commentary, in his *Aristotle's Categories and De Interpretatione*, Oxford, Clarendon, 1963. Cf. also J. Lukasiewicz, 'On determinism', in S. McCall (ed.), *Polish Logic 1920–1939*, Oxford, Clarendon, 1967; reprinted in Lukasiewicz's *Selected Works* (ed. L. Borkowski, Amsterdam, N. Holland, 1970).)

Richard Taylor, *Metaphysics*, Englewood Cliffs, N.J., Prentice-Hall, 1963 (revised 1974), Chapter 6. (Defends logical determinism.)

G. Ryle, *Dilemmas*, Cambridge University Press, 1954, Chapter 2. (Attacks logical determinism.)

Bibliography

W. V. Quine, *Word and Object*, New York, Technology Press of MIT, and London, John Wiley, 1960. (Eternal sentences; see index.)

Chapter 2

J. E. Wiredu, 'Deducibility and inferability', *Mind*, 1973. (See middle of p. 36 for brief reference to his view that the ascription of truth involves reference to a point of view. The article as a whole is in tune with this.)

R. M. Hare, *The Language of Morals*, Oxford University Press, 1952. (See index for phrastics and neustics. He adds a further notion ('tropics') in his *Practical Inferences*, London, Macmillan, 1971, pp. 89ff.)

G. Pitcher (ed.), *Truth*, Englewood Cliffs, N.J., Prentice-Hall, 1964. (Contains items by Ramsey, Austin, Strawson, and Dummett, *inter alia*, with an 'Introduction', where in particular see pp. 5–7 on phrastics and propositions. Strawson extends his discussion of Austin in 'Truth: a reconsideration of Austin's views', *Philosophical Quarterly*, 1965. Dummett's 'Truth' is also printed, with a postcript, in M. A. E. Dummett, *Truth and Other Enigmas*, London, Duckworth, 1978.)

G. Frege, 'Negation', in P. Geach and M. Black (eds), *Translations from the Philosophical Writings of Gottlob Frege*, Oxford, Blackwell, 1952, original 1919. (Negation and denying.)

D. Odegard, 'Truth and redundancy', *Mind*, 1977. (Mainly discusses redundancy and correspondence theories.)

D. Davidson, 'True to the facts', *Journal of Philosophy*, 1969. (Develops a kind of correspondence theory using Tarski's notion of satisfaction.)

A. Tarski, 'The semantic conception of truth and the foundations of semantics', *Philosophy and Phenomenological Research*, 1943–4. (Reasonably accessible exposition, with discussion of objections. For full version see 'The concept of truth in formalised languages', in his *Logic, Semantics, Metamathematics*, Oxford, Clarendon, 1956; and for more elementary exposition see M. Black, 'The semantic definition of truth', *Analysis*, vol. 8, 1947–8.)

D. J. O'Connor, *The Correspondence Theory of Truth*, London, Hutchinson, 1975. (Part I discusses, *inter alia*, the bearers of truth. Part II discusses Tarski and the Austin/Strawson debate.)

P. F. Strawson, *Individuals*, London, Methuen, 1959. (See index for 'feature-placing'.)

M. A. E. Dummett, *Frege: Philosophy of Language*, London, Duckworth, 1973. (See Chapter 2 for Frege on quantification.)

I. M. Copi, *The Theory of Logical Types*, London, Routledge & Kegan Paul, 1971. (Russell's theory of types.)

B. Russell, 'On denoting', *Mind*, 1905, often reprinted. (Source of Russell's 'theory of descriptions', which he uses to deal with cases like the 'King of France' example.)

P. F. Strawson, *Introduction to Logical Theory*, London, Methuen, 1952, Chapter 6. (Criticises Russell's theory of descriptions. Cf. also Strawson's 'On referring', *Mind*, 1950; and for development of his views on falsity and truth-value gaps see his 'Identifying reference and truth-values', *Theoria*, 1964. The last two are reprinted, along with his discussions of Austin, in his *Logico-Linguistic Papers*, London, Methuen, 1971.)

L. Linsky, *Referring*, London, Routledge & Kegan Paul, 1967. (See p. 94 for his criticism of Strawson on presupposition.)

Chapter 3

C. L. Stevenson, *Ethics and Language*, New Haven, Conn., Yale University Press, 1944.

R. M. Hare, *The Language of Morals*, Oxford University Press, 1952. (Two classic statements of non-cognitivist positions. Hare develops his views and answers criticisms in 'Meaning and speech acts', *Philosophical Review*, 1970.)

C. Beck, 'Utterances which incorporate a value statement', *American Philosophical Quarterly*, 1967.

R. W. Newell, 'Ethics and description', *Philosophy*, 1968. (Two attacks on fact/value distinction.)

M. A. E. Dummett, *Frege: Philosophy of Language*, London, Duckworth, 1973, pp. 351–4. (Discusses Frege's point about denying and negation, attributing its ethical application to Geach, pp. 327ff.)

G. E. Moore, *Principia Ethica*, Cambridge University Press, 1903, Chapter 1, especially §B. (Naturalistic fallacy christened and attacked.)

G. E. Moore, 'The refutation of idealism', *Mind*, 1903, reprinted in *Philosophical Studies*, Routledge & Kegan Paul, 1922.

D. Hume, *A Treatise of Human Nature*, 1739–40, Book III, Part I, Section I, last para. ('Is' and 'ought'.)

F. Foot (ed.), *Theories of Ethics*, Oxford University Press, 1967.

W. D. Hudson (ed.), *The Is/Ought Question*, London, Macmillan, 1969. (Two sets of discussions mainly of topics in area of naturalistic fallacy.)

J. R. Searl, 'How to derive "ought" from "is" ', *Philosophical Review*, 1964, reprinted in Foot and Hudson (above). (Promise-keeping. Cf. also his 'Meaning and speech sets', *Philosophical Review*, 1962, reprinted with additions in C. D. Rollins (ed.), *Knowledge and Experience*, Pittsburgh University Press, 1962, and cf. Searle's *Speech Acts*, Cambridge University Press, 1969.)

P. Foot, 'Moral beliefs', *Proceedings of the Aristotelian Society*, 1958–9, reprinted in Foot (above). (How arbitrary can moral beliefs be? Cf. also R. Norman, *Reasons for Actions*, Oxford, Blackwell, 1971, Chapter 3, on how arbitrary wants can be.)

G. E. M. Anscombe, 'On brute facts', *Analysis*, vol. 18, 1958. (Different kinds of fact.)

B. A. O. Williams, 'Morality and the emotions' (pamphlet of inaugural lecture), London, Bedford College, 1965. ('Blasted tricycle.')

J. L. Austin, *How to Do Things with Words*, Oxford, Clarendon, 1962. (See index under 'Infelicities' for discussion of problems about assessment.)

Chapter 4

L. Simons, 'Intuition and implication', *Mind*, 1965.
J. A. Faris, *Truth-Functional Logic*, London, Routledge & Kegan Paul, 1962, pp. 109–19. (Two attempts to assimilate 'if' and '⊃'. For discussions see A. J. Baker, 'If and ⊃', *Mind*, 1967; L. J. Russell, 'If and ⊃', *Mind*, 1970; G. Iseminger, 'The connection argument', *Mind*, 1972; G. Hunter, ' "Not both p and not q, therefore if p then q" is not a valid form of argument', *Mind*, 1973; L. Norreklit, 'On if and ⊃', *ibid.*)
P. F. Strawson, *Introduction to Logical Theory*, London, Methuen, 1952, Chapter 3, Part II. (His views on 'if' and ' ⊃', etc. See p. 89 for 'Dutchman' example. He has developed his views in a lecture so far unpublished.)
H. P. Grice, 'Logic and conversation', in D. Davidson and G. Harman (eds), *The Logic of Grammar*, Encino and Belmont, Cal., Dickenson, 1975. (Implicatures. Cf. also his 'The causal theory of perception', §3, *Proceedings of the Aristotelian Society*, supplementary volume, 1961.)
R. C. S. Walker, 'Conversational implicatures', in S. Blackburn (ed.), *Meaning, Reference and Necessity*, Cambridge University Press, 1975. (Tentative defence of a Gricean position. For point about truth-values see especially pp. 139, 140–1, 144, top.)
I. Hungerland, 'Contextual implication', *Inquiry*, 1960. (See p. 255 for quotation.)
A. N. Whitehead and B. Russell, *Principia Mathematica*, Cambridge University Press, vol. 1, 1913. (See pp. 7 and 20 for material and formal implication. For Russell's view that only material implication is needed for logic see his *Introduction to Mathematical Philosophy*, London, Allen & Unwin, 1919, pp. 152 last line–154.)
C. I. Lewis and C. H. Langford, *Symbolic Logic*, New York and London, Century, 1932, Chapter 8. (Strict implication and its relation to entailment.)
J. Bennett, 'Entailment', *Philosophical Review*, 1969. (Historical survey of entailment/strict implication issue, ending with defence of Lewis.)
G. E. Moore, 'External and internal relations', *Proceedings of the Aristotelian Society*, 1919–20, p. 53, reprinted with slight revisions in his *Philosophical Studies*, London, Kegan Paul, Trench, Trubner, 1922, p. 291. (Introduction of 'entailment'.)

Chapter 5

E. Sosa (ed.), *Causation and Conditionals*, Oxford University Press, 1975. (Articles on these topics.)
S. E. Toulmin, *The Philosophy of Science*, London, Hutchinson, 1953. (Instrumentalist approach to laws of nature; i.e., treats them as instruments

the scientist uses rather than as fundamental truths. Cf. especially Chapter 3 for discussion of other views.)

S. P. Schwartz (ed.), *Naming, Necessity, and Natural Kinds*, Ithaca, N.Y., Cornell University Press, 1977. (Contains *inter alia* important articles by Kripke, Putnam, and Quine, with excellent 'Introduction'. Cf. also W. V. Quine, *From a Logical Point of View*, Cambridge, Mass., Harvard University Press, 1953, revised 1961, Chapter 2 ('Two dogmas of empiricism') for his famous attack on the sacrosanctity of any necessity.)

D. K. Lewis, *Counterfactuals*, Oxford, Blackwell, 1973. (Elaboration of a 'possible worlds' approach; see especially Chapters 1, 3, 4. For another version see R. Stalnaker, 'A theory of conditionals', in Sosa (above), and for some discussion of possible worlds see Kripke, 'Identity and necessity', in Schwartz (above), and S. Kripke, *Naming and Necessity*, Oxford, Blackwell, 1980, especially pp. 15ff.)

I. Lakatos, *Proofs and Refutations*, Cambridge University Press, 1976. (Brings out the problems of formulating one's results even in a subject like mathematics.)

F. L. Will, 'The contrary-to-fact conditional', *Mind*, 1947. (Explores difficulties of one approach to counterfactuals. His book *Induction and Justification*, Ithaca, N.Y., Cornell University Press, 1974, develops his views.)

G. W. Leibniz, *Discourse on Metaphysics*, 1846 (written 1685–6). (This world as the best possible. He develops his views on possible worlds in his letters to A. Arnauld. For Voltaire's response see his *Candide* (1759).)

D. Hume, *A Treatise of Human Nature*, 1739–40, Book I, Part III. (Hume's main treatment of causation. Cf. also his *Enquiry concerning Human Understanding*, §§4, 7. For Kant, see 'Causality' in index to N. Kemp Smith's translation of Kant's *Critique of Pure Reason* (London, Macmillan, 1929; original 1781 and 1787).)

W. A. Davis, 'Indicative and subjunctive conditionals', *Philosophical Review*, 1979. (See especially p. 554.)

E. J. Lowe, 'Indicative and counterfactual conditionals', *Analysis*, vol. 39, 1979. (Problems in correlating them with each other.)

Chapter 6

J. S. Mill, *A System of Logic Ratiocinative and Inductive*, London, Longmans, Green, 1843, Book 1, Chapter 2, especially §5. (Classic theory of meaning of proper names.)

G. Frege, 'On sense and reference' in P. Geach and M. Black, *Translations from the Philosophical Writings of Gottlob Frege*, Oxford, Blackwell, 1952 (original 1892), often reprinted elsewhere. (Includes rival view to Mill's.)

B. Russell, *Logic and Knowledge*, London, Allen & Unwin, 1956, pp. 200–2. (Brief account of Russell's theory of proper names, including quoted phrase.)

J. R. Searle, 'Proper names', *Mind*, 1958. (Modification of Frege's approach, Cf. also his *Speech Acts*, Cambridge University Press, 1969, pp. 162ff. For criticism see Kripke item below, and for criticism of Kripke see P. Ziff, 'About proper names', *Mind*, 1977.)

L. Wittgenstein, *Philosophical Investigations*, Oxford, Blackwell, 1953, especially Part 1, §§1–43. (Criticises idea that meaning of name is its bearer.)

G. Evans, 'The causal theory of names', *Proceedings of the Aristotelian Society*, supplementary volume, 1973; reprinted in S. P. Schwartz (ed.), *Naming, Necessity, and Natural Kinds*, Ithaca, N.Y., Cornell University Press, 1977.

P. Strawson, 'On referring', *Mind*, 1950, often reprinted. (Includes discussion of how names are related to other words.)

J. Aitchison, *Linguistics*, London, Hodder & Stoughton, 1978, pp. 64ff. (Originally published 1972 as *General Linguistics*. Difficulties over what counts as a word.)

G. Frege, *The Foundations of Arithmetic*, transl. J. L. Austin, Oxford, Blackwell, 1950 (original 1884), §60. (Word has meaning only in context of proposition.)

J. L. Austin, *How to Do Things with Words*, Oxford, Clarendon, 1962. (Illocutions and perlocutions.)

R. G. Collingwood, *An Essay on Metaphysics*, Oxford, Clarendon, 1940. (Questions as prior to assertions.)

A. J. Ayer, *Language, Truth and Logic*, London, Gollancz, 1936, 2nd edition with important new 'Introduction', 1946. (Classic exposition in English of logical positivism. On 'statement' see p. 8 of 2nd edition. Ayer has also edited a set of essays called *Logical Positivism*, New York, Free Press, 1959.)

M. Schlick, 'Meaning and Verification', *Philosophical Review*, 1936. (Another version of logical positivism. For quotation see p. 351, emphasis his.)

I. Berlin, 'Verification', also listed as 'Verifiability in principle', *Proceedings of the Aristotelian Society*, 1938–9, reprinted in G. H. R. Parkinson (ed.), *The Theory of Meaning*, Oxford University Press, 1968 (which also contains Strawson's 'On referring'). (Criticises logical positivism. For further criticisms see A. C. Ewing, 'Meaninglessness', *Mind*, 1937; J. L. Evans, 'On meaning and verification', *Mind*, 1953.)

P. Nidditch, 'A defence of Ayer's verifiability principle against Church's criticism', *Mind*, 1961. (States Ayer's and Church's positions and criticises latter, all in less than two pages. In turn criticised by D. Makinson, 'Nidditch's definition of verifiability', *Mind*, 1965. Cf. also G. Schlesinger, *Religion and Scientific Method*, Dordrecht, Reidel, 1977, p. 154.)

W. V. O. Quine, 'Two dogmas of empiricism', in his *From a Logical Point of View*, Cambridge, Mass., Harvard University Press, 1953, revised 1961, often reprinted. (Classic attack on analytic/synthetic distinction. For Quine's views on radical translation see his *Word and Object*, New York, Technology Press of MIT, and London, John Wiley, 1960, Chapter 2.)

L. Wittgenstein, *Tractatus Logico-Philosophicus*, London, Routledge & Kegan Paul, 1921, transl. 1922 and (better) 1961. (A very difficult work giving one version of the philosophy called logical atomism. For quotation see §4.024. Frege's version of the view comes in his *Grundgesetze der Arithmetik*, vol. I, Hildesheim, Olms, 1893, §32, transl. in G. Frege, *The Basic Laws of*

Arithmetic: Exposition of the System, transl. and ed. by M. Furth, Berkeley, California University Press, 1964, pp. 89–90. Wittgenstein's (later) work influencing Dummett is primarily his *Remarks on the Foundations of Mathematics*, Oxford, Blackwell, 1956.)

D. Davidson, 'Truth and meaning', *Synthèse*, vol. 17, 1967; 'On saying that', *Synthèse*, vol. 19, 1968–9; 'Radical interpretation', *Dialectica*, 1973; 'Reply to Foster' in Evans and McDowell (below). Other relevant writings of Davidson include 'Semantics for natural languages', in D. Davidson and G. Harman (eds), *The Logic of Grammar*, Encino and Belmont, Cal., Dickenson, 1975 (which also contains 'On saying that'); 'True to the facts', *Journal of Philosophy*, 1969 (examines the extent to which a Tarskiesque account of truth involves correspondence); 'Theories of meaning and learnable languages', in Y. Bar-Hillel (ed.), *Logic, Methodology and Philosophy of Science*, Amsterdam, N. Holland, 1965 (for criticism of this last see R. J. Haack, 'Davidson on learnable languages', *Mind*, 1978).

G. Evans and J. McDowell (eds), *Truth and Meaning*, Oxford, Clarendon, 1976. (Essays based on Davidson's programme, mainly difficult. The 'Introduction' is useful, though not elementary.)

M. A. E. Dummett, 'What is a theory of meaning?' in S. Guttenplan (ed.), *Mind and Language*, Oxford, Clarendon, 1975; 'What is a theory of meaning? (II)' in Evans and McDowell (above). *Truth and Other Enigmas*, London, Duckworth, 1978. (Contains his article 'Truth' with a postscript, and many other developments of his outlook, with an important 'Preface'.)

A. Tarski, *Logic, Semantics, Metamathematics*, Oxford, Clarendon, 1956, pp. 187–8. (Convention T.)

J. McDowell, 'On the sense and reference of a proper name', *Mind*, 1977, reprinted in Platts (below). (Discusses proper names in light of Davidson/ Dummett issue. For quotation see p. 182; p. 160 in Platts.)

M. Platts (ed.), *Reference, Truth and Reality*, London, Routledge & Kegan Paul, 1980. (Further essays in the Davidson/Dummett area. For helpful critique of Dummett see C. McGinn, 'Truth and use'.)

P. Benacerraf and H. Putnam (eds), *Philosophy of Mathematics*, Oxford, Blackwell, 1964. (Contains two essays by Brouwer, as well as one by Dummett on Wittgenstein's philosophy of mathematics, and Quine's 'Two dogmas of empiricism'.)

B. Harrison, *An Introduction to the Philosophy of Language*, London, Macmillan, 1979, Chapter 8. (Treats Davidson.)

I. Hacking, *Why Does Language Matter to Philosophy?*, Cambridge University Press, 1975. (Chapter 12 treats Davidson in a historical context, in a book to be recommended on other grounds as well.)

P. F. Strawson, 'Scruton and Wright on anti-realism, etc.', *Proceedings of the Aristotelian Society*, 1976–7. (Brief but illuminating discussion of anti-realism. D. M. MacKinnon, 'Idealism and realism: an old controversy renewed', in the same volume, is also worth reading.)

A. Millar, 'Truth and understanding', *Mind*, 1977. (Suggests replacing realism/ anti-realism contrast by another one.)

227

S. Kripke, *Naming and Necessity*, Oxford, Blackwell, 1980 (original version 1972).

H. Putnam, 'Is semantics possible?', 'Meaning and reference', both in S. P. Schwartz (ed.), *Naming, Necessity, and Natural Kinds*, Ithaca, N.Y., Cornell University Press, 1977, and in Putnam's *Philosophical Papers*, Cambridge University Press, 1975, vol. 2; latter in *Journal of Philosophy*, 1973. (See also his 'What is realism?', *Proceedings of the Aristotelian Society*, 1975–6, for a discussion of realism in the context of the philosophy of science, and his *Meaning and the Moral Sciences*, London, Routledge & Kegan Paul, 1978, especially Part 4, where he distinguishes between an empirical and a metaphysical version of realism; P. Pettit's review in *The Times Higher Education Supplement* for 17 March 1978 is helpful here.)

R. Descartes, *Discourse on Method*, 1637, end of Part 5. (Descartes on animals – but interpretation of him is admittedly difficult.)

Chapter 7

Plato, *Phaedo*, 380 BC (approx.)

R. Descartes, *Meditations on the First Philosophy*, 1641, especially Meditation 6. (Two dualists, Cf. also Descartes's *The Principles of Philosophy*, 1644, Part 4, especially principles 189–97 (in the 1912 Everyman edition numbered as principles 2–10); *The Passions of the Soul*, 1649, especially articles 30–47.)

G. Ryle, *The Concept of Mind*, London, Hutchinson, 1949, especially Chapter 1. (Famous attack on Descartes's dualism, treated as involving 'ghost in machine'.)

G. Frege, 'The thought: a logical inquiry', *Mind*, 1956 (original 1918–19); K. R. Popper, *Objective Knowledge*, Oxford, Clarendon, 1972 (see index). (Third realm/third world.)

W. J. Ginnane, 'Thoughts', *Mind*, 1960. (What actually happens when a thought suddenly occurs to us? Cf. further discussion in D. L. Mouton, 'Thinking and time', *Mind*, 1969.)

B. Spinoza, *Ethics*, 1677. (His main philosophical work, including his anticipation of identity theory, normally called 'double aspect theory'.)

C. V. Borst (ed.), *The Mind/Brain Identity Theory*, London, Macmillan, 1970. (Collection of papers, including those by Smart, Nagel, Cornman, Rorty, Taylor, and Malcolm. Other collections include C. F. Presley (ed.), *The Identity Theory of Mind*, St Lucia, Queensland University Press, 1967; J. O'Connor (ed.), *Modern Materialism*, New York, Harcourt, Brace and World, 1969.

K. Campbell, *Body and Mind*, London, Macmillan, 1970, Chapters 5, 6. (Elementary discussion.)

D. Davidson, 'Mental Events', in L. Foster and J. W. Swanson (eds), *Experience and Theory*, London, Duckworth, 1970.

C. McGinn, 'Mental states, natural kinds and psychophysical laws', *Proceedings of the Aristotelian Society*, supplementary volume, 1978. (Develops Davidson.)

S. Kripke, *Naming and Necessity*, Oxford, Blackwell, 1980, pp. 144–55 (original version 1972, pp. 334–42).

Aristotle, *On the Soul* (also called *De Anima*), 330 BC (approx.), especially Books 2 and 3. (Main treatment of mind/body problem in Aristotle.)

P. F. Strawson, *Individuals*, London, Methuen, 1959 Chapter 3. (Strawson's view that 'person' is an irreducible concept. See also his 'Self, mind and body', in his *Freedom and Resentment*, London, Methuen, 1974, for criticism of dualism.)

S. Williams, 'Pains, brain states and scientific identities', *Mind*, 1978. (See p. 87 note for quotation.)

Chapter 8

L. Wittgenstein, *Philosophical Investigations*, Oxford, Blackwell, 1953, Part I, §§243–315. (Main attack on private languages.)

O. R. Jones (ed.), *The Private Language Argument*, London, Macmillan, 1970. (Collection of papers, including those by Mundle, J. J. Thomson, Malcolm, Ayer, Castañeda, Kenny, Garver, Holborow.)

J. T. Saunders and D. F. Henze, *The Private Language Problem*, New York, Random House, 1967. (Discussion of the problem in dialogue form, originating in real debate between authors.)

R. Descartes, *Meditations on the First Philosophy*, 1641. (See Meditation 2 for the Cogito argument, and Meditation 1 for the argument about dreaming, to which Descartes gives his final answer in the last paragraph of Meditation 6. For the dream argument in Plato see his *Theaetetus*, §158.)

B. Russell, *The Problems of Philosophy*, Oxford University Press, 1912. (See opening chapters for example of Russell's views on our knowledge of the external world. The book as a whole, which represents an early stage in Russell's thought, is still an excellent introduction to philosophy, despite being out of fashion in some of its conclusions.)

W. K. C. Guthrie, *A History of Greek Philosophy*, Cambridge University Press, vol. 1, 1967. (See Chapters 6 and 7 for introductions to Xenophanes and Heraclitus.)

N. R. Hanson, 'On having the same visual experiences', *Mind*, 1960. (Might red things seem to you as green things seem to me? Cf. also D. M. Taylor, 'The incommunicability of content', *Mind*, 1966.)

J. W. Cornman, 'Private languages and private entities', *Australasian Journal of Philosophy*, 1968. (See pp. 125–6 for point that 'I am in pain' may be a report even if pains are not private.)

J. W. Cook, 'Wittgenstein on privacy', *Philosophical Review*, 1965. (Relations between knowing about pains and experiencing them.)

D. Locke, *Myself and Others*, Oxford, Clarendon, 1968, Chapter 5. (Emphasises difference between knowing the meaning and knowing the truth-value of statements about pains.)

G. E. Moore, 'The refutation of idealism', *Mind*, 1903, reprinted in his *Philosophical Studies*, London, Kegan Paul, Trench, Trubner, 1922. (Sensation and its objects. The article was influential in leading to the decline of idealism in Britain.)

Chapter 9

H. Sidgwick *The Methods of Ethics*, London, Macmillan, 1874, final revision 1901. (Utilitarianism, or close approach to it, in its heyday. Claims to reconcile utilitarianism with common-sense morality. For elaborate commentary on it and its background see J. B. Schneewind, *Sidgwick's Ethics and Victorian Moral Philosophy*, Oxford, Clarendon, 1977.)

J. J. C. Smart and B. Williams, *Utilitarianism For and Against*, Cambridge University Press, 1973. (Debate, with annotated bibliography.)

D. Lyons, *Forms and Limits of Utilitarianism*, Oxford, Clarendon, 1965. (Discusses relations between versions of act and rule utilitarianism. Cf. also B. A. Brody, 'The equivalence of act and rule utilitarianism', *Philosophical Studies*, 1967, and M. D. Bayles (ed.), *Contemporary Utilitarianism*, New York, Doubleday (Anchor), 1968.)

J. Raz, 'Principles of equality', *Mind*, 1978. (Kinds and significance of egalitarianism.)

G. E. Moore, *Principia Ethica*, Cambridge University Press, 1903. (See Chapter 6 for his own list of goods.)

G. F. Fisher. (His remark on equality was made at Blantyre on 25 April 1955, and reported in the *Nyasaland Times* the next day.)

Plato, *Republic*, 375 BC (approx.), Book 1, §331c. (Returning knives to maniacs.)

G. R. Grice, *The Grounds of Moral Judgment*, Cambridge University Press, 1967.

J. Rawls, *A Theory of Justice*, Oxford, Clarendon, 1972. (For his 'Justice as fairness' see *Philosophical Review*, 1958. The secondary literature includes N. Daniels (ed.), *Reading Rawls*, Oxford, Blackwell, 1975, and R. P. Wolff, *Understanding Rawls*, Princeton, N.J., Princeton University Press 1977. B. Barry's *The Liberal Theory of Justice*, Oxford, Clarendon, 1973, is itself a commentary on Rawls.)

Plato, *Crito*, 390 BC (approx.); T. Hobbes, *Leviathan*, 1651; J. Locke, *Two Treatises of Government*, 1690 (see the second); J. J. Rousseau, *The Social Contract*, 1762. (Social contract theories.)

I. Kant, *Groundwork (or Fundamental Principles) of the Metaphysic of Morals*, 1785; *Critique of Practical Reason*, 1788. (Kant's main works on ethics. For the duty to execute murderers see his *Metaphysic of Morals*, 1797, Part 1, General Remarks (after §49) E 1, p. 333 in standard paging, transl. in H. Reiss (ed.), *Kant's Political Writings*, Cambridge University Press, 1970,

p. 156; and by J. Ladd in *Kant: The Metaphysical Elements of Justice*, Indianapolis, Bobbs-Merrill, 1965, p. 102.)

R. Nozick, *Anarchy, State, and Utopia*, Oxford, Blackwell, 1974. (Develops political system based on principles of justice that involve severe restrictions on governmental interference.)

Chapter 10

W. Charlton, *Aesthetics: An Introduction*, London, Hutchinson, 1970. (Includes some connections of aesthetics with metaphysics.)

R. L. Meager, 'The uniqueness of a work of art', *Proceedings of the Aristotelian Society*, 1958–9. (Discusses some of the issues of this chapter.)

H. M. Jones, 'The relevance of the artist's intentions'; J. Kemp, 'The work of art and the artist's intentions', both in *The British Journal of Aesthetics*, 1964.

C. Radford, 'Fakes', *Mind*, 1978. (Ought we to value a work less highly when we find it is a fake?)

R. A. Sharpe, 'Type, token, interpretation and performance', *Mind*, 1979. (Applies type/token distinction, which is rather like that between universals and particulars, to discussion of music.)

G. Vlastos, *Platonic Studies*, Princeton, N.J., Princeton University Press, 1973, Chapter 10, §3. (Pauline prediction.)

Part Two

N.B.: References given previously are not repeated here unless there is a point in doing so.

Chapter 11

R. Grossmann, *Meinong*, London, Routledge & Kegan Paul, 1974. (See pp. 226 and 228 for passages from Meinong on subsistence.)

M. J. Woods, 'Scepticism and natural knowledge', *Proceedings of the Aristotelian Society*, 1979–80. (Naturalised epistemology.)

W. J. Ginnane, 'Thoughts', *Mind*, 1960. (Metaphysical approach.)

S. Blackburn and J. Heal, 'Thoughts and things', *Proceedings of the Aristotelian Society*, supplementary volume, 1979. (logical approach.)

S. E. Toulmin, *The Uses of Argument*, Cambridge University Press, 1958, Chapter 2. (Probability.)

Chapter 12

D. Hume, *Enquiry into the Principles of Human Understanding*, 1748. (For quotation see its closing words.)

B. Russell, *My Philosophical Development*, London, Allen & Unwin, 1959. (See last chapter for Russell's reactions to Wittgenstein and to the rise of linguistic philosophy.)

D. F. Pears, *Bertrand Russell and the British Tradition in Philosophy*, London, Collins (Fontana), 1967. (See especially index under 'Atomism' for logical atomism.)

L. Wittgenstein, *Philosophical Investigations*, Oxford, Blackwell, 1953. (See Part I, §270 for metaphor of idling knob, and §309 for fly-bottle.)

L. Kolakowski, *Positivist Philosophy from Hume to the Vienna Circle*, Harmondsworth, Middx., Penguin, 1966 (transl. from Polish 1968). (Treats Comte and Mach *inter alia*.)

Aristotle, *Protrepticus*, 360–50 BC? (Only fragments remain. For one discussion of it see W. Jaeger, *Aristotle*, Oxford, Clarendon, 1934 (German original 1923), Chapter 4.)

G. Ryle (ed.), *The Revolution in Philosophy*, London, Macmillan, 1956. (One of the manifestoes of linguistic philosophy.)

P. H. Nowell-Smith, *Ethics*, Harmondsworth, Middx., Penguin, 1954. (Minor classic of linguistic philosophy.)

A. Flew, 'Divine omnipotence and human freedom', in A. Flew and A. MacIntyre (eds), *New Essays in Philosophical Theology*, London, S.C.M., 1955. (Paradigm case of freewill.)

H. A. Prichard, 'The obligation to keep a promise', in his *Moral Obligation*, Oxford, Clarendon, 1949.

L. J. Cohen, 'The causal theory of perception', *Proceedings of the Aristotelian Society*, supplementary volume, 1977. (See p. 133 for quotation.)

E. Gettier, 'Is justified true belief knowledge?' *Analysis*, vol. 23, 1962–3, reprinted in A. P. Griffiths (ed.), *Knowledge and Belief*, Oxford University Press, 1967, with references to later discussions; to which add A. I. Goldman, 'A causal theory of knowing', *Journal of Philosophy*, 1967; B. Skyrms, 'The explication of "X knows that p" ' (*ibid.*); and B. Grant, 'Knowledge, luck and charity', *Mind*, 1980.

J. L. Austin, 'Pretending', *Proceedings of the Aristotelian Society*, supplementary volume, 1958.

F. Waismann, 'Analytic', *Analysis*, vols 10–3, 1949–53, reprinted in his *How I See Philosophy*, London, Macmillan, 1968.

W. V. Quine, *Word and Object*, New York, Technology Press of MIT and London, John Wiley, 1960, Chapter 2. (Indeterminacy of translation. 'Gavagai!', etc.) For discussions of Quine see D. Davidson and J. Hintikka (eds), *Words and Objections*, Dordrecht, Reidel, 1969 (which incidentally contains Davidson's 'On saying that'); and also P. Roth, 'Theories of nature and the nature of theories', *Mind*, 1980.)

A. Gewirth, 'Metaethics and moral neutrality', *Ethics*, vol. 18, 1967–8.

(Example of breakdown of ethics/meta-ethics borderline. Cf. also J. Rawls, *A Theory of Justice*, Oxford, Clarendon, 1972, §75.)

F. H. Bradley, *Ethical Studies*, Oxford, Clarendon, 1876. (For ethics and meta-ethics see p. 193 in second edition, and cf. the comments on it by J. B. Schneewind in his *Sidgwick's Ethics and Victorian Moral Philosophy*, Oxford, Clarendon, 1977, pp. 398–411, to which I owe the reference.)

W. James, *Pragmatism*, London, Longmans, Green, 1907, lecture 1. (Tough- and tender-minded.)

G. E. Moore, *Principia Ethica*, Cambridge University Press, 1903, §50. (Beautiful desert. See Chapter 6 for his list of most valuable things, and P. A. Schilpp (ed.), *The Philosophy of G. E. Moore*, Evanston, Ill., Northwestern University Press, 1942, p. 618, for withdrawal.)

D. R. P. Wiggins, 'Truth, invention, and the meaning of life', *Proceedings of the British Academy*, 1976, especially §§V, XII.

P. F. Strawson, *Individuals*, London, Methuen, 1959. (See p. 9 for quotations.)

I. Kant, *Critique of Pure Reason*, 1781, revised 1787. (His main work on metaphysics.)

G. Berkeley, *A Treatise concerning the Principles of Human Knowledge*, 1710. (His main work on metaphysics.)

G. W. Leibniz, *Discourse on Metaphysics*, 1685–6 (published 1846), *Monadology*, 1714 (published 1720). (His main works on metaphysics.)

G. E. Moore, 'A defence of common sense' in J. H. Muirhead (ed.), *Contemporary British Philosophy* (2nd series), London, Allen & Unwin, 1925, reprinted in Moore's *Philosophical Papers*, London, Allen & Unwin, 1959. (Cf. also his *Some Main Problems in Philosophy*, London, Allen & Unwin, 1953 (composed 1910) for his metaphysics in general.)

K. R. Popper, *The Logic of Scientific Discovery*, London, Hutchinson, 1959 (German original 1934–5). (His main work on philosophy of science.)

C. Kirwan, 'How strong are the objections to essence?', *Proceedings of the Aristotelian Society*, 1970–1.

J. Lyons, *Chomsky*, London, Collins (Fontana), 1970, revised and expanded 1977. (Elementary introduction to him. Cf. also G. Harman (ed.), *On Noam Chomsky: Critical Essays*, Garden City, N.Y., Anchor Press, 1974 (which, incidentally, includes Davidson's 'Semantics for natural languages'). For Chomsky's criticism of Kripke see his *Reflections on Language*, London, Collins (Fontana), 1976, pp. 46–52.)

J. Locke, *An Essay concerning Human Understanding*, 1690. (His main philosophical work. On our knowledge of morals see III 11 xvi, IV 3 xviii, IV 12 viii.)

Chapter 13

O. Neurath, 'Protocol sentences' in A. J. Ayer (ed.), *Logical Positivism*, New York, Free Press, 1959. (Coherence theory of truth; see especially p. 203, and for criticism ensuing paper by Schlick, §III. See also C. G. Hempel, 'On the logical positivists' theory of truth', *Analysis*, vol. 2, 1934–5, which criticises Schlick in turn.)

A. J. Ayer, *The Origins of Pragmatism*, London, Macmillan, 1968. (Treats Peirce and James.)

B. Aune, *Rationalism, Empiricism, and Pragmatism*, New York, Random House, 1970. (Chapters 4 and 5 discuss modern versions of pragmatism.) Cf. also D. H. Mellor (ed.), *Prospects for Pragmatism*, Cambridge University Press, 1980.

Conclusion

T. S. Kuhn, *The Structure of Scientific Revolutions*, Chicago University Press, 1962; 2nd edition with 'Postscript' 1970. (Revolutionary view of scientific revolutions. For criticism and discussion see I. Lakatos and A. Musgrave (eds), *Criticism and the Growth of Knowledge*, Cambridge University Press, 1970.)

J. A. Passmore, *100 Years of Philosophy*, London, Duckworth, 1957, expanded 1966. (Philosophy from John Stuart Mill onwards.)

A. Flew, *An Introduction to Western Philosophy*, London, Thames and Hudson, 1971. (Based on extensive quotation mainly from the philosophical classics.)

Philosophy and Public Affairs. (Quarterly journal linking philosophy to current issues.)

Index

This index does not cover the Preface or Bibliography. Numbers in parentheses refer to places where a term appears only by implication; only a few such references are included.

sentences, 38, 85, 87; and
statements, 29, 87; *see also*
functions; sentences; statements
psychology: philosophical, 183;
social, 185
Ptolemy, 10
purple cow (example), 47, 48, 53, 105,
106–7
Putnam, H., 79, 81, 108, 114–16

quantification, quantifier, 38–9
questions, 86
Quine, W.V.O., 207; on analytic/
synthetic, 88, 206; on eternal
sentences, 25; as pragmatist, 218;
on radical translation,
indeterminacy of translation, 101,
(102), 105–6; on revisability of
laws, 79, 206

rabbit (example), 207
rationalism, 195, 214, 216
rationality, 131, 160, 179; *see also*
reasoning
Rawls, J., 158, 159, 160–5, 185, 187
real and true, 27, 29
realism, 47, 104, 105, 107–8, 180,
209, 216–17, 218; in ethics, 53,
218; medieval, 218; *see also* anti-
realism
reasoning, 178, 185; *see also*
rationality
recursive, 38, 91
reductionism: and anti-realism, 217;
and empiricism, 217, 219; and
logical atomism, 194; and logical
positivism, 193, 218; and meaning
and truth, 104, 195; relativity of,
195; and Wittgenstein, 194, 199
reference: theory of, 104, 133; *see
also* meaning
relativism, 54
religion, 95, 108, 201, 209, 215;
philosophy of, 186; *see also* God
representation: in art, 173; kinds of,
30

revelation, 48, 53, 57
Richards, I. A., 95
right and good, 160
rights, 154, 155, 158, 161
rigour, 7, 8
romanticism, 11
Rorty, R., 128
Rousseau, J.-J., 158
rule-following, 143, 144–5, 146, 194
Russell, B. A. W., 8, 206; and
egocentric predicament, 137; and
hook symbol, 59; and linguistic
philosophy, 199, 200; and logical
atomism, 194, 217; and material
implication, 65–6; and names, 109;
and ordinary language, 199; and
referring to the non-existent, 42,
43–5, 46; and theory of
descriptions, 109; and theory of
types, 41; and Wittgenstein, 194,
199

satisfaction, 38, 39–40; of desire, 211
Satz, 85
scepticism, 136–51, 179, 190, 201;
forms of, 137–8
Schlick, M., 86, 87, 95, 198
science, 11, 42, 70, 199, 214; *see also*
philosophy
Searle, J. R., 57–8, 110
semantic, 37, 91, 108; *see also* truth
sensations, 124–9, 133–5, 139, 140,
141–50
sense, 63, 109–10
sense-data, 137, 191, 205, 216
sentences, 218; as bearers of truth-
values, 27–8, 29–30; and
conventions, 35; eternal, 25, 29;
open, 38, 39; and statements and
propositions, 29–30, 33, 34, 38, 85,
87; and thoughts, 130; and words,
80–1, 103; *see also* functions;
general statements or sentences;
meaning; propositions; statements;
T; truth

181, 186, 187, 188, 197, 218; and
art 173; and assertibility, 106,
107–8, 194; and assertion, 86;
bearers of, 27–30, 42; coherence
theory of, 42, 217–18; -conditions,
37, 103, 187, 195, 217;
correspondence theory of, 30–42,
46–7, 48, 50; defined by
satisfaction, 40; indeterminate
truth-values, 37, 43–7, (64); logical
and factual, 205; and meaning, 86,
95–108; meaning of, 30–42;
performative theory of, 36–7; and
philosophy, 10–11, 178, 181,
200–201, 219–20; and place, 23,
24–5; pragmatic theory of, 42,
(218); -preserving, 45; redundancy
(or 'no truth') theory of, 36;
semantic theory of, 37–42; and
time, 20–5, 184; true and correct,
29; true-in-L, 42; true and real, 27,
29, 208; vacuous, 45, 72, 74,
144–5; -value, 38, 43, 44, 45, 46,
63, 72, 74; -value gap, 43, 44, 72,
see also non-cognitivism; weak
correspondence theory of, 35–6,
36–7, 37–42, 48; *see also*
designate; determinism, logical;
theory of truth
Tully/Cicero (example), 109, 110,
111, 113, 116
two-colour problem, 150
type, 132–3
types: theory of, 41
typical and average, 170

understanding: theory of, 104
universalisability, 204–5
universals, 110, 118, 180, 191, 218,
219; family resemblance view of,
110; model-, 173; nature of, 84,
169, 218; and sensation, 150; and
works of art, 169, 171
utilitarianism, 152–8, 163, 165,
210–11; act- and rule-, 157–8;
ideal, 152

valid, 45, 58, 64
value, 180, 181, 205, 210–11; kinds
of, 165, 185; *see also* fact
value judgments, 48–58, 69, 103, 177,
200; examples of, 55; strict sense
of, 57
Van Meegheren, J., 172
variable, 39
veil of ignorance, 161, 162, 163, 164
Venus de Milo, 167, 168
verification: ambiguities in, 87, 89,
90; difficulties in, 89–95, 143
verification theory of meaning, 47,
86–95, 192–3, 195, 199, 200, 213,
217; applied to itself, 196–8; and
Dummett, 105, 106, (179), 217;
and Frege, 95; and Popper, 214;
and private language argument,
143, 149, 194; and Wittgenstein,
95, 143, 194; *see also* logical
positivism
Vermeer, J., 172
Vienna Circle, 192, 194, 206
Voltaire, 75

Waismann, F., 206, 207, 208
Walker, R. C. S., 63
water (example), 114–15
Wegener, A., 220
Whitehead, A. N., 10
Wiggins, D. R. P., 211
Will, F. L., 74
Williams, B. A. O., 51
Williams, S., 135, 151
wisdom: concept of, 4; and
knowledge, 2
Wittgenstein, L., 136, 143, 194; and
dualism, 205; and linguistic
philosophy, 194, 198–9; and
logical atomism, 194; and logical
positivism, 194; and mathematics,
194–5; on meaning of names,
82–4, 145; on meaning of
sentences, 95; on meaning as use,
105; on mind/body problem, 151;
on philosophy, 198–9; and private